Global Youth in Digital Trajectories

This is a fascinating and thought provoking volume on youth engagement with digital technology and one that is genuinely transnational and transdisciplinary in flavour. Studies of gaming, video production and social media show how new technologies are woven into the lives of young people, supporting their developing sense of agency and civic engagement. An important contribution to the field.
Guy Merchant, *Professor of Literacy in Education, Sheffield Hallam University, UK*

Global Youth in Digital Trajectories explores the most recent developments regarding youth and media in a global perspective. Representing an innovative contribution to virtual research methods, this book presents research carried out in areas as diverse as Greece, the Netherlands, Germany, Brazil, Russia, and India. The volume examines which new anthropological and cultural-historical conditions and changes arise in connection with the widespread presence of digital media in the lives of the networked teens. Indeed, it is highlighted that the differentiation between an offline world and an online world is inapplicable to the lives of most young people.

Exploring youth's imaginary productions, personal sense-making processes and cross-media dialogues in today's multimedia worlds, *Global Youth in Digital Trajectories* will be of particular interest to undergraduates and postgraduates in the fields of sociology, anthropology, education studies, media research, and cultural studies. It may also appeal to practitioners in social work and schools.

Michalis Kontopodis is a Senior Lecturer in Educational Psychology, University of Sheffield, UK.

Christos Varvantakis is a Research Fellow at the School of Education & Social Work, University of Sussex, UK.

Christoph Wulf is Professor for Anthropology and Education at Free University Berlin, Germany.

Routledge Research in Information Technology and Society

Global Youth in Digital Trajectories
*Edited by Michalis Kontopodis, Christos Varvantakis
and Christoph Wulf*

Global Youth in Digital Trajectories

Edited by Michalis Kontopodis,
Christos Varvantakis and
Christoph Wulf

LONDON AND NEW YORK

First published 2017
by Routledge
2 Park Square, Milton Park, Abingdon, Oxon OX14 4RN

and by Routledge
711 Third Avenue, New York, NY 10017

Routledge is an imprint of the Taylor & Francis Group, an informa business

© 2017 Michalis Kontopodis, Christos Varvantakis and Christoph Wulf

© 2017 selection and editorial matter, Michalis Kontopodis, Christos Varvantakis and Christoph Wulf; individual chapters, the contributors

All rights reserved. No part of this book may be reprinted or reproduced or utilised in any form or by any electronic, mechanical, or other means, now known or hereafter invented, including photocopying and recording, or in any information storage or retrieval system, without permission in writing from the publishers.

Trademark notice: Product or corporate names may be trademarks or registered trademarks, and are used only for identification and explanation without intent to infringe.

British Library Cataloguing-in-Publication Data
A catalogue record for this book is available from the British Library

Library of Congress Cataloging-in-Publication Data
Names: Kontopodis, Michalis, editor. | Varvantakis, Christos, editor. | Wulf, Christoph, 1944– editor.
Title: Global youth in digital trajectories / [edited by] Michalis Kontopodis, Christos Varvantakis and Christoph Wulf.
Description: Abingdon, Oxon ; New York, NY : Routledge, 2017. | Series: Routledge research in information technology and society ; 19 | Includes bibliographical references and index.
Identifiers: LCCN 2016045680 | ISBN 9781138236035 (hardback)
Subjects: LCSH: Internet and youth. | Mass media and youth. | Information technology—Social aspects.
Classification: LCC HQ799.9.I58 G56 2017 | DDC 004.67/8083—dc23
LC record available at https://lccn.loc.gov/2016045680

ISBN: 978-1-138-23603-5 (hbk)
ISBN: 978-1-315-30323-9 (ebk)

Typeset in Times New Roman
by Apex CoVantage, LLC

Contents

List of figures vii
List of tables viii
Notes on contributors ix
Acknowledgements xvii

Introduction:
Exploring global youth in digital trajectories 1
MICHALIS KONTOPODIS, CHRISTOS VARVANTAKIS, AND
  CHRISTOPH WULF

1 **Digital identity building: A dialogue with Berlin technology
  and computer science students** 12
  NIKA DARYAN AND CHRISTOPH WULF

2 **Young people, Facebook, and pedagogy: Recognizing
  contemporary forms of multimodal text making** 22
  JEFF BEZEMER AND GUNTHER KRESS

3 **Playing sports with Nintendo Wii in Berlin: Technography,
  interactivity, and imagination** 39
  NINO FERRIN AND MICHALIS KONTOPODIS

4 **Digital filmmaking as a means for the development
  of reflection: A case study of a disabled university
  student in Moscow** 53
  OLGA RUBTSOVA AND NATALYA ULANOVA

5 **Youth tubing the Greek crisis: A cultural-historical perspective** 69
  MANOLIS DAFERMOS, SOFIA TRILIVA, AND CHRISTOS VARVANTAKIS

6 **Dove YouTube campaign "the pressure on young girls and women to fit an artificial body ideal": A sequential analysis** 97
ALEXIOS BRAILAS, GIORGOS ALEXIAS, AND
 KONSTANTINOS KOSKINAS

7 **Youth, Facebook, and mediated protest in India: A cross-media exploration** 110
SUPRIYA CHOTANI

8 **Enhancing multimedia use in state secondary schools in São Paulo: A critical collaborative perspective** 127
FERNANDA LIBERALI, MARIA CECÍLIA MAGALHÃES,
 MARIA CRISTINA MEANEY, CAMILA SANTIAGO, MAURÍCIO
 CANUTO, FELICIANA AMARAL, BRUNA CABABE, AND
 JÉSSICA ALINE ALMEIDA DOS SANTOS

**Instead of an epilogue:
Iconophagy: Impact and impulses for global youth and education** 146
NORVAL BAITELLO JUN.

Index 151

Figures

1.1	Focus-group discussion with the students	17
2.1	Daan's status update on Facebook	29
2.2	Status update interface on Facebook app for iPhone	30
3.1	Evasive maneuver	44
3.2	Jubilation	45
5.1	Metadata collection example	79
5.2	One of the five texts-on-texts	79
5.3	Example of code-categorizing and processing of the cultural-historical theme of the data corpus	80
5.4	Student chained to the school desk	87
5.5	Still from the video "Greek Financial Crisis: Youth React"	89
6.1	Coding scheme categories and relative observed frequencies	102
7.1	Trends in corruption coverage (2005–2011) in six news channels	114
8.1	Various media presented in a didactic unit suggested by the researchers	134
8.2	Various media used by one school in the didactic unit presented	139

Tables

2.1	Number of 'posts' on Daan's wall, per type and term	28
4.1	Data collection schedule	58
5.1	The set of concepts of cultural-historical theory used in this study and their definitions	73
5.2	The five videos used in the analyses, their titles and genres, dates of production, producers, and descriptions	77
6.1	Coding scheme categories and relative observed frequencies	101
6.2	Absolute frequencies of observed coding scheme categories	104
6.3	Transitional probabilities of observed coding scheme categories	105
7.1	News capsules on protests in two channels (April 2011–March 2012)	113
7.2	Pages and followers of protests on Facebook (accessed on June 10, 2013)	113
7.3	User created Facebook pages on corruption in India	115
7.4	Total prime-time (7–11 PM) coverage of gang rape cases and related issues (Dec 17–31, 2012)	116
7.5	Facebook pages opened after December 16, 2012	117

Notes on contributors

Editors

Michalis Kontopodis's research interests concern youth development, education, and mutual understanding in the era of global uncertainty. Michalis Kontopodis accomplished his PhD at the Free University Berlin and is currently directing the MSc in Psychology and Education at the University of Sheffield. Before that he worked and/or was a visiting staff member at University of Roehampton, Humboldt University Berlin, City University of New York, New York University, Moscow State University, Pontifical Catholic University of São Paulo, and Jawaharlal Nehru University. He has until currently coordinated the international research project *Global Perspectives on Learning and Development with Digital Video-Editing Media*. His book *Neoliberalism, Pedagogy and Human Development* was published as a paperback (second edition) with Routledge in 2014.

For updated information, visit: http://mkontopodis.wordpress.com/

Contact Details: Dr. Michalis Kontopodis, School of Education, University of Sheffield, 388 Glossop Road, Sheffield S10 2JA.
Email: michaliskonto@googlemail.com

Christos Varvantakis is an anthropologist and research fellow for the CONNECTORS Study (University of Sussex/ERC). He completed his PhD at the Freie Universität in Berlin, having previously been trained as a sociologist (University of Crete) and visual anthropologist (Goldsmiths College). He has undertaken research in Germany, South India, and Greece and has until recently worked as a research associate in the University of Crete and as a visiting scholar in the Jawaharlal Nehru University in Delhi. He has received research, writing, and travel grants by funding bodies such as DFG and DAAD. He is member of the editorial board of *Sensate: Journal for Experiments with Critical Media* and he is a curator for the Athens Ethnographic Film Festival since 2008. He has produced several ethnographic films and published papers on the de-politicization of memory, ritual and community dynamics, the history of ethnographic film, video and youth activism.

x *Notes on contributors*

Contact Details: Dr. Christos Varvantakis, School of Education and Social Work, Room 121, University of Sussex, Falmer BN1 6HD.
Email: c.varvantakis@sussex.ac.uk

Christoph Wulf is Professor of Anthropology and Education and a member of the Interdisciplinary Centre for Historical Anthropology and the Graduate School "InterArts" at the Free University Berlin. His books have been translated into fifteen languages. He is Vice President of the German Commission for UNESCO. He has received research stays and invited professorships at many universities all over the world. Major research areas: historical and cultural anthropology, educational anthropology, rituals, gestures, emotions, intercultural communication, mimesis, aesthetics. Latest book publications with: University of Chicago Press (2013), Routledge (2009, 2011, 2012, 2014), Springer (2011, 2014), and transcript (2014). Christoph Wulf is also editor, coeditor, and member of the editorial staff of several national and international journals such as *Paragrana* and *Zeitschrift fuer Erziehungswissenschaften*.

Contact details: Prof. Dr. Christoph Wulf, Free University of Berlin, Department of Anthropology and Education, Habelschwerdter Allee 45, 14195 Berlin, Germany.
Email: chrwulf@zedat.fu-berlin.de

Authors

Giorgos Alexias is an associate professor at the Department of Psychology, Panteion University in Athens, Greece. His research interests focus on sociology of the body and health. More specifically, he studies the social dimension of health, illness and death in online and offline spaces. He is the author of *Sociology of Human Body: From Homo Neanderthal to the Terminator* (in Greek, Pedio, 2011).

Contact Details: Dr. Giorgos Alexias, Panteion University, School of Social Sciences and Psychology, Department of Psychology, New Building, Room C13, 136 Sygrou Avenue, GR 176 71, Greece.
Email: galexias@panteion.gr

Feliciana Amaral holds a Master's Degree in Applied Linguistics from the Pontifical Catholic University of São Paulo. She has worked as a Portuguese teacher at a prominent bilingual school in São Paulo as well as at a public state school. She is a member of the research group LACE (Language in Activities in School Contexts). Her main interests concern students' and teachers' agency as well as collaboration in school contexts.

Contact Details: Feliciana Amaral, Rua Hanna Abduch, 126, Vila Palmeira-Freguesia do Ó-SP, 02726–020, Brazil.
Email: feliciana@mail.stance.com.br

Norval Baitello Jun. is Professor of Media Theory, Communication, and Cultural Sciences of Culture at the Pontific Catholic University of São Paulo and Director of the Interdisciplinary Research Centre for Cultural Semiotics and Media Theory. He has been visiting professor at the University of Vienna, at the Universidad de Sevilla, Universidad Autonoma de Barcelona, University St. Petersburg, and University of Évora. His books include: *Flussers Völlerei* (Flusser's gluttony) (2007); *A serpente, a maçã e o holograma* (The serpent, the apple and the hologram) (2010); *O pensamento sentado* (Thinking while seated); *A era da iconofagia* (The era of iconophagy) (2014).

Contact Details: Prof. Dr. Norval Baitello Jun., Rua Itapicuru, 333 ap 124, 05006–000, São Paulo, Brasil.
Email: norvalbaitello@pucsp.br

Jeff Bezemer is Co-Director of the Centre for Multimodal Research at the Institute of Education, University of London. He is interested in multimodal perspectives on learning, communication, and identity. His research stretches across a range of sites, including schools, work places, and print-based and digital platforms for text production. This work is funded by the Economic and Social Research Council and published in linguistic, educational, and medical journals. His most recent publication is the book *Multimodality, Learning and Communication: A Social Semiotic Frame* co-authored with Gunther Kress (Routledge, 2015).

Contact details: Dr. Jeff Bezemer, London Knowledge Lab, 23–29 Emerald Street, London WC1N 3QS, UK.
Email: j.bezemer@ioe.ac.uk

Alexios Brailas is a post-doc researcher at the Department of Psychology, Panteion University in Athens, Greece. Through his research he strives to bring insights from complexity theory and network approaches to both formal and informal teaching. Research interests and recent projects include: remodeling of Grounded Theory (Networked Grounded Theory); research methods in cyberspace; complexity theory and learning. He is the author of *Learning at the Internet Chronotope: Communities, Digital Cultures, Wikipedia and MOOCs* (Vrlab, 2015). For further and updated information, visit: http://abrailas.github.io/

Contact Details: Dr. Alexios Brailas, Panteion University, School of Social Sciences and Psychology, Department of Psychology, New Building, Room C13, 136 Sygrou Avenue, GR 176 71, Greece.
Email: abrailas@panteion.gr

Notes on contributors

Bruna Cababe holds a Master's Degree in Applied Linguistics from the Pontifical Catholic University of São Paulo. She was a Fulbright Portuguese Language Teaching Assistant at the University of Notre Dame in 2011–2012. She has worked at a Brazilian publishing house on the developing of digital and printed language textbooks, and she currently works as a Portuguese foreign language teacher at the Armando Álvares Penteado Foundation College in São Paulo (FAAP). As a member of the research group LACE (Language in Activities in School Contexts), her main research interests are multimodality, multiculturality, and the role of argumentation in learning processes.

Contact Details: Bruna Cababe, Av. Itaboraí, n.457, APT 91, Saúde, 04135–000, São Paulo-SP, Brasil.
Email: brunacababe@gmail.com.

Maurício Canuto holds a Master's Degree in Applied Linguistics from the Pontifical Catholic University of São Paulo. He is a member of the research group LACE (Language in Activities in School Contexts). Currently, he works as a Portuguese teacher and an extra activities coordinator at a public elementary school in Secretariat of Education in São Paulo. He also teaches some education-related courses at the post-graduation center of PUC/SP, COGEAE.

Contact Details: Maurício Canuto, Rua Domenico Montella, 335 – Parque Nações Unidas, 02996–080, São Paulo, Brasil.
Email: mau.canuto@gmail.com

Supriya Chotani has recently finished her PhD thesis at the Centre for the Study of Social Systems, Jawaharlal Nehru University, Delhi, titled "Between the Street and the Screen: A Study of Protest and Representation in Contemporary India". She works as a Guest Faculty at the Centre for Culture, Media and Governance, Jamia Millia Islamia. Her interests are in media and social movements, media development, and gender studies.

Contact Details: Dr. Supriya Chotani, Centre for Culture, Media and Governance, Jamia Millia Islamia University, New Delhi, 110025, India.
Email: supriyachotani@gmail.com

Manolis Dafermos is an Associate Professor in Epistemology of Psychology at the Department of Psychology at the University of Crete. He holds a PhD in Philosophy from the Lomonosov Moscow State University. His interests include cultural-historical psychology, critical psychology, history of psychology, and methodological and epistemological issues in the social sciences. He has authored or co-authored papers in these areas for *Theory & Psychology*, *European Journal of Psychotherapy and Counseling*, *Journal of Community & Applied Social Psychology*, *Forum Kritische Psychologie*, etc. He is a member of the Editorial Board of journals *Dialogical Pedagogy* and *Teoría y Crítica de la Psicología*. He has been a guest editor of two special issues of the journal *Annual Review of Critical Psychology*.

Contact Details: Dr. Manolis Dafermos, Department of Psychology, University of Crete, Gallos University Campus, Rethymno, GR 74100, Greece.
Email: mdafermo@uoc.gr

Nika Daryan works as a researcher and lecturer at the Department of Anthropology and Education at the Faculty of Educational Science and Psychology at the Free University of Berlin, as well as at the Institute of Educational Sciences at Leuphana University. Research interests: historical and cultural anthropology, educational anthropology, theory of practice and imagination, mediology.

Contact details: Dr. Nika Daryan, Leuphana Universität Lüneburg, Institute of Bildungswissenschaft, Scharnhorststr.1, C1.203, 21335 Lüneburg, Germany.
Email: nika.daryan@leuphana.de

Nino Ferrin studied educational science, sociology, psychology, and philosophy at Free University Berlin and at University of Barcelona and completed his PhD in 2011 at the Faculty of Education and Psychology of Free University Berlin, Germany. He worked as research assistant at the Institute of Anthropology and Education, Faculty of Education and Psychology, Free University, Berlin and currently is a research associate in the same faculty. His interests concern theory and philosophy of education and media as well as pedagogical anthropology and reconstructive ethnography. His publications include coedited books from the *Berlin Ritual and Gesture Study* as well as the book *Selbstkultur und mediale Körper* (Culture of the self and the medial body)(2013).

Contact Details: Dr. Nino Ferrin, Faculty of Education and Psychology, FU Berlin, Habelschwerdter Allee 45 (Silberlaube: Raum KL 23/129a), 14195 Berlin, Germany.
Email: nino.ferrin@fu-berlin.de

Konstantinos Koskinas is a professor at the Department of Psychology, Panteion University in Athens, Greece. He is the founder and director of the Virtual Reality, Internet Research and eLearning Laboratory (http://vrlab.panteion.gr) and the director of the postgraduate program in "Virtual Communities: Socio-Psychological Approaches and Technical Applications". He is the coeditor of the collective volume *Virtual Communities and the Internet: Psychosocial Approaches and Technical Applications* (in Greek, Klidarithmos, 2009).

Contact Details: Prof. Konstantinos Koskinas, Panteion University, School of Social Sciences and Psychology, Department of Psychology, New Building, Room C13, 136 Sygrou Avenue, GR 176 71, Greece.
Email: kkoski@panteion.gr

xiv Notes on contributors

Gunther Kress is Professor of Semiotics and Education at the Institute of Education, University of London. His interests are in communication and meaning (making) in contemporary environments. His two broad aims are to continue developing a social semiotic theory of multimodal communication, and, in that, to develop an apt theory of learning and apt means for the 'recognition' and 'valuation of learning'. He is the author of *Literacy in the New Media Age* (2003); *Multimodality: A Social Semiotic Approach to Contemporary Communication* (2009); *Multimodality, Learning and Communication: A Social Semiotic Frame* (2015, with J. Bezemer), and other books published by Routledge.

Contact Details: Prof. Gunther Kress, Institute of Education, 20 Bedford Way, London WC1H 0AL, UK.
Email: g.kress@ioe.ac.uk

Fernanda Liberali holds a doctorate degree from the Applied Linguistics and Language Studies Program at the Pontifical Catholic University of São Paulo, where she has worked as a professor and researcher since 2000. She has recently concluded two post-doctoral studies: one at the University of Helsinki, and another one at the Freie Universität Berlin. She holds a fellowship from CNPq, a national funding agency. Together with Maria Cecília Magalhães, she coordinates the research group LACE (Language in Activities in School Contexts/ Linguagem em Atividade no Contexto Escolar). In a socio-historical-cultural perspective, her extramural, consultancy, and research concerns are related to school management, teachers' and teacher-educators' development, teaching-learning issues, multiliteracy, citizenship education, multilingual education, multiculturalism, and argumentation. She is the author of "Argumentação em contexto escolar" (Argumentation in the school context) (2013), "Formação crítica de Educadores: Questões fundamentais" (Critical teacher education: fundamental issues) (2012, 2010, 2018).

Contact Details: Dr. Fernanda Liberali, Rua Ministro Ferreira Alves, N° 1031 APT 182 A, 05009–000, Perdizes-São Paulo, Brasil.
Email: liberali@uol.com.br

Maria Cecília Magalhães holds a Doctorate Degree in Education from Virginia Tech University. She is currently a Professor at the Linguistic Department and the Applied Linguistics and Language Studies Post-Graduation Program of the Pontifical Catholic University of São Paulo, Brasil. She works with theoretical-methodological issues in teacher education, mainly focused on critical collaborative research within the theoretical frame of the Socio-Historical-Cultural Activity Theory. Her main research interests are related to school teaching-learning processes, citizenship education, and community building. She is the author of "Questões de método e de linguagem na formação docente" (Questions of method and language in teacher education) (2011) and *A formação do professor como um profissional crítico: Linguagem e reflexão* (Educating teachers as critical professionals: Language and reflection) (2004, 2009).

Contact Details: Prof. Maria Cecília Magalhães, Rua Dr. Artur Neiva 330, 05359–200, São Paulo, SP, Brasil.
Email: cicamaga@gmail.com.

Maria Cristina Meaney holds a Master's Degree in Applied Linguistics from the Pontifical Catholic University of São Paulo. She has worked as an English teacher and pedagogical coordinator at prominent language and bilingual schools in São Paulo. She also works as a teacher educator for both public and private schools and develops didactic materials for teaching English as an international language through social activities within a multiliteracy perspective. As a member of the research group LACE (Language in Activities in School Contexts), her interests include the role of argumentation in learning processes, bilingual education, and multiliteracy.

Contact Details: Maria Cristina Meaney, Rua Trajano de Morais, 124. São Paulo, SP, 02630–050, Brasil.
Email: crismeaney@hotmail.com

Olga Rubtsova, is Associate Professor of the Department of Educational Psychology and Head of the Center for Foreign Languages Psy-Lingua at Moscow State University of Psychology and Education. Her research interests concern adolescent crisis and its underlying inner conflicts, psychological peculiarities of the development of contemporary teenagers, identity formation in adolescence, as well as psychological aspects of the widespread use of new technologies.

Contact details: Dr. Olga Rubtsova, Department of Educational Psychology, 29 Sretenka Str., Moscow 127051, Russia.
Email: ovrubsova@mail.ru

Camila Santiago holds a Master's Degree in Applied Linguistics from the Pontifical Catholic University of São Paulo. She has taught students from all ages and levels in different language institutes. She has been working as a languages, linguistics, and scientific methodology professor in face-to-face and distance graduation and post-graduation courses and also as an assistant coordinator in the Languages Center at UMESP (Methodist University of São Paulo). She is a member of LACE (Language in Activities in School Contexts) and, in a social-historical-cultural perspective, her main research interests include knowledge production through critical collaboration and argumentation, English teaching-learning, and multiliteracy.

Contact Details: Camila Santiago Rua Curitiba, N° 341, Parque Erasmo Assunção, Santo André-SP, 09271–480, Brasil.
Email: santiago.camila@gmail.com

Jéssica Aline Almeida Dos Santos has graduated in Portuguese and Spanish Languages at the Faculdade Eça de Queirós. She has worked as a Portuguese teacher at Cursinho Popular Chico Mendes, in Itapevi-SP. She is a member of the research group LACE (Language in Activities in School Contexts).

Contact Details: Jéssica Aline Almeida Dos Santos Bonifácio de Abreu, Bairro dos Abreus N° 1202, 06654–000, Itapevi-São Paulo, Brasil.
Email: jessica.almeidas@ymail.com

Sofia Triliva is an Associate Professor at the University of Crete where she has been teaching for the last 25 years. Her research focuses on community mental health and the ways to promote it. She is the author of several books on promoting mental health in schools and communities. She has published her work in peer-reviewed journals and has coedited collective volumes such as: "Critical Psychology in a Changing World" (*Annual Review of Critical Psychology*, 2006), "Doing Psychology under New Conditions" (2013), etc.

Contact Details: Dr. Sofia Triliva, Department of Psychology, University of Crete, Gallos University Campus, Rethymno, GR 74100, Greece.
Email: triliva@uoc.gr

Natalya Ulanova accomplished her PhD at the Moscow State University of Psychology and Education where she consequently worked as research fellow, educational program coordinator, and UNESCO Chair of Cultural-historical Psychology of Childhood from 2010 to 2014. She is currently leading the research project "Struggle for School and Struggle at School: School Education in the Context of Confessional and Regional Policy in East and South Africa", at the Institute for African Studies of the Russian Academy of Sciences. Her research interests and recent publications focus on comparative studies in education, cultural-historical and educational psychological theory, contemporary education systems, and digital technologies in education.

Contact details: Dr. Natalya Ulanova, 16–4, Marshala Biruzova, Moscow, Russia 123060.
Email: natalya.ulanova@gmail.com

Acknowledgements

The research presented in this volume was supported by a Marie Curie International Research Staff Exchange Scheme (IRSES) Grant within the 7th European Community Framework Program (PIRSES-GA-2012–318909). Under the coordination of Dr. M. Kontopodis, "Global Perspectives on Learning and Development with Digital Video-Editing Media" explored the potential of digital filming and multimedia use for school, youth development, and community life through a partnership between a three-member European consortium (University of Crete, Free University Berlin & Institute of Education, University College London), the Moscow State University of Psychology and Education, the Jawaharlal Nehru University, and the Pontifical Catholic University of São Paulo.

We acknowledge the significant contribution to methodology development, data collection and analysis, discussion of results, and theory building of all members of the IRSES network who do not appear as authors in the present volume, and especially of: Martin Bittner, Maitrayee Chaudhuri, Carey Jewitt, Nadia Lebedev, Angela Lessa, Vinod Kumar, Anil Kumar Patel, Lev Kuravsky, Wellington de Oliveira, Gurram Srinivas, and most importantly: Vitaly Rubtsov. Furthermore, we would like to thank the members of the External Advisory Ethics Board: Despina Anagnostopoulou, Jackie Marsh, and Anja Kraus, who monitored closely all research activities of the exchange scheme according to the relevant national, European, and international ethical guidelines. Last but not least, a special thanks is due to the project advisers in the REA office of the European Commission: Desislava Kolarova and Eleftheria Lykouressi for their great patience and support in dealing with all our queries and requests throughout the duration of the project.

Introduction
Exploring global youth in digital trajectories

Michalis Kontopodis, Christos Varvantakis, and Christoph Wulf

Setting the stage: youth, globalization, and digital media

In 1996 (i.e., before the emergence of YouTube and Facebook and before mobile internet devices such as tablets and smartphones were widely available) Arjun Appadurai, in his seminal book *Modernity at Large: Cultural Dimensions of Globalization*, described how the world has become *interconnected* through the flow of capital, technologies, populations, media images, and ideas to an unprecedented extent. When so-called "new media" emerged, this development was intensified with the world becoming increasingly *hyperconnected*: global communication is nowadays taking place through interactive, fast, and mobile media that enable the distributed production and peer-to-peer circulation of advanced audio-visual designs and bits of information across the most different geographical areas.

These developments concern today's young people more than anybody else. In 2001, Marc Prensky was already arguing that due to digital technologies, a physiological transformation of the brain structure is taking place and that young "digital natives" think in different ways compared to older generations (2001a, 2001b). However simplified this position may be because of the single focus on generational differences (cf. Helsper & Eynon, 2010), much scholarship has explored the major influences of digital technologies on young people. Terms such as *the Net generation* (Tapscott, 2009), *digital youth* (Subrahmanyam & Šmahel, 2011), *the app generation* (Gardner & Davis, 2013), and *networked teens* (boyd, 2014) have been introduced in this context to describe a radical shift in the lives of the young in the "new media" era.

Another designation often employed in the same context is the term *global children* or *global youth* (de Block & Buckingham, 2007; Nilan & Feixa, 2006). Maintaining critical distance from Eurocentric and neoliberal understandings of "globalization" (cf. Andreotti, 2011; Kontopodis, 2012; McFarlane, 2009), we should acknowledge here that even if technology hyperconnects the most diverse and distant locations, it is discernibly unequally accessible and distributed across geographical areas (Apperley, 2010) and there are significant differences in media practices depending on the young people's gender, class, race, and socio-cultural and ethnic backgrounds (Brown & Davis, 2004; Walkerdine, 2007). Still, youths all around the globe seem to increasingly express themselves in public internet forums (Buckingham & Willett, 2006), come of age in virtual social worlds (Boellstorff, 2008), make friends on social networking sites (de Haan & Pijpers, 2010; Livingstone, 2010), play games (Burn & Richards, 2014), and consume online (Buckingham & Tingstad, 2010).

Much research has also explored the role digital technologies may play globally with regard to young people's formal and informal education inside and outside of school, in virtual learning environments, and/or through mobile interfaces (Davies, Coleman & Livingstone, 2014; Pachler, Bachmair, Cook & Kress, 2010; Potter, 2012; Renninger & Shumar, 2002; Selwyn, 2013). Literacy in this context has been redefined as the capacity to participate in the processes of locating, creating, filtering, and/or reusing and remixing audio-visual and written material and web-design so as to be able to engage meaningfully, and if needed critically, with digital contents, whilst protecting oneself against unwanted exposure or offensive behavior. According to the white paper *Confronting the Challenges of Participatory Culture* (Jenkins, Clinton, Purushotma, Robison & Weigel, 2009), this set of skills can be described as *new media literacies*, or as scholars such as Andrew Burn (2009) and Dustin Summey (2013) propose, *digital literacies*, or simply *new literacies* (Lankshear & Knobel, 2011). Further advancing this scholarship with regard to newer and more complex interfaces and designs, Guy Merchant, Julia Gillen, Jackie Marsh, and Julia Davies (2012) have introduced the term *virtual literacies* while Cathy Burnett, Guy Merchant, Julia Davies and Jennifer Rowsell (2014) have explored the global dimension and responsibilities of literacy studies in the 21st century.

While the first wave of scholarship, referred to above, mostly explored *online* youth practices, a second wave of research argues that the boundaries between life *online* and life *offline* are increasingly blurred, to an extent that the original meanings of the words *online* and *offline* seem to be diffused, both in theory and in practice. Luciano Floridi (2014), for instance, has recently introduced the term *onlife* to account for the contemporary ways of living in which humans are endlessly surrounded by smart, responsive objects when they play, shop, learn, entertain themselves, and conduct relationships or even wars. At the same time, it seems that media scholars are moving from a focus on "new" media to exploring how "older" and "newer" media worlds may be intertwined in terms of theory as well as in terms of methodology (Debray, 2000; Jenkins, 2006 Leander, 2008; Zielinski, 2006).

Even if this scholarship has a "global" appeal, it is mostly produced in the so-called "global North" – with only a few exceptions such as the recent edited volume by Anastacia Kurylo and Tatyana Dumova (2016), exploring the similarities, distinctions, and specific characteristics of social media networks in diverse settings including not only the US and the UK but also Spain, Turkey, and China. *Global Youth in Digital Trajectories* aims to address this gap in the literature; it not only presents empirical case studies from areas as diverse as the Netherlands, Germany, Brazil, Greece, Russia, and India but also engages in dialogue with relevant local theories and research traditions that are not often referred to in Anglo-Saxon media studies such as cultural-historical theory (Kontopodis, Wulf & Fichtner,

2011; Vygotsky, 1934/1987), critical collaborative research (Fidalgo & Shimoura, 2007; Liberali-Coehlo, Damianovic, Guimares Ninin, Mateus & Guerra, 2016), mediology (Debray, 2000), and historical anthropology (Wulf, 2013).

The research presented in this volume was enabled by a Marie Curie grant for International Research Staff Exchange (IRSES) within the 7th European Community Framework Program (PIRSES-GA-2012-318909), which supported the partnership between a three-member European consortium (University of Crete, Free University Berlin, and University College London), the Moscow State University of Psychology and Education, the Jawaharlal Nehru University, and the Pontifical Catholic University of São Paulo. Resulting from long-term visiting scholarships, research stays, and repeated meetings among researchers from three continents, *Global Youth in Digital Trajectories* pursues therefore an adventurous research path: the volume explores emotions, imaginary productions, personal sense-making processes, and cross-media dialogues by youth in today's interactive, sensuous, smart, non-linear, multimodal, multimedia arrangements across diverse cultural settings and geographical areas while cutting across a wide range of case studies, disciplines, and approaches. It contributes to the relevant research in five respects as follows:

First of all, we demonstrate, with the help of several case studies on the experiences of youth on three continents, that the differentiation between an *offline* world and an *online* world is inapplicable to the lives of most young people. *Being online* is a fundamental dimension of the everyday lives of youths – particularly of those in urban settings. The special character of the *online* world, that some research accentuates, no longer correlates with the experience of youths today. Doing things *online* and *offline* is merely a matter of swiftly switching between the different modalities of the everyday life. Youth communities in this context are not only *virtual communities* in the widespread sense of virtual, i.e., *made to appear to exist by software* (cf. Rheingold, 2000) but as integral parts of the youth's living worlds (in German "Lebenswelt"). Youths rely on virtual communication while dealing with all possible everyday offline *and* online tasks. This communication enables them to share feelings and thoughts, discuss questions and problems, and arrange meetings with each other – often developing new forms of social interaction (see Chapter 1). The interconnections between the *online* and the *offline* are part of the living worlds of youths and offer them speedy and straightforward communication. For many youths, the return to a world without nonstop communication is barely imaginable and indeed undesirable. Most youths want to be constantly reachable, in the same way that they want other youths to be immediately reachable. One's own availability and the availability of others as well as the requisite flexibility are sought-after qualities. Young people are, as some express it, constantly ready – so to say "pready" – for communication.

Secondly, our book examines which new anthropological and cultural-historical conditions and changes arise in connection with the widespread presence of digital media in the lives of the *networked teens* (cf. Beyes, Schipper & Leeker, 2016; boyd, 2014). These contemporary changes are as fundamental as the development of script in ancient times, which led to far-reaching transformations in the human mental structure and society. In Plato's dialogues, where philosophizing still takes place in terms of oral speech, the transition from the spoken word to the written text is indicated. The emergence of script resulted in new forms of rational and argumentative speech (Gebauer & Wulf, 1995; Havelock, 1985; Ong, 2002). In this context, repetition, which was still of central importance to the aesthetic layout of the Homeric epics, became rather superfluous for the purpose of clearly unfolding of a thread of thoughts. Of similarly incisive effect is the discovery and dispersion of the press two thousand years later (Giesecke, 1998). In our multicultural study, we carve out a row of similarly drastic changes that can be reconstructed from the statements of the young people and our observations, which provide hints as to how far reaching these changes are.

The virtual communication among young people is *multimodal* as Carey Jewitt, Jeff Bezemer and Kay O'Halloran (2016) have also recently argued. Our case studies demonstrate through the analysis of interviews, focus-group discussions, and digital productions by young people as well as by means of participant observation, that images, script, sound, and spoken language assume new ties nowadays that were hitherto impossible. These have repercussions on the visual, written, and oral youth culture. Images – including the whole spectrum from *selfies* to *screenshots* – are becoming a fundamental means of communication between young people. Ever more frequently, youths resort to images as to communicate their feelings, hopes, fears, dreams, fantasies, and concerns (see Chapter 2). They become *digital makers*, that is to say youths who are productive in the sense of locating, filtering, and/or editing pictures, and who at the same time use their own productions thereby undermining the difference between *producer* and *consumer* (Potter, 2012). By means of pictures, iconic information that can only partly be expressed through language is communicated while certain sensibilities and competences are developed among youths – and others may be vanished as Norval Baitello warns in the last section of the volume. As pictures become part of the youth imaginary, traditional differences between *subject* and *object* shift, or even cease to exist (see Chapters 1 and 3).

Thirdly, our research reveals not only that digital technologies have become a steadfast part of the lives of youths, but also that herein lies significant potential for their upbringing and education. Without adopting too quickly an either cyberutopian or cyber-critical position, in two case studies, our research demonstrates the pedagogic potential of digital media to achieve inclusive and quality education for all (Chapters 4 and 8; cf. also United Nations, 2015). The youths of our research participate with their *extended bodies* in virtual, interactive, sensuous, smart, multimodal arrangements. With the help of digital operations, they attain new forms of expression and modes of belonging and make positive social experiences, thus redefining what may be understood as "inclusion/exclusion", "disability", or "learning difficulties". They are thereby recognized and valued. As the case studies reveal, digital technologies facilitate dealing with new learning tools, which in turn fosters not only the development of new skills but also the development of new psychological functions (Vygotsky, 1934/1987). Employed in combination with other forms and means of education, digital technologies – as our school study in Brazil (Chapter 8) demonstrates – fascinate many students. They can support processes of decentralization of pedagogic action and creativity overcoming the restraints of *banking education* (Freire, 1970). They can also contribute to the development of various forms of literacy and therefore to human development – especially when the established ways of formal teaching and learning are extended to embrace globally emerging mobile, smart and sensuous technologies, online gaming cultures, and multimodal designs (cf. Beavis & O'Mara, 2016; Bezemer & Kress, 2015; Marsh, 2015).

Fourthly, *Global Youth in Digital Trajectories* displays the great political potential of digital culture. Digital culture enables the formation and negotiation of political views, insights, knowledge, and beliefs in emerging virtual public spaces. By analyzing the digital productions and virtual communication of young people, we obtain for example insights into contexts and situations of social crises, such as in Greece, where youth's hopes for the future have been crushed, and a young *precariat* is emerging (Chapter 5). Here youths try, through the production of digital videos and films, to bring to expression the political, economic, social, and emotional turmoil they live in. In further case studies, we demonstrate how views and opinions circulate between YouTube, Facebook, and traditional media such as TV or newspapers with regard to corruption, gender-related violence, and beauty ideals (Chapters 6 and 7). Our research explores how virtual communication processes, multimodal representations, and interpretations of the political situation develop and are mutually intensified in the virtual public sphere. A bottom-up process of political participation emerges, through which the views of many youths are expressed, sometimes in agreement with and other times in opposition to mainstream media expanding the existing forms of political participation (cf. Cammaerts, Bruter, Banaji, Harrison & Anstead, 2015). By way of commentaries disseminated via virtual networks, youth engagement with micro- and macro-political problems is strengthened while certain emotions are shared and intensified through mimetic practices – a process that entails risks as well as possibilities (cf. Hüppauf & Wulf, 2009).

Fifthly, our research delivers a multidimensional contribution to the debate on digital and virtual research methods (Hine, 2013; Jewitt, Domingo, Flewitt, Price & Sakr, 2017). The methods developed and presented in the edited volume are manifold and complementary. In addition to (offline) interviews and focus-group discussions, which explored the youth experience from a first-person perspective, Chapter 3 for example, introduces *technography* – a methodology that extends ethnography by documenting and interpreting the interconnectedness between players and avatars in complex socio-technical constellations. Chapters 2, 5, and 6 introduce innovative methods (multimodal analysis, sequential analysis, etc.) that explore Facebook and YouTube posts, user profiles, hits, likes, and comments and their interconnections. In turn, Chapter 7 evaluates inter-channel and cross-media differences by mapping the number and frequency of daily references to certain news items and their reception. Whilst the internet is a widespread medium that more and more young people around the globe have a share of, our volume explores by means of innovative case studies the cultural diversity and multiplicity of digital media. Thereby we learn a lot about the challenges and problems that young people face in diverse socio-cultural settings, whilst simultaneously exploring the globally hybrid and emerging forms of youth life.

Case studies and organization of chapters

In line with the above, the first chapter of our book, "Digital Identity Building: A Dialogue with Berlin Technology and Computer Science Students" by Nika Daryan and Christoph Wulf, explores the most recent effects of technological transformation on youth identity formation. Envisaging present-day technology and computer science students as tomorrow's average youth, the authors, by way of dialogue with such students, explore how youth identity formation develops on the basis of constant Wi-Fi access. The analysis reveals that young people can have no participation in their peer group, college settings, and other everyday life undertakings without Wi-Fi access. Digital media are interwoven with daily life, and in this sense, all identity is "digital identity", i.e., there is no separate *online* identity developed in addition to an *offline* one. Consequently, there is a shift with regard to the efficiency of traditional pedagogical institutions, and a need to rethink pedagogical theory and practice.

A central question that poses itself in this frame is what counts as text – not as seen from the perspectives of existing theories or school curricula, but as seen from the perspectives of the young. The second chapter of the volume, "Young People, Facebook, and Pedagogy: Recognizing Contemporary Forms of Multimodal Text Making" by Jeff Bezemer and Gunther Kress, explores how young people draw on several modes of representation in their communication. In many of their texts, writing is not the central medium for making meaning. Departing from a case study of a 12-year-old boy's text making on Facebook in the Netherlands, the authors propose a social semiotic framework to account for the recent changes in text making and outline what a "pedagogy of multimodal text making" could be.

How various modes of representation merge into each other is also explored in the third chapter of the volume: "Playing Sports with Nintendo Wii in Berlin: Technography, Interactivity, and Imagination" by Nino Ferrin and Michalis Kontopodis. The authors explore media sporting activities with the game console "Nintendo Wii", in which games such as boxing or bowling are handled by haptic corporal movements. The links between the *off-screen* body movements and the image of the body *on-screen* are explored through a detailed technography. The analysis of the empirical research examples opens into a broader discussion about the notions of self-image and imagination with regard to sensuous media.

Turning the reader's attention to another media practice, that of digital filmmaking, the fourth chapter of the volume, "Digital Filmmaking as a Means for the Development of Reflection: A Case Study of a Disabled University Student in Moscow" by Olga Rubtsova and Natalya Ulanova, explores the micro-dynamics of the development of reflection in the case of a young student with cerebral palsy. The research team accompanies the student during the last semester of his studies, which is devoted to shooting a short digital movie as a graduation project.

Following a cultural-historical approach, the chapter investigates how digital filmmaking was turned into a meaningful activity of creating new cultural signs and meanings for this student, on-screen as well as off-screen. It also explores how this activity unfolded as an essential part of a broader attempt to cope with his emotionally intense and challenging everyday life.

In turn, Manolis Dafermos, Sofia Triliva, and Christos Varvantakis in the fifth chapter of the volume, "Youth Tubing the Greek Crisis: A Cultural-Historical Perspective", shed light on the processes and the outcomes of psychological development in the case of young people producing and circulating YouTube films and relevant posts about the current financial and socio-political crisis taking place in Greece. The authors introduce an innovative method for the analysis of the videos, user profiles, hits, likes and dislikes, and their related descriptions and commentaries. They contextualize this within the broader everyday life settings of the youngsters. The analysis explores how producing and circulating YouTube films offers the young people the means to re-appropriate and combine cultural signs and meanings from a wide range of virtual symbolic resources, and in doing so deal with the crisis. The young people express their fears and hopes, whilst intervening and participating in society at a moment when social integration is breaking down.

The sixth chapter, "Dove YouTube Campaign 'The Pressure On Young Girls and Women to Fit an Artificial Body Ideal': A Sequential Analysis" by Alexios Brailas, Giorgos Alexias, and Konstantinos Koskinas, explores the discussion on a YouTube video by Dove. By counting two-comment sequences, reporting frequencies, and computing probabilities for all coded comments, meaningful patterns of user interaction were recognized. The findings indicate that insulting comments were more likely to occur following a disagreement regarding the prevailing opinion. The chapter concludes with a broader discussion on the significance and limitations of sequential analysis in exploring virtual discussion spaces.

Virtual discussion platforms, online forums, and micro-blogging apps provide young people with enriched possibilities for decentralized and distributed production and peer-to-peer circulation of advanced audio-visual designs. However, as becomes evident in the chapters above, this production is linked to and entails images, ideas, and symbols circulated through older audio-visual media such as TV channels or mainstream cinema. In this frame, the following chapter, "Youth, Facebook, and Mediated Protest in India: A Cross-Media Analysis" by Supriya Chotani, focuses on two recent protest campaigns, namely the India Against Corruption campaign (2011) and the Anti Rape protests (2012). The author explores whether the television news media broadcasting had an influence on which issues of protest became dominant on Facebook. The data indeed reveals that the social movements and campaigns given the most coverage by the television news media had a correspondingly high proportion of social media response. On the basis of this data, the author discusses the emergent mediation between older and newer media and its implications with regard to the political engagement of young people in India.

While certain interfaces, web-designs, and media privilege particular forms of communication, memory, and imagination but constrain others (cf. Kress, 2010;

New London Group, 1996), *Global Youth in Digital Trajectories* explores how collaborative, participatory, and sustainable futures can be imagined and implemented by creatively engaging with the interfaces and designs that the information society offers (Chau, 2010; de Block & Sefton-Green, 2004; Fuchs & Sandoval, 2014). The eighth chapter of our book, "Enhancing Multimedia Use in State Secondary Schools in São Paulo: A Critical Collaborative Perspective" by Fernanda Liberali, Maria Cecília Magalhães, Maria Cristina Meaney, Camila Santiago, Maurício Canuto, Feliciana Amaral, Bruna Cababe, and Jéssica Aline Almeida Dos Santos explores this question in dialogue with teachers and students of state/public secondary schools in Brazil's major city. Through a detailed analysis of video-recorded participatory workshops with teachers and pupils, the authors oppose top-down and curricula-based approaches to employing technology in the school. They suggest that *argumentation* – which may entail opposition and clashes of ideas as well as joint decisions – is the foundation for the innovative and sustainable introduction of novel technologies in educational settings, especially when taking under consideration the educational and broader socioeconomic discrepancies of contemporary Brazil (Kontopodis, Magalhães & Coracini, 2016).

The edited volume comes to an end with Norval Baitello Jun.'s "Instead of an Epilogue", a critical reflection on contemporary *iconophagy* and its implications with regard to global youth and education. According to the author, iconophagy refers both to the operation of constantly "feeding" the flow of images, and to the process in which the images "feed" human lives, time, space, and bodies. Iconophagy becomes the regulating principle of the traffic between humans and images today – a vicious circle of quick consumption, superficial loss, and rapid replacement by new images. Taking critical distance from approaches that claim that pedagogical interaction is no longer needed in the global digital era, Norval Baitello argues in this context that a pedagogy, which encourages deeper engagement with the historicity of the senses, is indispensable for contemporary youth.

Even if media practices have received much attention in the last decade across a wide range of fields, their dynamic development as well as their globalized presence pose challenging questions that cannot be easily addressed through the lenses of a single theory or approach. The present volume invites the interested reader to accompany contemporary youth in their digital trajectories and virtual adventures; we hope that the broad spectrum of investigated fields in combination with the innovative theoretical and methodological frameworks introduced by renowned and engaged scholars from the UK, Germany, Greece, Brazil, Russia, and India add depth and breadth to current discussions on the involvement of digital technologies in youth everyday life practices, socialization, and education.

References

Andreotti, V. (2011). *Actionable postcolonial theory in education*. New York: Palgrave Macmillan.
Appadurai, A. (1996). *Modernity at large: Cultural dimensions of globalization*. Minneapolis and London: University of Minnesota Press.

Apperley, T. (2010). *Gaming rhythms: Play and counterplay from the situated to the global*. Amsterdam: Institute of Network Cultures.
Beavis, C., & O'Mara, J. (2016). Shifting practices and frames: Literacy, learning and computer games. In G. Johnson & N. Dempster (Eds.), *Leadership in diverse learning contexts* (pp. 239–253). Cham: Springer.
Beyes, T., Schipper, I., & Leeker, M. (Eds.). (2016). *Performing the digital: Performance studies and performances in digital cultures*. Bielefeld: Transcript.
Bezemer, J., & Kress, G. (2015). *Multimodality, learning and communication: A social semiotic frame*. London and New York: Routledge.
Boellstorff, T. (2008). *Coming of age in Second Life: An anthropologist explores the virtually human*. Princeton: Princeton University Press.
boyd, d. (2014). *It's complicated: The social lives of networked teens*. New Haven: Yale University Press.
Brown, A. J., & Davis, N. E. (Eds.). (2004). Digital technology, communities and education (World yearbook of education 2004). London: Routledge Falmer.
Buckingham, D., & Tingstad, V. (Eds.). (2010). *Childhood and consumer culture*. New York: Palgrave Macmillan.
Buckingham, D., & Willett, R. (Eds.). (2006). *Digital generations: Children, young people and new media*. London: Lawrence Erlbaum.
Burn, A. (2009). *Making new media: Creative production and digital literacies*. New York: Peter Lang.
Burn, A., & Richards, C. O. (Eds.). (2014). *Children's games in the new media age: Childlore, media and the playground*. Burlington: Ashgate.
Burnett, C.; Merchant, G.; Davies, J. & Rowsell, J. (Eds.). (2014). *New Literacies around the Globe: Policy and Pedagogy*. London: Routledge.
Cammaerts, B., Bruter, M., Banaji, S., Harrison, S., & Anstead, N. (2015). Participation of youth in and through media: Traditional and new media. In B. Cammaerts, M. Bruter, S. Banaji, S. Harrison, & N. Anstead (Eds.), *Youth participation in democratic life: Stories of hope and disillusion* (pp. 133–166). Basingstoke and New York: Palgrave MacMillan.
Chau, C. (2010). YouTube as a participatory culture. *New Directions for Youth Development*, 2010(128), 65–74.
Davies, C., Coleman, J., & Livingstone, S. (Eds.). (2014). *Digital technologies in the lives of young people*. London and New York: Routledge/Taylor & Francis.
de Block, L., & Buckingham, D. (2007). *Global children, global media: Migration, media and childhood*. Basingstoke and New York: Palgrave MacMillan.
de Block, L., & Sefton-Green, J. (2004). Refugee children in a virtual world: Intercultural online communication and community. In A. J. Brown & N. E. Davis (Eds.), *Digital technology, communities and education (World yearbook of education 2004)* (pp. 196–210). London: Routledge Falmer.
de Haan, J., & Pijpers, R. (Eds.). (2010). *Contact! Kinderen en nieuwe media*. Houten: Bohn Stafleu van Loghum.
Debray, R. (2000). *Introduction à la médiologie*. Paris: Presses Universitaires de France.
Fidalgo, S. S., & Shimoura, d. S. A. (Eds.). (2007). *Pesquisa crítica de colaboração: Um percurso na formação docente*. São Paulo: Ductor.
Floridi, L. (2014). *The fourth revolution: How the infosphere is reshaping human reality*. Oxford: Oxford University Press.
Freire, P. (1970). *Pedagogy of the oppressed*. New York: Herder and Herder.
Fuchs, C., & Sandoval, M. (Eds.). (2014). *Critique, social media & the information society*. London and New York: Routledge.

Gardner, H., & Davis, K. (2013). *The App generation: How today's youth navigate identity, intimacy, and imagination in a digital world.* New Haven: Yale University Press.

Gebauer, G., & Wulf, C. (1995). *Mimesis: Art, culture, society.* Berkeley: University of California Press.

Giesecke, M. (1998). *Der Buchdruck in der frühen Neuzeit.* Frankfurt am Main: Suhrkamp.

Havelock, D. A. (1985). *The muse learns to write: Reflections on orality and literacy from antiquity to the presence.* New Haven and London: Yale University Press.

Helsper, E. J., & Eynon, R. (2010). Digital natives: Where is the evidence? *British Educational Research Journal, 36*(3), 503–520.

Hine, C. (Ed.). (2013). *Virtual research methods.* London: Sage.

Hüppauf, B., & Wulf, C. (Eds.). (2009). *Dynamics and performativity of imagination: The image between the visible and the invisible.* New York: Routledge.

Jenkins, H. (2006). *Convergence culture: Where old and new media collide.* New York: New York University Press.

Jenkins, H., Clinton, K., Purushotma, R., Robison, A. J., & Weigel, M. (2009). *Confronting the challenges of participatory culture: Media education for the 21st century.* Chicago: MacArthur Foundation.

Jewitt, C., Bezemer, J., & O'Halloran, K. (2016). *Introducing multimodality.* London and New York: Routledge.

Jewitt, C., Domingo, M., Flewitt, R., Price, S., & Sakr, M. (Eds.). (2017). *Digital research methods: A multimodal approach.* London and New York: Routledge.

Kontopodis, M. (2012). *Neoliberalism, pedagogy and human development: Exploring time, mediation and collectivity in contemporary schools.* London and New York: Routledge/Taylor & Francis.

Kontopodis, M., Magalhães, M. C., & Coracini, M. J. (Eds.). (2016). *Facing poverty and marginalization: 50 years of critical research in Brazil.* Bern, Oxford and New York: Peter Lang.

Kontopodis, M., Wulf, C., & Fichtner, B. (Eds.). (2011). *Children, development and education: Cultural, historical, anthropological perspectives.* Dordrecht, London, New Delhi and New York: Springer.

Kress, G. (2010). *Multimodality: A social semiotic approach to contemporary communication.* London and New York: Routledge.

Kurylo, A., & Dumova, T. (Eds.). (2016). *Social networking: Redefining communication in the digital age.* London: Rowan & Littlefield.

Lankshear, C., & Knobel, M. (2011). *New literacies: Everyday practices and social learning.* Berkshire: Open University Press.

Leander, K. (2008). Toward a connective ethnography of online/offline literacy networks. In J. Coiro, M. Knobel, C. Lankshear, & D. Leu (Eds.), *Handbook of research on new literacies* (pp. 33–65). London and New York: Routledge.

Liberali-Coehlo, F., Damianovic, C. M., Guimares Ninin, M. O., Mateus, E., & Guerra, M. (Eds.). (2016). *Argumentacao em contexto escolar: Relatos de pesquisa.* São Paolo: Pontes.

Livingstone, S. (2010). Taking risky opportunities in youthful content creation: Teenagers' use of social networking sites for intimacy, privacy and self-expression. *New Media & Society, 10*(3), 393–411.

Marsh, J. (2015). *Making literacy real: Theories and practices for learning and teaching* (second revisited edition). London: Sage.

McFarlane, C. (2009). Translocal assemblages: Space, power and social movements. *Geoforum, 40*(4), 561–567.

Merchant, G., Gillen, J., Marsh, J., & Davies, J. (Eds.). (2012). *Virtual literacies: Interactive spaces for children and young people*. London and New York: Routledge.

New London Group. (1996). A pedagogy of multiliteracies: Designing social futures. *Harvard Educational Review*, 66(1), 60–92.

Nilan, P., & Feixa, C. (Eds.). (2006). *Global youth? Hybrid identities, plural worlds*. London and New York: Routledge.

Ong, W. J. (2002). *Orality and literacy: The technologizing of the world*. London and New York: Routledge.

Pachler, N., Bachmair, B., Cook, J., & Kress, G. R. (2010). *Mobile learning: Structures, agency, practices*. New York: Springer.

Potter, J. (2012). *Digital media and learner identity: The new curatorship*. New York: Palgrave MacMillan.

Prensky, M. (2001a). Digital natives, digital immigrants: Part 1. *On the Horizon*, 9(5), 1–6.

Prensky, M. (2001b). Digital natives, digital immigrants: Part 2. *On the Horizon*, 9(6), 1–6.

Renninger, A., & Shumar, W. (Eds.). (2002). *Building virtual communities: Learning and change in cyberspace*. Cambridge: Cambridge University Press.

Rheingold, H. (2000). *The virtual community: Homesteading on the electronic frontier*. Cambridge: MIT Press.

Selwyn, N. (2013). *Education in a digital world: Global perspectives on technology and education*. London: Routledge.

Subrahmanyam, K., & Šmahel, D. (Eds.). (2011). *Digital youth: The role of media in development*. Dordrecht: Springer.

Summey, D. C. (2013). *Developing digital literacies: A framework for professional learning*. London: Sage.

Tapscott, D. (2009). *Grown up digital: How the Net generation is changing your world*. New York and London: McGraw-Hill.

United Nations. (2015). *Sustainable development goals*. New York: United Nations.

Vygotsky, L. S. (1934/1987). Thinking and speech (N. Minick, Trans.). In R. Rieber (Ed.), *The collected works of Vygotsky, Vol. 1 Problems of general psychology* (pp. 39–288). New York and London: Plenum Press.

Walkerdine, V. (2007). *Children, gender, video games: Towards a relational approach to multimedia*. London: Palgrave MacMillan.

Wulf, C. (2013). *Anthropology: A continental perspective*. Chicago: University of Chicago Press.

Zielinski, S. (2006). *Deep time of the media: Toward an archaeology of hearing and seeing by technical means*. Cambridge: MIT Press.

1 Digital identity building

A dialogue with Berlin technology and computer science students

Nika Daryan and Christoph Wulf

Humans, things, and hyperspherical practice

The relationship between the "non-human" and the "human" has recently attracted much research interest (cf. Latour, 2008; cf. also Ferrin & Kontopodis, 2017). The traditional dualism between "subject" and "object" has been questioned, the "subjectivity" and the "agency" of "objects" has been propagated, and the "object-character" of "subjects" has been explored. The German language distinguishes different concepts in this regard: *Objekt, Gegenstand, Ding, and Sache* are basic terms to describe the "non-human" within the world perceived by "humans." According to classic media-anthropological approaches, "objects" are designated as "extensions" (McLuhan, 1965) or as "prosthetics" (Leroi-Gourhan, 1984) of historically and culturally shaped human bodies. Media studies and aesthetic philosophy have examined the subject-formation power of objects, i.e., their ability to evoke memories, affect imagination, and shape human perception. Walter Benjamin, for example, describes the appropriation of the world as a mimetic correspondence between the world of objects and the human body (cf. Gebauer & Wulf, 1995; Wulf, 2013a, 2013b, 2014).

The subject-object relationship is indeed a highly complex multidimensional phenomenon. Régis Debray (2003) speaks of the *double body of a medium*, thereby placing the relationship between subject and object at the center of attention. Debray's concept of *mediasphere* is a mediological concept (Debray, 2003, 2007) that refers to the general living conditions of humans, whose existence intrinsically depends on a series of technological and institutional configurations. Four subtypes of the *media sphere* can be distinguished here: the *logosphere* (based on oral culture), the *graphosphere* (based on book culture), the *videosphere* (based on TV culture), and the ever-expanding *hypersphere* (based on digital culture). Nowadays one can observe a simultaneous presence of all these forms.

Many people acquire *hyperspherical* forms of practice during their childhood and youth, and internet-based digital technologies become completely incorporated into their everyday lives. Hyperspherical practices do not arise from the use of television. They are shaped by new forms of digital collectivity, such as virtual communities.[1] The *digital natives*[2] of these virtual communities are not mere spectators or participants in a digital community, they are *users* surfing through the digital sphere (Reckwitz, 2006; Westphal & Jörissen, 2013). During their school and university education many young people acquire advanced technological knowledge. Media are conceived as an intrinsic part of almost every learning process, and media competence is seen as a key qualification important for the future of the so-called *entrepreneurial self* (Bröckling, 2007). With the advent of digital technologies such as Facebook and Instagram, further new forms of learning manifest themselves. Numerous studies on today's living conditions depict profound changes in the social conditions present in today's educational institutions and educational practices, as referred to in the introduction to this book (Kontopodis, Varvantakis, and Wulf, 2017).

The concept of *digital media competence* has been proposed in this context, which understands the human as a subject making use of digital technologies as manageable objects. Taking critical distance from the subject-object dualism implied in popular definitions of *digital media competence*, in the following we explore the effects the technological transformations of recent decades have had on emergent learning cultures (cf. Wulf et al., 2008; Wulf & Zirfas, 2014) through focus-group discussions with young technology and computer science students. Taking the analysis of this data as a point of departure, the paper discusses the above-mentioned theoretical positions and revisits the concept of media competence.

Methodology: focus-group discussions with young experts

Two groups of 20 to 24-year-old *digital natives* were selected and invited to participate in focus-group discussions at the Free University Berlin in December 2013. One group (A) was composed of four students of a technical post-secondary school; the other group (B) consisted of four students enrolled in a university computer science program. All participants lived in Berlin, Germany. The majority of the participants were male. For this particular study, gender was not a particular focus, since it has been widely explored in other digital media research (cf. Walkerdine, 2007).

The focus-group discussions were initiated with the following statement from the participant researchers: "We are interested in the attitudes young people have towards digital media and we would like to know which roles these media play in your lives" (in German). Each focus-group discussion lasted about one hour. The focus-group discussions were video-recorded and transcribed in terms of verbal and non-verbal expressions (in German). The young students were seen as "experts" in the digital field, and their talk was analyzed following general principles of qualitative content analysis (Gläser & Laudel, 2004). Selected extracts were translated from German to English and cross-checked by a native speaker of both languages for the purposes of the presentation below. In addition, back-up data from participant observation were taken under consideration for purposes of analysis and interpretation. Furthermore, a year after the first collection of data we talked again with some of the participants. At that time, no significant change had taken place regarding the students' hyperspherical practices.

Digital identity formation

Interrelating humans with personal computers, laptops, tablets, and smartphones leads to novel forms of media competence; these in turn shape young people's identity formation. The interviewed young people seem to need to maintain permanent access to the digital world in their everyday lives. The idea that there is a "private" or "professional" life outside the media does not do justice to the existential dependence of the young people on media, and to the central roles that PCs, laptops, tablets, and smartphones play in their lives. Young people can have no participation in today's world without internet-based digital technologies. These technologies create worlds of existential importance for the young. In this sense, one could say that all identity is "digital identity," and that there is no separate online world existing *in addition to* an offline, non-digital world. Digital media are interwoven with daily life.

The following sequence from the focus-group discussion demonstrates how the young computer science students experience this situation, and how they depend on the digital world:

(B) S2: So your computer is there when you're home. It's a ritual. So you come home, turn your computer on. *I* have to say that I have that very much under control, but I know other people who say things like, "If you are at a party and the battery of your smartphone runs out, then the party is over."

The following extracts also manifest how important the access to computers is for the social life of the young people in question:

(B) S3: It is of course the case that internet is *fundamental* for us. That is to say, all homework, all information is updated and renewed daily on the internet. That is, someone who has no internet access *cannot really take part* in such an academic program.

(B) S2: So if someone would tell me he has no internet at home, I'd just ask: "How can it be that you have no internet at home?"

Statements such as "I'm constantly on" or "without internet nothing happens" and "I'm online 24 hours a day" permeated the focus-group discussions. When we accompanied some of the participants into their private realm indeed we could see that digital technologies had replaced many other object references for them. The young students' smartphones were omnipresent in almost every situation, and most bodily movements in the social space were shaped by this presence. Digital technologies seemed to constitute the center of the young people's social and educational lives. They were not a mere addition or partial extension, but *the* focus. In a few cases, this centrality could be classified as compulsive or even addictive.

Another important dimension of digital identity is related to *egocentricity* or the sense of the self (cf. Plessner, 1967):

(B) S4: We had such a hunger for this. Our generation had a hunger for it. We wanted to get on the internet. We got onto the internet. We were then like, "We want this. We – we live with this," and so on.

In these quotations the interaction with media is seen as central for the young person's sense of self and self-relation. At the same time, we can see an extension of one's own life sphere into the global. During the focus-group discussions, the students did not refer to a national identity but almost exclusively to a digital collective identity:

(B) S2: It does not depend on how old you are, but on which side you are on. And since the internet connects us all, it is also the case that you communicate in English, because it's the main language. It is just normal that one discusses one's opinions with people from all over the world, or (that you) just joke around or meet up.

The fact that national identity is no longer of primary importance to young people goes along with internet access and dealing with international/intercultural digital collectives that are independent of the nation-states.

The globalization of human living conditions seems thus to lead to a *homogeneous interobjectivity* and a *hybrid intersubjectivity* (cf. Daryan, 2012). The fusion of different media innovations in the twentieth century (audio media, visual media, text media, and their hybrid forms) leads to a *homogeneous mediality*. This is a physical practice with a screen-based flat object which, through its networking potential, contributes to reducing societal obstacles and resistance against practices of international intersubjectivity. This transformation leads to the emergence of a global society that has positive potential, but that also increases competitive pressure:

(B) S2: So we simply have competition, you know. And you are competing against the *entire* world. That is, if I make an artwork, then those who are criticizing it are (today) not just my friends or my family, but perhaps also artists from America or elsewhere. That means communication is everywhere.

At the same time, new microforms of social practice are created and new practices of recognition and appreciation are developed:

(B) S2: The phenomenon of Facebook is of course particularly interesting, because right now people are using it on their smartphones. And then it is always along these lines: "I haven't been online for five minutes, for six hours." And of course it's always like that now, if you look you can

	see who is already asleep, who is still awake – oh, I can still call them. He is still online. Or also if you are sitting (somewhere) in a lecture hall: "Where are you sitting?" and then you answer something quickly over the internet. You *constantly* have the *opportunity* to communicate something with somebody else. If I am contacted and I do not respond, then that is also somehow a sign that I do not want to call.
(B) S4:	That's just how things are, the way you are in social behavior – you do not say no. You simply don't respond.
(B) S3:	There are people who then become restless. You always see "read," a checkmark. You see that the other person got the message, clicked on it, and read it. And there are so many friends who will then be impatient if this "read" sign is there and you have not already answered after five minutes. With some people it is OK. You've read it. You wait a bit, think of an answer, and then write back a day later or so.
(B) S2:	So sometimes it's also the case that you are *unintentionally* online. For example, you head out to the bakery. And then you come back and read, "Why are you not writing me? You're online!" and things like that. But I was really not there. So when you are online, it is expected that you answer immediately. Because people think that when you're online you're at your computer. But I'm the kind of person, my computer is often on. And you are really online almost twenty-four hours a day.

Indeed, a lot of research on digital technologies and education often implies that personal computing devices are data-storage devices (Debray, 2007). Our data on hyperspherical practices reveal a reduced archiving strategy in today's young people. Being constantly online and thus circulating all kinds of up-to-date data and metadata (such as one's geo-location) constitutes a much more important principle of contemporary media practices than archiving and the search for information.

Digital role models, gestures, and mimetic learning

A series of significant changes with regard to informal educational practices are currently taking place. Mimetic references (cf. Gebauer & Wulf, 1995) are increasingly oriented toward videos and comics, i.e., digital, computer-generated role models and images. Sites like *9gag.com* or *reddit.com* are image-distribution platforms that break with every traditional image arrangement. We can see there that various types of images are presented at the same time, on the same space. Because of this simultaneity, they are not perceived as separate images. These pages and their pictures are designed to follow the principle of "scrolling." The user is supposed to scroll down in a seemingly endless manner looking at the different images. At the same time, there is no specific sense of visual order.

The following sequence from the focus-group discussion with group (B) refers to this new form of digital knowledge conveyance:

(B) S2:	There are also sites where there are just hundreds of pictures, and they are always very fast. You scroll down and then you get *tiger* photos (and

Digital identity building 17

Figure 1.1 Focus-group discussion with the students

then they have) flowers, cars, weapons, women, men. And then you have an input which is so enormous, and that causes it to change a bit, the *ideal*. You end up in an apathetic state of mind. "I've seen it all. You can't shock me anymore." You've actually seen it all before.

Images that function as role models in education are therefore subject to many variations and stimulations. In this context, the media also constitute a mimetic reference point for the configuration and meaning of gestures (cf. Wulf, 2013b).

In Figure 1.1, the participant on the right quickly moves his arm up and down and imitates the reopening of an imaginary laptop while talking about closing his laptop:

(B) S4: So what do I do? I close the computer; I briefly pace around my room, because I'm working in my head. If I have an idea, I open it up right away and continue. So closing your laptop is *really* a cool thing.

The gesture in this case adapts to the digital technologies that play such a central role in the student's daily life.

Outlook: emerging forms of media competence & educational perspectives

The concept of *competence*, which has recently gained much institutional importance and a legitimizing function, is intrinsically connected to *upbringing*, *education*, and *learning*. If the identity formation, mimetic referencing, and everything in the lives of young students are changing as described above, then the concept of *competence* must be significantly criticized and modified as well. Existing understandings of *media competence* insufficiently encompass the new qualities of hyperspherical practices.

Especially with reference to *digital natives* such as the young students who participated in our qualitative research project, a "Net logic" is emerging that cannot be described as *knowledge* relating to computer science or mathematics, but must be understood as a *practice in the digital space*, as an *interface*. The logic of the Net is not the same as computer logic. While computer logic would presume programming competence, the logic of the Net is similar to the practical knowledge of a driver, whose ability to drive a car does not require electro-technical knowledge. The driver does not need to know how the engine of his/her vehicle works, but s/he must master the traffic laws and terms of use and behave strategically in traffic. We want to identify this form of knowledge as the *practical sense* of the partially digitized human.

Even if our sample is small, it becomes quite clear that a new type of media competence is what enables a person to develop a synthetic form of identity that can endure the boundlessness of the digital space and reshape the need for self-expression. The competence to develop a digital identity is not yet accepted as a general social task. We assume, however, that this kind of media competence will soon become more important than it is today. It will become a necessary prerequisite for many institutionalized forms of life, not only the usual fields of technology and computer science. A social appreciation of cultural practices with digital technologies is necessary for this. The aim of future educational efforts should be to create conditions that allow people to form a *sustainable* digital identity for living in the hypersphere.

While envisaging the present-day technology and computer science student as tomorrow's average young person, we would like to conclude our study with the following propositions for future research and debate:

- *Digital technologies have created new ways of accessing the world.* There is a constitutive relationship between practice and digital technologies. Digital technologies are not just additional media for work and communication. They are the starting points from where young people relate to the world; they constitute the centers of their everyday practices through their professional and private lives. Traditional differentiations between public and private spheres do not have the same effects on *digital natives* as they had on "traditional" young people and the development of their identities. For *digital natives*, their home is not just a private place, it is also a place where internet and smart-phone-based public actions take place. This changes the character of privacy.
- *A homogeneous mediality is spreading.* We are facing a previously unimagined homogenization of learning processes, especially with regard to secondary and post-secondary education. Audio-visual media are at the center of learning. Written words, for example, are increasingly consumed more as pictures and less as texts. Although the participants in the study only refer to their own dependency on digital technologies, it is obvious that today nobody

can study in post-secondary or higher education without internet access and the necessary devices; tools such as pen and paper are no longer sufficient. Most BA and MA programs presume students' access to digital infrastructure and rather advanced digital technologies. To do the necessary coursework, personal computers are needed. Much of the communication with students takes place via email and messenger systems.

- *Through the use of digital technologies, social relationships take place in digital spaces.* One's relationship to the Other changes, because the perception of the Other is shaped within the digital space of the digital technologies. A transformation of one's relationship with the Other and thus the emergence of new forms of intersubjective relations are the result. Educational research has the task to create new categories and new categorical instruments in this regard. This is necessary in order for a coherent institutional frame to be provided, which in turn can facilitate the understanding of the new role of digital media in the development of educational and social relationships.
- *How young people relate to their bodies is increasingly configured in relation to digital technologies.* Basic elements of identity formation are determined by digital technologies. Digital technologies are central to the identity formation of individuals and to the processes of enculturation and appropriation. These processes increasingly take place through digital technologies, that is, in a hybrid way. Based on McLuhans's mediological considerations (1965), digital technologies should be understood as an extension of the human body. This means that digital technologies are experienced as part of the body and that their absence produces an incomplete self-awareness. This absence is experienced as a form of physical disability. Educational research should take into account this so-to-speak "pathological" condition of young people.
- *The transformation of role models* upends conventional pedagogical and educational concepts (Wulf, 2014). New digital role models have emerged; their meaning is difficult to interpret because they are very different from traditional role models; mimetic reference points are now discovered in new forms of representation. Hyperspherical image practices are no longer subject to the traditional institutional control of images. In contrast to the old institutional practice of an iconic dealing with images or the legal handling of images, today's image practice is *indexical*. This means that a recipient consumes images detached from traditional symbolic contexts. Iconological, symbolic, and indexical ways of dealing with images mix and overlap, while the influence of the image is still not given adequate consideration in education.
- *The fusion of digital and non-digital worlds leads to new digital forms of human life.* This has far-reaching consequences for social relations. In the 20th century, many efforts were made to understand the internal logic and fundamental effects of new technologies, thereby emphasizing the digitality of culture and society (Faßler, 2002). Through digital media practices, not only the speed of information dissemination, but also a transformation of the relationship of people to the world is taking place. These transformations can

be assessed as educational processes that contribute to the development of new forms of subjectivity, as well as to enormous psychosomatic pressure for being continuously updated.

- *Young people's practical sense is increasingly based on hyperspherical practices.* Digital natives orient themselves less and less towards the objectives and incentives of traditional institutions. Hyperspherical forms of practice are detached from these institutions. We refer to this as the *practical sense of hyperspherical habitus.* Digital technologies release people from a particular form of standstill. Every form of media can be used almost anywhere. Symbolically laden places like the phonebooth, the workplace, and the armchair lose their structuring effect. In accordance with the practical sense of hyperspherical habitus, any place can become a "workplace" or an "armchair."

It is evident that the above-described changes have strong implications for education not only with regard to Berlin technology and computer science students, but for most young people and future generations around the globe. The change of perspective regarding the young people's relationships to one's self, to the Other, and to things represents a significant change in the processes of young people's identity formation and in the consequent employment of the term "media competence." Goals and values previously mediated in offline spaces and times through social practices are no longer handed down to the same extent as before; however, the new digital technologies open space for practices and processes we cannot yet thoroughly understand and evaluate.

Notes

1 For a concise introduction to the internal logic of digital collectivity, see Jörissen (2007).
2 *Digital natives* refer to people who were born into a digitalized world. Marc Prensky (2001), who conceived the term, includes everyone born in highly industrialized countries in 1980 or later; cf. also Kontopodis, Varvantakis and Wulf 2017
3 Here the associated principle of the image is "Forever Alone No More!"; see http://9gag.com or also http://www.reddit.com/. For an explanation of the comics, see http://knowyourmeme.com/memes/rage-comics.

References

Bröckling, U. (2007). *Das unternehmerische Selbst: Soziologie einer Subjektivierungsform.* Frankfurt am Main: Suhrkamp.
Daryan, N. (2012). Mediologische Grundlagen von Bildung (PhD Dissertation). Berlin: Free University Berlin.
Debray, R. (2003). *Einführung in die Mediologie.* Berne: Haupt.
Debray, R. (2007). *Jenseits der Bilder. Eine Geschichte der Bildbetrachtung im Abendland.* Berlin: Avinus-Verlag.
Faßler, M. (2002). *Bildlichkeit: Navigationen durch das Repertoire der Sichtbarkeit.* Wien-Köln-Weimar: Böhlau Verlag.

Ferrin, N., & Kontopodis, M. (2017). Playing sports with Nintendo Wii in Berlin: Technography, interactivity, and imagination. In M. Kontopodis, C. Varvantakis, & C. Wulf (Eds.), *Global youth in digital trajectories*. London: Routledge.

Gebauer, G., & Wulf, C. (1995). *Mimesis: Art, culture, society*. Berkeley: University of California Press.

Gläser, J., & Laudel, G. (2004). *Experteninterviews und qualitative Inhaltsanalyse als Instrumente rekonstruierender Untersuchungen*. Wiesbaden: Verlag für Sozialwissenschaften.

Jörissen, B. (2007). Informelle Lernkulturen in online-communities: Mediale Rahmungen und rituelle Gestaltungweisen. In C. Wulf, B. Althans, G. Blaschke, N. Ferrin, M. Göhlich, B. Jörissen, R. Mattig, I. Nentwig-Gesemann, S. Schinkel, A. Tervooren, & M. Wagner-Willi (Eds.), *Lernkulturen im Umbruch: Rituelle Praktiken in Schule, Medien, Familie und Jugend* (pp. 184–219). Wiesbaden: VS-Verlag.

Kontopodis, M., Varvantakis, C., & Wulf, C. (2017). Exploring global youth in digital trajectories. In M. Kontopodis, C. Varvantakis, & C. Wulf (Eds.), *Global youth in digital trajectories*. London: Routledge.

Latour, B. (2008). *Wir sind nie modern gewesen: Versuch einer symmetrischen Anthropologie*. Frankfurt am Main: Suhrkamp.

Leroi-Gourhan, A. (1984). *Hand und Wort: Die Evolution von Technik, Sprache und Kunst*. Frankfurt am Main: Suhrkamp.

McLuhan, M. (1965). *Understanding media: The extensions of man*. New York: McGraw-Hill.

Plessner, H. (1967). Der Mensch als Lebewesen. In W. Schüßler (Ed.), *Philosophische anthropologie* (pp. 71–84). München: Alber.

Prensky, M. (2001). Digital natives, digital immigrants. *On the Horizon*, 9(5). Retrieved from http://www.marcprensky.com/writing/Prensky%20-%20Digital%20Natives,%20 Digital%20Immigrants%20-%20Part1.pdf (date of access: 07/09/2014).

Reckwitz, A. (2006). *Das hybride Subjekt: Eine Theorie der Subjektkulturen von der bürgerlichen Moderne zur Postmoderne*. Göttingen: Velbrück Wissenschaft.

Walkerdine, V. (2007). *Children, gender, video games: Towards a relational approach to multimedia*. London: Palgrave MacMillan.

Westphal, K., & Jörissen, B. (Eds.). (2013). Mediale Erfahrungen: Vom Straßenkind zum Medienkind. Raum- und Medienforschung im 21. Jahrhundert. Weinheim: Juventa/Beltz.

Wulf, C. (2013a). Die mimetische Aneignung der Welt. *Zeitschrift für Erziehungswissenschaft - Sonderheft*, 25, 15–26.

Wulf, C. (2013b). *Anthropology: A continental perspective*. Chicago: University of Chicago Press.

Wulf, C. (2014). *Bilder des Menschen: Imaginäre und performative Grundlagen der Kultur*. Bielefeld: Transcript.

Wulf, C., Althans, B., Blaschke, G., Ferrin, N., Göhlich, M., Jörissen, B., Mattig, R., Nentwig-Gesemann, I., Schinkel, S., Tervooren, A., & Wagner-Willi, M. (2008). *Lernkulturen im Umbruch: Rituelle Praktiken in Schule, Medien, Familie und Jugend*. Wiesbaden: VS-Verlag.

Wulf, C., & Zirfas, J. (Eds.). (2014). *Handbuch Pädagogische Anthropologie*. Wiesbaden: VS-Verlag.

2 Young people, Facebook, and pedagogy

Recognizing contemporary forms of multimodal text making

Jeff Bezemer and Gunther Kress

Text making in a changing social and semiotic world

The contemporary semiotic world poses sharp questions about text making. Whether we look at text made by young children (Kress, 1997; Mavers, 2011), students in secondary school (Burn, 2014; Ranker, 2012; Yandell, 2013) and in higher education (Archer, 2010), or YouTube users (Adami, 2014), what becomes visible is that text makers draw on several modes of representation, and in many texts writing is not the central means for making meaning. People, including young people, have always drawn on a range of different 'modes' – writing and image foremost among them – yet a combination of social change and new technologies have given rise to the possibilities for an increase in the use of more and other modes than these, in new 'ensembles' of modes, and with differently distributed functions. Hence text making is no longer organised around separate modes; the question is no longer whether to, say, 'write' or to present something via image, but what to use writing for and what to use image for, where to place written components and images, and how to articulate the connections between them.

In this chapter we aim to begin to develop theoretical and methodological tools to account for these changes in text making. While changes in and contemporary usage of writing in digital environments have attracted significant attention from sociolinguists with an interest in new media (see Androutsopoulos [2011] for an overview), we propose to develop an encompassing framework for understanding how (young) people use a range of modes of representation – writing, typography, image, moving image, speech, colour, etc. – to make text. Instead of studying changes in the use of each of these in isolation, or studying (changes in) some modes and not others, we aim to develop an integrated account of contemporary text making. Such an account attends to the socially, culturally, and materially shaped potential of modes and multimodal ensembles.

Our framework recognizes changes in text making in relation to the technological affordances of contemporary platforms for text making, as well as current social change; more specifically, changes in power and in principles and agencies of control. These are – among others – about a shift from vertical to horizontal social structures, from hierarchical to more open, participatory relations. The shift has effects in many ways: such as the disintegration of formerly stable social frames, leading to changes in genres; or in changes of access to and notions of authorship and canonicity. This wholesale change in social relations means that participation in semiotic production now describes the characteristics of communication more accurately than, for instance, the traditional sender-message-receiver model. With former structures of power, the characterization of the relation of 'audience' to 'author' had been that of 'consumption' or 'acquisition' in the domain of 'education'. With present distributions of power, *production* and *participation* are the ruling dispositions of many of those who had previously been seen as 'audience'.

These social changes have significant effects on text making. Where previously text making rested on relatively stable notions of 'author' and 'reader', it now involves a wide and diversified range of meaning makers. Where previously routines of convention were expressed in dichotomies such as 'formal-informal', 'standard-vernacular', serving as reliable guides in composition, in the contemporary world there is a need to assess on each *occasion* of text making what the social relations with an audience are, what *platforms* and *resources* there are for making and disseminating the text, what *local norms* are operating, and how these fit with what is to be communicated and with a clear understanding of the characteristics of the audience. Smartphones and tablets are now ubiquitous, alongside platforms for producing and/or disseminating multimodal text – Facebook, WhatsApp, YouTube, Powerpoint, Movie Maker, and so forth. These platforms equip (young) people with resources for producing and disseminating multimodal texts on a much wider range of occasions than before, across different institutional and non-institutional contexts.

Divergent, contradictory, confusing views dominate debates on contemporary practices in text making. One frequently voiced concern is that as young people are using image more, their writing skills have declined, as 'evidenced', for instance, in non-standard spelling and new orthographic forms, and the absence of complete and complex sentences in, for instance, text messaging or 'chatting'. Another concern is that young people's 'creative', 'authentic', 'original' writing has declined, as 'evidenced', for instance, in frequent 'copying and pasting' (but see Mavers, 2011). All this leads some to conclude that literacy skills are under threat or declining, and that contemporary text making practice must inevitably lead to the 'loss' of a profound kind, not just for literacy (see, e.g., Baron, 2008) and text making but for all of culture and, by a further effect, is bound to have deleterious effects on economic performance, as witnessed in OECD sponsored studies such as the Programme for International Student Assessment (PISA), a triennial survey aimed at evaluating education worldwide by testing knowledge skills of 15-year-old students.

These concerns fail to consider seriously and to attempt to recognize the practices, aesthetics, ethics, and epistemologies of contemporary forms of text production. New theoretical means are needed for making sense of these to replace the 19th century models underpinning those concerns. Where up to two decades ago maybe, competence in relation to one mode, *writing*, was seen as sufficient for the task of the composition of a text, we now need to understand the semiotic potentials of all resources and platforms involved in the design and production of *multimodal* text. Where previously competence in a relatively small set of relevant genres was seen as sufficient for participating effectively in different social domains, we now need to understand how text makers respond to the specific demands and social conditions of a much wider range of different occasions for text making.

There is an urgent and pressing need to produce apt accounts of contemporary multimodal text making. First, texts are social and cultural artefacts, i.e., signs of engagement with the contemporary world, which need to be recognized and documented. Second, in order to prepare young people for participation in that world they need an apt semiotic 'toolkit'. For instance, the 'meta-language' (e.g., 'grammar') traditionally taught at school, does not account for image, moving image, and other modes of representation now central to text making. Indeed the school curriculum may need considerable rethinking (Cope & Kalantzis, 2009). Some curricula maintain strong boundaries between sets of resources typically used in combination. For instance, the 'attainment targets' for primary education in the Netherlands, which is the setting for the case study we present in this paper, mention 'layout', 'image', and 'colour' in the margin of one of six targets for writing, while some notion of multimodality is introduced under the heading of 'artistic expression' (this target translates as 'the students learn to use image, language, music, play and movement to express feelings and experiences and to communicate) (Greven & Letschert, 2006). Yet others are rethinking the curriculum from a multimodal perspective, redefining traditional boundaries between language, visual, music, and performance arts, and drawing out principles of composition across those formerly separate subject areas (Albers & Sanders, 2010). Third, a multimodal perspective opens the full range of different contexts for text making, both inside and outside school, allowing teachers to consider connections, disconnections, and gaps between these two domains.

The multimodal approach we introduce and illustrate in this paper is set within a *social semiotic* framework. We give an outline of this theoretical framework in the next section, followed by a discussion of the materials and methods we have used for this paper. Following that, we give an account of a 12-year-old boy's text making on Facebook, in two parts. In the first part, we explore the types of texts he produces and their occurrences in the course of his first year on Facebook. In the second part, we zoom in on one specific text, investigating the ways in which he uses the resources available to him to construct a multimodal text. Our aim is – among other issues – to show what might be gained from a theoretical and empirical focus on multimodal *text*, namely, the recognition of the 'semiotic resourcefulness' (Mavers, 2007) of text makers as they address an audience, using the means of representation and communication made available by a digital platform. In the closing section, we consider the pedagogic implications of such a multimodal social semiotic account.

A social semiotic approach to text making

The theoretical frame of our account of contemporary text making is social semiotics. A social semiotic approach to text places multimodality and agency in meaning *making* at the centre of attention (Hodge & Kress, 1988; Kress, 2010). It ascribes meaning to all modes of communication, including image, writing, typography, layout. It treats signs of any kind as reflecting the *interests* of the makers of these signs – here, young people. In each of the modes used, *semiotic work* – attending, engaging, selecting, transforming, integrating, ordering – is done by both makers and 'readers' (-as-remakers/transformers) of text. In one mode certain semiotic work is to be done *by* the reader (the layout of a modular text, say), in another, simultaneously present mode, certain work has been done *for* the reader by the designer (in continuous segments of writing, say). Contemporary (multimodal) text design is based on such 'division of labour', and only by looking at the entire, multimodal design can we reconstruct these complex social relations which are evident in the text.

In this perspective, *producers* are regarded as *sign-makers* as are *users-as-interpreters* of text, and, in that, both are seen as *meaning makers*. Signs are elements in which meaning and form have been brought together in a relation motivated by the interest of the sign-maker. A sign made by a text 'designer' is *re-made* ('interpreted') by a 'user'/'reader' (who may or may not represent the audience imagined by the text maker). Sign-*making* is always subject to the availability of semiotic resources and to the aptness of the resources to the meanings which the sign-maker wishes to realize. In principle, limitations of resources apply always and everywhere, even if not with the same severity: different *platforms* make available different sets of resources. Nevertheless, the design of a text is treated by us as the sign-maker's apt representation of her or his interest, given the resources available in the circumstances which prevail. This means that the signs made by the text 'makers' are never exact replicas when they are *re*-made by its 'users'. This points to a significant difference between our social semiotic theory of communication and theories which assume that 'messages' are 'encoded', 'transferred', and then 'decoded'.

The interest of the producer of the texts at issue here is rhetorical. Rhetorical interest responds to the rhetor's question "what is my preferred social relation with my imagined audience and how can I best realise it?" The producer's as well as the audience's interests are shaped by the social, cultural, economic, political, and technological environments in which signs are made; the design is the result of the interaction between all of these. At the same time, sign-makers have to be aware of the *media* of distribution for their signs. These are now usually spoken of as 'platforms', especially in the case of digital environments – and the rhetor's awareness is factored into the making of the sign.

Signs are made using the resources of *modes*. A *mode* is a socially and culturally shaped resource for making meaning. Modes can be used to represent what the world is like, how people relate in social settings, and how semiotic entities are connected. *Image, writing, layout, colour, typography, music* are examples of *modes* used in (contemporary) text. Modes each offer differing representational resources. Writing for instance, has syntactic, grammatical, and lexical as well as typographical resources such as type size, font, and letter fit. *Speech* and *writing* share certain aspects of *grammar, syntax,* and *lexis*. Beyond these, *speech* has resources specific to sound: of intonation for instance, of loudness, length, tone of voice. *Image* has resources such as pictorial detail, size, colour, spatial relation of depicted entities, placement in a framed space, shape. These different resources can be used to do different kinds of semiotic work or to do broadly similar semiotic work through the differential use of (elements of) resources. Modes, that is, have different material bases, which have been shaped, over time, by their social users, to become tools with which to 'mean'. Each mode enables sign-makers to do specific semiotic work in relation to their interests and their rhetorical intentions for designs and communication of meaning; which, in modal ensembles, best meet the rhetor's interest and sense of the needs of the actual or imagined audience. That is, by drawing on the specific affordances of each mode in the making of modal ensembles, sign-makers can achieve the complex, often contradictory demands of their own interest, of the needs of the matter to be communicated, of characteristics of the audience, and of their relation to that audience in terms of power.

Given the complex relation of modal affordance, rhetor's interest, and the variability and complexity of social environments, *design* moves into the centre of attention in the making of complex signs-as-texts. The shift, conceptually, from *composition* to *design* mirrors a social shift from competence in a specific practice conceived in terms of understanding of and adherence to convention governing the use of a mode – writing, say – to a focus on the interest and agency of the designer in the making of signs-as-texts. Design is the practice where modes, media, and platforms on the one hand, and rhetorical purposes, the designer's interests, and the characteristics of the audience on the other are brought into (some) coherence with each other. From the designer's perspective, design is the (intermediary) process of giving shape to the interests, purposes and intentions of the rhetor in relation to the semiotic resources, which are available for realizing these purposes as apt material signs, texts for the assumed characteristics of a specific audience.

Methods and materials

The examples we present in this paper are drawn from a case study of a 12-year-old Dutch boy's text making on Facebook. He and his parents have consented to the research. Our corpus of texts made by the boy, whom we call Daan, consists of all the 28 posts he produced in the first year of his Facebook life, as well as his 'profile' pages. Our methods of analysis are focused on the textual fine grain. We aim to render visible what 'stuff' and 'tools' (young) people use to conjoin meaning and form, drawing on socially and culturally shaped histories of meaning making. Through detailed analysis of *text*, as with the analysis (or 'deciphering') of other cultural artefacts, such as old inscriptions in a cave, we reconstruct the principles underpinning their composition. Thus the focus of our analytical efforts is directed towards the multimodal design of the texts produced. This is a deliberate methodological choice; following Halliday and Hasan (1976), and building on social semiotics (Kress, 2010), we engage with text as cultural artefacts, documenting

Young people, Facebook, and pedagogy 27

the means that text makers use and the choice they make in re-presenting the world, in constructing social relations with their audience, and in bringing signs together to form coherent textual entities.

In all modes we attended to principles of selection (what is selected for representation, what is left out), highlighting (what is foregrounded, what is backgrounded), and arrangement (how are semiotic entities ordered). In *writing* we attended to generic structure, information structure, lexis, and syntax, drawing on Halliday and Hasan (1976) and Hodge and Kress (1988). In image, we attended to the notions of concept and narrative, drawing on Kress and Van Leeuwen (2006). In *video*, we attended to frame, shot and angle, drawing on Burn (2014). In *layout* we attended to placement, orientation, and alignment of constituent text elements. We also explored the relations between the constituent elements of text, drawing on Barthes (1973) and Martinec and Salway (2005); the functional distribution of modes, drawing on Kress, (2010); and cross-modal cohesion, drawing on Halliday and Hasan (1976).

As we analyse texts we also consider the platforms and wider social context that shape their production. Thus we attend to the ways in which the platform – in this case, Facebook – and the resources it makes available, as well as the social conditions in which it and its users live their lives, shape the texts we analysed. In short interviews with Daan we discussed his experiences on Facebook, and mapped his connections to his Facebook Friends.

Text making on Facebook

Daan joined Facebook in January 2013, when he was 12 years old. Facebook's official age limit is 13, but this can be circumvented by entering a false date of birth. One year on, he has 33 'Friends' on Facebook: this is his 'audience' on this platform. They include 20 'peers' (13 boys, seven girls), including classmates, other friends from the neighbourhood, and his sister; three cousins, all 16+; and 10 adults, including his mother, six uncles, and one aunt, and two female adult friends of the family. Except for three of his uncles and the aunt, all 'Friends' live in the same city, the majority in the same neighbourhood, where he meets them face-to-face on a daily basis. He himself does not (yet) post frequently on Facebook – 23 posts in the first year – but he reads what his Friends post every day. Most of the time, he accesses Facebook on his iPhone 5, using a Facebook app.

After one year of being on Facebook, Daan's 'wall' shows 28 'texts'. Of those, 23 were posted by himself; one was a 'status update' of someone else who had 'tagged' him (i.e., added a link to Daan's profile in a post created by that other person). Of the 23 self-initiated posts, 15 are 'status updates', four are posts created through other platforms, four are 'links' shared. Four more texts appeared on his wall, all 'authored' by Facebook: one notification of Daan joining Facebook, and three notifications of a change of his profile picture. Table 2.1 maps the number of each type of post on a timeline.

28 *Bezemer and Kress*

Table 2.1 Number of 'posts' on Daan's wall, per type and term

	Jan–March	April–June	Jul–Sept	Oct–Dec	Total
FB notification	2		2		4
Tagged by Friend		1			1
Shared link	1	3	1		5
Via other platform		2			2
Status update		3	12	1	16
Total	3	9	15	1	28

Thus the most common type of text is the 'status update'. The status update on Facebook is

> an update feature which allows users to discuss their thoughts, whereabouts, or important information with their friends. Similar to a tweet on the social networking site Twitter, a status update is usually short and generally gives information without going into too much detail. When a status is updated, it posts on the user's personal wall, as well as in the news feeds of their friends. Statuses can be updated from a web browser, mobile site, or through text message.
>
> (whatis.techtarget.com)

Daan posted his first *status update* in June. In the following six months, his updates change in form. The first three updates, all posted in June, consist of writing only: 'cool', 'cool', and 'nice more friends'. In the second half of the year he begins to use the 'event report', reporting what he is up to, using self-made pictures and one written sentence ('on way to beach', 'Enjoying having a drink with Jaap', 'I am going to Sweet hurray').

The four *posts created through other platforms* are pictures and videos Daan made himself which are then edited automatically by the other platform to create special effects, making someone look old (AgingBooth), or making someone have a moustache (Boothstache), or in 'Action Movie', even suggesting that the person featured in the video is being shot at. All these posts created in other platforms were made in the first six months of Daan's Facebook life. Only one is accompanied by a written comment by Daan ('Yo this is my little brother'). The other pictures are of himself, with special effects but still recognizably 'Daan'.

The four *links shared* are a YouTube film of a cat watching TV titled 'dramatic cat' that was posted twice (perhaps a sign of trying to work out how to share links); a picture of a woman with 'can I eat more' superimposed; and a link to an online game to which Daan had signed up ('Online Soccer Manager'). These four posts were also made in the first half of the year. Note that these posts re-use materials produced by others, while the other 19 posts he made are based on pictures, videos, and written text produced by Daan. A total of 20 posts include image or video. Of those, 14 include image or video produced by Daan himself. In two posts he uses videos or image produced by others, as in the example we will discuss in the next section. In another post, produced by a Friend, he was 'tagged'.

Taken together, the 23 posts he produced himself show a development from creating 'funny' pictures made on external platforms and sharing links to stuff on other external platforms (YouTube) to creating a typical type of status update: reporting an event – one example is the 'koermeten' post we will discuss in the next section. We understand this development as a change in Daan's interest, prompting a gradual *expansion of his repertoire* of text types. We might say that for him the resources for text making on Facebook have been augmented. Learning has taken place: Daan has achieved an augmentation of his capacities for representation, through his making of signs. An augmentation of resources constitutes at the same time a change in potentials for action, and, in this, a change in identity.

Designing a multimodal status update

We will now look at one of Daan's texts on Facebook in more detail. We picked the most recent status update, posted on the 31st of December, exactly one year after he joined Facebook, to explore the semiotic resources he draws on after 23 posts, and 16 status updates on this platform. A snapshot of the post is presented here as Figure 2.1.

The post contains a written component and a (still from a) video that can be played by readers of the update. The written component is placed above the video,

Figure 2.1 Daan's status update on Facebook (reprinted with permission from Daan and Facebook)

as a 'heading', prompting the reader to engage with the writing before playing the video. This *reading path* does not reflect the order of production. Daan first made a video in one platform – iPhone camera – then moved it to another – Facebook. In Facebook, the post was created, using the video and writing. Figure 2.2 shows what the *site of production* for updating your status on (the English version of) a Facebook app for iPhone looks like.

The example illustrates the expansion of the range of occasions for text making: in the pre-mobile phone era one would not have written on occasions such as these, let alone composed a text using writing and video. At the same time we might consider the constraints of the size and touch-screen keyboard and its effects

Figure 2.2 Status update interface on Facebook app for iPhone (reprinted with permission from Daan)

on the length of texts made on a smartphone. One factor leads to an increase in the number of texts being produced; another factor leads to a limitation on the size of written text elements that can be produced – though the limits on the size of the text are different again. There are also limitations on the resources made available by Facebook for composing a text. For instance, the size, type, colour, weight, and other features of the font are fixed by Facebook, and there are limitations on the placement of text elements, the length of the written elements, and so forth. These limitations have changed significantly since Facebook was launched in 2004, and are likely to continue to change, with the further effect of increasing the possibilities for text making, for instance, in the editing of photographs.

Before we explore the writing and the video in this post and the relations between them in more detail, we consider the 'interest' of the text maker (Kress, 1997). 'Interest' arises out of the text maker's social, cultural, affective, material position in the world, shaping attention to and engagement with the world. Daan's post demonstrates an interest in a particular occasion and an interest in communicating selected features of the occasion to a known audience of friends and family as the featured event is unfolding. Put differently, his attention is drawn to selected elements in the social, cultural, and material environment he is in; and he in turn draws the attention of his audience to (some of) those elements. In so doing Daan makes choices about what to select and how to represent it. Only what is 'criterial' is represented; other features are left out or are backgrounded. Only that which can be articulated with the resources available for representation is represented; other features are 'lost' in the process of text making. Hence only some of the people present in the environment that Daan was in are introduced, leaving others unnoticed. Readers get a glimpse of what selected parts of the environment looks like, while they can only imagine what it smelled like.

In 'entextualising' the world around him, Daan made choices about meaning and form. One choice is about the *platform* to be used for the production and dissemination of his text. For instance, Daan also frequently uses WhatsApp (now owned by Facebook). The potentials and constraints for text making on each differs significantly, and so does the audience he can reach on each. Hence making text now requires an assessment of the aptness of fit between platform, which has implications for resources available for text making and audience, and the text maker's interest.

Another choice is about the *type* of text. Daan's post takes the form of a common type of 'status update' on Facebook and other social networks: the live report of an event in which the author is taking part. The report is brief, so that it can be produced, disseminated, and read instantly, with relatively little effort (Lee, 2011). In this case, Daan wrote:

(1) Leuk met oom en vader en neef koermeten

In English, this would translate roughly to, 'Enjoying dining with uncle and father and cousin' (a word-by-word translation would be, 'Nice with uncle and father and cousin dining').

The adverb in first position, 'Leuk', ('nice') modifies what follows: *met oom en vader en neef koermeten*. The prepositional phrase in second position, *met oom* and *vader* and *neef*, describes a *selection* of the people around him. Other people co-present, including his siblings, are excluded. He describes the participants in relational terms, well suited for an audience that is not familiar with the proper names of his relatives. The verb in last position, *koermeten* (spelled as a non-standard variation of 'gourmetten'), refers to cooking on a raclette, which in the Netherlands is typically done on special occasions, e.g., during the festive season. Participants grill different kinds of charcuterie, vegetables, as well as pancakes (not so much cheese, as in the Swiss version), each guest using their own little pan. Thus, *koermeten* describes a well-understood, culturally shaped social event.

Daan also made a choice about the *order of the constituent written elements*. He placed the verb describing the activity in finite position, which is an entirely unmarked order in Dutch. He could also have chosen any one of the following 'grammatical' alternatives:

(2)   Leuk koermeten met oom en vader en neef
(3)   Met oom en vader en neef koermeten, leuk
(4)   Koermeten met oom en vader en neef, leuk

As well as that, he could have varied the order of the named participants:

(5)   met vader en oom en neef
(6)   met neef en oom en vader
(7)   met vader en neef en oom

So why did Daan choose (1), and not any of the other possibilities? One possible principle Daan may have followed is 'I put the elements in order of significance': 'I place that which is most important to me first'. Hence 'leuk' – a description of his mood/appraisal of the reported event – is placed in first position; and (selected) participants, starting with the host (his uncle), in second position, before the activity in which they are engaged, suggesting that to Daan, being 'with' others was more significant than what they did. He uses this structure in other status updates too; e.g., in 'lekker met Jaap aan het drinken' ('enjoying – with Jaap – having a drink'); indeed the appraisal-participants-activity structure appears to be the *preferred* structure for the written component of his reporting of social events.

The *video* is 12 seconds long and made by Daan with his iPhone. The camera work is shaky. The frame moves from right to left and back, giving a 'panoramic', 180-degree close-up view of the camera holder's surroundings from a low/eye-level angle. The video shows parts of some people in a room, where in the room they are, and what they orient to. In the foreground, one adult is shown standing, orienting to an object on the table; a child tries to get in frame of the camera. In the background, some people are on a sofa. The TV is on. Two lights are visible, including one star-shaped light hanging in front of a window. It is night-time. In the dimmed light the people appear as silhouettes; the vision is blurry; and as the camera moves quickly it is all the more difficult to identify people and objects. Fragments of speech are audible: one adult refers to food ('shoarma'), a child calls for mama; and there's sizzling of some kind.

Having explored the written element and the video, we can now consider how the two are semiotically related. If we assume that 'readers' of the post will have engaged with Daan's writing before playing the video, we might say that the writing *frames* the video. Indeed without having read the written texts (as 'heading') first, the video is difficult to interpret (in Barthes' (1973) terms, the writing *anchors* the image; it "*directs* the reader through the signifieds of the image"). There are other signs shaping the meaning-making work of readers too: above the text written by Daan are the elements automatically generated by Facebook, i.e., the author's name and the date and means of posting. As posts are often read immediately or soon after they've come in, readers will also place the post, which the writing suggests is a 'live update' of an ongoing event, in the context of the festive season: it is New Year's Eve, and people are celebrating, engaging in more or less predictable activities.

Knowing it is (or was) New Year's Eve, and, having read Daan's writing first, readers are likely to interpret the adult's actions, the sizzling sound and the reference to 'shoarma' in the video as relating to the grilling of food on a raclette; and assumptions may be made about the identity of the adult in the foreground – uncle or father. In other words, readers make links between the various components of the post, expecting *cohesion*: "a potential for relating one element in the text to another, wherever they are and without any implication that everything in the text has some part in it" (Halliday & Hasan, 1976, p. 27). In Daan's text, the writing names an activity ('koermeten') which is coherent with the actions depicted in the video. The writing introduces an uncle, father, and cousin; the moving image shows an adult and two children, leaving some room for uncertainty about how they map onto each other.

These cross-modal 'repetitions' of selected participants represented in writing and moving image produce cohesion: an element in one mode can be related to another; they are part of a single integrated text. How writing and the video operate in a single frame can also be explored by asking: What if the video was left out, or what if readers chose not to play the video? What does the video provide that the written sentence doesn't? Here we might say that the writing is an 'abstraction': concrete events are transcribed into generic categories, selecting some of its constituent elements while leaving out others. In this case, the writing doesn't describe many of the specifics of the circumstances, such as features of the setting or indeed characteristics of the participants: what they look like, how they sound, etc. – yet above all to give an 'impression' of the atmosphere (in Kress and Van Leeuwen's [2006] terms: a 'symbolic suggestive process'), depicting a 'generalized essence', the gist rather than the detail, complementing the description given in the writing, 'leuk' ('nice').

This shows how modes operate in ensembles serving complementary *functions*: writing describes the social relations between the text maker and the people represented in the text, the occasion of the gathering, and it provides an appraisal of the situation from the text maker's point of view. None of this information is provided by the moving image, by speech, or other mode in the video. The video shows some of the more specific actions involved in the event, and some of the characteristics of the participants not mentioned in the written sentence, including visual and vocal features, giving an impression of mood or atmosphere. Without one or the other, the text wouldn't be the same; they are mutually modifying.

We can extend our account of the post by exploring how it is placed in the 'news feeds' of Daan's Facebook friends. When Daan posted the text he had created, it was 'slotted in' a range of different texts, generated by Facebook algorithms and partially shaped by the settings ('customisations') of Daan's Friends/audience and the devices they use to read these texts. On this level of appearance, text is composed through a complex interaction between different types of 'designers' (platform and algorithm designers and authors of individual texts) and readers, in ways typical of digital platforms (see, for instance Caple's [2013] account of online newspapers).

In Facebook terms, the 'encompassing' texts in which texts made by others are collated are so-called News Feeds, which, according to Facebook's 'glossary of terms', is "an ongoing list of updates on your homepage that shows you what's new with the friends and Pages you follow". On the News Feed, texts are organised vertically, indeed as a list, with the most recently posted text appearing on top. When scrolling down, older texts appear. The News Feed appears as an encompassing text as Facebook produces coherence across the posts: it fixes the layout, background colours, and font; pictures are cropped and so forth, so that different posts look the same, even though they are produced by different people and are different on many other levels.

On the News Feed, posts are separated by horizontal hairlines, and marked by a profile picture and two written elements generated by Facebook, providing the name of the *author* of the text, the date (in Daan's case, 31 December 2013), and the means of posting (in Daan's case, via iOS, i.e., with an iPhone). The author's name is highlighted by embolding. These elements appear above the texts produced by the Facebook users; below it appears the 'like/unlike – comment – share' bar, giving Friends an opportunity to 'interact' with the post. Thus on the News Feed each post is vertically, sequentially organised, with three 'slots'; text in the first slot is more or less fixed, the second slot is filled with the text produced by the author of the post, and the third slot is filled with evaluations and comments from Friends.

The text in first position serves significant framing functions. In Daan's case, it 'tells' readers that it is Daan who is reporting (and perhaps for that reason Daan leaves the subject position in his written text empty), and that he is reporting on New Year's Eve. That he uses his mobile phone for this could suggest that he is providing the report when the event reported is still ongoing, matching or substituting present continuous tense marking in writing (in Dutch present continuous can be transcribed using the preposition 'aan', as in 'aan het drinken'; it does not have an equivalent of the English inflectional suffix 'ing', as in, 'enjoying').

By looking at the placement of Daan's text in a News Feed, some of the effects of Daan's choices become visible: for instance, the effect of including a video. Without the video (or a picture), the salience of the post on a News Feed would have been lower. The video/still takes up more space than the single line of writing, so that it potentially stands out more, potentially 'luring' Friends in. With potentially many different posts by different people to compete with, such forms of highlighting (in this case perhaps not produced with that intention) may become essential for making oneself visible. At this point we might also ask what the effects are of using a video instead of a photo. One such effect is *inclusion*: you'd need several pictures to capture the 180 degrees view that Daan portrayed. Another effect is *sequentiality*: the video, when played, unfolds in time, potentially raising excitement on the part of the audience of not knowing what will be revealed (unlike a single picture, in which all elements are simultaneously available). It may also be that Daan had just learned how to post a video from iPhone directly onto Facebook.

Daan's post attracted 'likes' from six Facebook Friends, including four uncles, one adult neighbour and one neighbour friend. One of the (English-speaking) uncles also added a short comment ('Miss you Daan'). What these 'likes' and 'comments' show is that his post was noticed. They are signs of engagement with the post; indeed this post is the highest number of likes/comments he has received on any post in his first year on Facebook. These signs of engagement are likely to shape Daan's future text making; through these signs Daan might learn what types or features of a post his audience is drawn to.

Outlook: towards a pedagogy of multimodal text making

Our case study showed, first, that through a detailed analysis of multimodal text made by a 12-year-old on Facebook we are able to recognize some of the semiotic resources that the boy draws on, and some of the principles he follows when making text of this kind. These resources and principles could provide a useful starting point for an assessment of what he already knows and what might need to be taught and learned in school; for instance, how to make text on other social occasions, and with different platforms – for instance, a Powerpoint presentation about a curricular topic (cf. Yandell, 2013). The analysis of Daan's text making also shows what a 'meta-language' for text making ought to account for. For instance, it might draw attention to such issues as 'cohesion' across modes and the 'affordances' and 'functional distribution' of modes.

Lastly, the analysis renders visible competencies central to contemporary text making, such as filming, that may not yet be part of the curriculum. The principles of text making that we have here rendered visible demonstrate competence in multimodal design, including knowledge of the availability of some of the semiotic resources on Facebook; knowledge of the affordances of these resources; knowledge of a generic form commonly used on that platform and on the occasion he is experiencing; knowledge of writing, knowledge of video making; knowledge of multimodal composition; knowledge of audience; and knowledge of the 'aptness of fit' between interest on the one hand, and platforms, resources, and forms of text on the other. These competencies will continue to develop. For instance, as he continues to make text on Facebook, he might learn how to 'tag' Facebook Friends named in his posts.

We also recognize that in other contexts, young people make quite different types of text. For instance, we explored some short films produced by 15-year-old Greek students (see Dafermos, Triliva, and Varvantakis, 2017). Like the films studied by Gilje (2010), the 'machinimas' analysed by Burn (2014), and video-interactions discussed by Adami (2014), these texts were produced and disseminated in entirely different platforms (including film editing software, YouTube), involving different modes (including moving image, music, and different notions of timing and commitment. Our point is that young people today develop *repertoires* of text making competences in response to shifting social demands and technological affordances, with profound effects on what 'text' looks like. Where previously 'complexity' of text making lay primarily with the mode of writing, now complexity lies in the vastly extended range of different social occasions for text making on the one hand, in the (inter-) relations between these resources, in the vastly extended range of platforms and semiotic resources now available for text making on the other.

These new forms of complexity need to be recognized and documented. The future uses, shapes, potentials of text making as well as conceptions of text making pedagogies need to be considered within a clear sense of social environments. Pedagogy is a specific instance of a larger-level social practice with its relations, processes, and structures, characterized by a focus on particular selections and shaping of 'knowledge' (as 'curriculum') and learning (as engagement with and transformation of that 'curriculum' in relation to the learner's interest), in or out of institutions such as schools, university, etc. Social relations in pedagogic settings shape engagement with the cultural technologies of representation (modes), production ('tools'), and dissemination (media): they are active in selection and shaping of modes to be used in representation. In this way they shape valuations of *writing* (compared to *image* for instance), conceptions of 'canonicity' and shape individual dispositions, and make what was socially produced and is culturally available seem natural, normal, routinized, and grooved.

At the moment the school is caught between different conceptions of authority and agency in relation to production of knowledge, to the authoring of texts, the authority/canonicity of knowledge and of semiotic forms. But learning has long since left the confines of institutions such as school, university, college, etc. and forms of pedagogy have to accommodate to 'life-long', 'life-wide' learning, that is, learning at *all times*, by those who have every right for their interests to be taken with utmost seriousness, in *all sites*, in *all phases* of professional and personal life. In school, many young people see themselves as authors of the knowledge they want, of the kinds of texts that meet their social, personal, and affective needs and in that they come into conflict with the sharply differing conceptions and practices of the school. Hence conceptions of pedagogy held by 'the school' are at loggerheads with those held – however implicitly – by those in school. In that stand-off, conceptions of pedagogy will need to be developed which accommodate the conflicting interests of generation, of power, of politics, and of an ever more globalizing market-dominated economy. Clearly, the agency of learners has to be taken as the central plank. Equally clearly, the insights, understandings, values, pieces of knowledge which are the results of centuries and millennia of social and cultural work cannot and should not suddenly be ditched.

These considerations apply for pedagogies for/of *text making*. Pedagogically, the agency and the centrality of designers and of readers, of those who make meanings, has to be the starting point. Semiotically, *writing* has to be seen at all times as part of *multimodal design* arising from a specific *rhetorical interest*. In such designs the affordances of all modes are judged and used in relation to that. Given its long history of social preponderance, *writing* has present social valuations which are part of its social affordances. *Design* is prospective and therefore always necessarily innovative and transformative rather than competent implementation of conventionally given practices. Social agency and the interested process of design engage with the affordances – socially and semiotically – of the media and the means/resources of production.

In that context a pedagogy of *writing* has to be seen as an integral part of a framing pedagogy of text making, in which writing has a specific place. Components of that pedagogy are multimodal representation and sensitivity to media and their affordances. In a globalizing environment, both in local manifestations, e.g. London as a microcosm of the global, and in manifestations beyond the local – with profoundly different conceptions of social positions, semiotic resources, and notions of 'the public domain' – pedagogies of communication have to be sensitive to the particularities of the specific locality.

Acknowledgements

The research was supported by a Marie Curie International Research Staff Exchange Scheme Fellowship within the 7th European Community Framework Programme (PIRSES-GA-2012–318909) as well as with a grant from the United Kingdom's Economic and Social Research Council (RES-576-25-0027) for MODE, a node of the National Centre for Research Methods. We would like to thank Diane Mavers and Elisabetta Adami and all colleagues from the DIGIT-M-ED project for their very insightful comments on an earlier version of this chapter.

References

Adami, E. (2014). 'Why did dinosaurs evolve from water?': (In)coherent relatedness in YouTube video-interaction. *Text & Talk*, 34(3), 239–260.

Albers, P., & Sanders, J. (Eds.). (2010). *Literacies, the arts and multimodality*. Urbana: National Council of Teachers of English.

Androutsopoulos, J. (2011). Language change and digital media: A review of conceptions and evidence. In K. Tore & N. Coupland (Eds.), *Standard languages and language standards in a changing Europe* (pp. 145–161). Oslo: Novus.

Archer, A. (2010). Multimodal texts in higher education and the implications for writing pedagogy. *English in Education*, 44(3), 201–213.
Baron, N. S. (2008). *Always on: Language in an online and mobile world*. Oxford: Oxford University Press.
Barthes, R. (1973). *Mythologies*. St Albans: Paladin.
Burn, A. (2014). The kineikonic mode: Towards a multimodal approach to image-media. In C. Jewitt (Ed.), *The Routledge handbook of multimodal analysis* (pp. 375–385). London: Routledge.
Caple, H. (2013). *Photojournalism: A social semiotic approach*. Basingstoke: Palgrave MacMillan.
Cope, B., & Kalantzis, M. (2009). Multiliteracies: New literacies, new learning. *Pedagogies*, 4(3), 164–195.
Dafermos, M., Triliva, S., & Varvantakis, C. (2017). Youth tubing the Greek crisis: A cultural-historical perspective. In M. Kontopodis, C. Varvantakis, & C. Wulf (Eds.), Global youth in digital trajectories. London: Routledge.
Gilje, Ø. (2010). Multimodal redesign in filmmaking practices: An inquiry of young filmmakers' deployment of semiotic tools in their filmmaking practice. *Written Communication*, 27(4), 494–522.
Greven, J., & Letschert, J. (2006). *Kerndoelen Basisonderwijs*. Den Haag: DeltaHage.
Halliday, M. A. K., & Hasan, R. (1976). *Cohesion in English*. London: Longman.
Hodge, R., & Kress, G. (1988). *Social semiotics*. Cambridge: Polity Press.
Kress, G. (1997). *Before writing: Rethinking the paths to literacy*. London: Routledge.
Kress, G. (2010). *Multimodality: A social semiotic approach to contemporary communication*. London: Routledge.
Kress, G., & van Leeuwen, T. (2006). *Reading images: A grammar of visual design*. London: Routledge.
Lee, C. K. M. (2011). Micro-blogging and status updates on Facebook: Texts and practices. In C. Thurlow & K. Mroczek (Eds.), *Digital discourse: Language in new media* (pp. 110-130). Oxford: Oxford University Press.
Martinec, R., & Salway, M. (2005). A system for image-text relations in new (and old) media. *Visual Communication*, 4(3), 337–371.
Mavers, D. (2007). Semiotic resourcefulness: A young child's email exchange as design. *Journal of Early Childhood Literacy*, 7(2), 155–176.
Mavers, D. (2011). *Children's drawing and writing: The remarkable in the unremarkable*. London: Routledge.
Ranker, J. (2012). Young students' uses of visual composing resources in literacy classroom contexts: A cross-case analysis. *Visual Communication*, 11(4), 461–483.
Yandell, J. (2013). *The social construction of meaning: Reading literature in urban English classrooms*. London: Routledge.

3 Playing sports with Nintendo Wii in Berlin

Technography, interactivity, and imagination

Nino Ferrin and Michalis Kontopodis

Introduction

Research on gaming cultures may focus on several aspects. For instance, one may investigate the impact of video games on literacy, education, and everyday life (Beavis & O'Mara, 2016; Gee, 2003), how young people play video games within multiple spaces and rhythms (Apperley, 2010; Fields & Kafai, 2009), or to what extent newer forms of video games (augmented reality games, sensuous games, etc.) should be considered as an integrated part of the young people's living world, i.e., the German "Lebenswelt" (cf. Kontopodis, Varvantakis, and Wulf, 2017). The emphasis can also vary when it comes to deciding how to shift the research focus from individuals or multi-player groups to the software and the design of the devices and interfaces themselves (and vice versa) while maintaining the overview of the performativity and relationality of complex socio-technical arrangements and media ecologies (Beyes, Schipper & Leeker, 2016; Fuller, 2005; Leonardi, Nardi & Kallinikos, 2012).

Thomas Apperley and Darshana Jayemane (2012) reviewed a wide range of game studies that explored (a) the multiple contexts in which game play takes place, (b) the relevant codes, software, and devices as well as (c) the political economy of digital labor invested into gaming; they argued that a *material* or *materialist* turn had taken place in game studies, emphasizing the significance of the embodied and socio-material dimensions of gaming across a number of scholarship areas. Concluding their review, Apperley and Jayemane briefly discussed recent developments in the game industry – such as the Wii, PlayStation Move, and Microsoft Kinect – that reshape and transform human bodies and perceptions and proposed that

> more research in this area would be a welcome contribution to understanding [. . .] how games play a role in mediating our relationship with the world through their subtle and intimate relationship with our cognition, perception and subjectivity.
>
> (p. 17)

Our chapter below presents a case study into the ways in which performative off-screen body movements relate to the on-screen body images thus forming new hybrid imaginaries while playing sports with the Nintendo Wii. After a brief introduction to *technography*, a data set of gaming with the Nintendo Wii console is subjected to microanalysis: we reconstruct the socio-material dimensions of gaming through analyzing videotaped records and – departing from those results – revisit main themes of educational anthropology and psychology such as the concepts of *body* and *imagination* (cf. Wulf, 2013).

Indeed, with the integration of digital media into all of the different domains of socialization, new thinking about the human body, agency, and imagination is needed. To begin with a reflection on how to conceptualize the relationship between the "human" and the "things", we invoke the German lyric poet Rainer Maria Rilke, who artistically conceptualizes the statue of Apollo as a rather *active* counterpart to the observer:

> "We cannot know his incredible head,
> where the eyes ripened like apples,
> [. . .]
> or burst out from its confines and radiate like a star:
> for there is no angle from which it cannot see you.
> You have to change your life".
>
> (Rilke, 2010, online)

The agency and performativity that Rilke attributes to the statue of Apollo indicates that the "non-human" material world and "human" actions are interconnected and frame each other. Rilke, in this sonnet, creates an impact on the reader by attributing gaze to the statue itself – not to the observer. The statue of Apollo is presented as if it bears a subjective will and a potential for action (cf. Bilstein, 2004).

This poem counts as an early-modernity example of discussing *agency* as an attribute of the "non-human" world and of pointing to the implications of this position for art and philosophy (Parmentier, 2001, Schuster, 2011). It indicates a deep bond between images and the imagination, and points to the possibilities contained in the performative interconnection between "inner" thought and "external" stimulation (cf. Huppauf & Wulf, 2009b). Our examples below explore newer forms of such interconnections and demonstrate – even more clearly than Rilke's poem – how agencies can be attributed to "all the parties involved" and not only to "humans". In concrete, we will explore sensuous gaming interfaces, where bodies (in movement) actively participate in complex processes of technical registration and interact with the almost simultaneously reproduced images of their own movements so that the boundaries between the "human" and the "things" are blurred.

Technography

Much relational thinking in psychology and educational science as well as across the social sciences has explored the connections between "humans" and "things" in joint networks over the past 20 years (cf. Kontopodis & Perret-Clermont, 2015;

Latour, 1993, 1996). The actor is understood as a social being, part of social groups and communities.

But to do so, it does not limit itself to human individual *actors*, but extends the word *actor* – or *actant* – to non-human, non- individual entities.
(Latour, 1996, p. 369, italics by the authors)

Actants constitute symmetric constellations together with *actors*, and this is the point of departure for a so-called *symmetric* anthropology (cf. Latour, 1993, 2004). Net(-work)s of interactivity which bring together objects *and* subjects constitute everyday life situations. In those hybrid networks the emergent actions are based on the underlying histories of the actors *and* their environments. The "human" bodies and all other "things" have a constantly evolving and mutual history. It is therefore uncertain, to what extent "humans" are affected by and shaped by "things" or vice versa – which is the reason that we place all of those words in quotations marks. Symmetric anthropology thus provides the fundamental principles for the integration of material conditions into the research routine (cf. Kontopodis & Niewöhner, 2011).

Sociologist of technology, Werner Rammert, discusses these theses, referring to the *inter-agency between people and objects*, critiquing the fact that the role of technology is unattended to in most social-scientific research:

The inter-agency between people and objects is the strategic bridging concept between the two sides of human and material agency. These cross-relations of *interactivity* constitute the hybrid world of interfaces, human-computer interaction or socio-technical systems.
(Rammert, 2012, p. 101)

A whole agenda of social-scientific research is thus proposed, which focuses on the implicit forms of knowledge and the everyday uses of advanced technology. In a similar mode, Leonardi, Nardi, and Kallinikos (2012) explore the material dimensions of socio-technological systems across a wide range of settings and the effects of materiality for the organization of social life.

In this context, the classic ethnographic exploration of other cultures – developed by Malinowski for instance – has been modified to explore cultural spaces that are characterized by virtual components. Methodologies such as *online ethnography*, *digital ethnography*, *connective ethnography*, and *netnography* have been developed as to explore online as well as hybrid on-/offline cultural spaces (Jewitt, Domingo, Flewitt, Price & Sakr, 2017; Leander, 2008). Expanding the focus from internet interfaces to all media including ambivalent, smart, and sensuous technologies, which shape everyday life situations, the term *technography* has been proposed:

At its simplest, technography is an ethnography of technology. The term technography is derived from that of "ethnography", used in the social sciences to account for the detailed description of human × human interaction.
(Jansen & Vellema, 2011, p. 169)

Technography explores the "human × machine/tool interaction" (Jansen & Vellema, 2011; Kien, 2008) while a *symmetric* distribution of choreographies concerning "human" actors and technical agency is proposed (cf. Rammert, 2007, p. 24–28).

Gaming with the Nintendo Wii remote in Berlin, Germany

Following a technographic approach, we explore below empirical examples from video-supported observations of gaming with the console "Nintendo Wii". First, we explore the body movements and speech acts by "human" actors. Then, we identify reciprocal gestures of the various *actors* and *actants* as a becoming-significant movement in the process of a further allocation of meaning and interpretation (which entails how the sensors of the console interpret the movements of the "human" bodies). The specificity of the media field as a field of socialization and sharing of meaning is subsequently revealed. In contrast to a mouse, joystick, or keyboard, the Wii console is mainly characterized by an innovative handling by means of a multi-sensorial controller. In this controller – the "Wii remote" – sensors have been implemented that transmit its position in the room as well as register movement through its location/direction in relation to the infrared camera in the device and two additional sensors near to the screen. This data is simultaneously recoded into analogous movements on the screen. This already shows that meaning is produced in this case through the technical recording, conversion, and playback of data. The console defines itself as a *controlling body*, since it actively re-shapes the player's positions and changing direction by carrying out the allocation of meaning within the socio-technical arrangement, whereby the image on the screen can be given the quality of a synchronicity in relation to the parallel body movements. In other words, movements carried out in real space are staged almost simultaneously on the screen. This is implemented by the just mentioned "Wii Remote", which is marketed by the manufacturer as follows:

> Gaming with motion controls is a fun, active, and intuitive experience, and nobody does it quite like Wii. With games that give you the feeling of playing your favorite sports activities, and adventures that put a sword in your hand like never before, your own body's movements are used to interact with the games in fun and delightful ways – thanks to the Wii Remote Plus controller in your hand. [. . .] It responds to motion and rotation for enhanced control as you swing, swipe, thrust, or turn the controller. With Wii Remote Plus, your gaming experience becomes more active and immersive than you ever thought possible.
>
> (Nintendo, 2014, online)

The controller can operate, for example, as a tennis racket which is held, like a real tennis racket, in the hand. The head of the racket, which the controller lacks, has to be imagined, while the swing of the racket is "carried out" with the controller. The special nature of this game is primarily the enhanced physical activity during play.

The subsequent empirical scenes show the qualities of these image-generated gestures by demonstrating the power of body images over movements in real space. It culminates in the question: who controls whom or what? The videotapes were recorded at a family event to celebrate a christening in the year 2008 in Berlin, Germany. This was part of a broader piece of research that is presented in German in the book *Culture of the Self and the Medial Body* (Ferrin, 2013), where the focus is laid on the conceptualization of media aspects in the transformation of self- and world- views. Approximately 80 people were present at the festivity, and about half of them were relatives of the baptized child. The actual group of players included 16 people, most of whom were 8 to 16 years old and only few older than 35 years, like the 40-year-old Fred, the owner of the Wii. While the rest of the players originate from Berlin and the rural area around Oldenburg, the youngest player (see below in the first scene) comes from London, and the only two women playing (cf. second example with the female commentator) originate from the USA. Because of this international setting, most of the German participants spoke in English some of the time and at other times in German – while the British and US participants spoke English most of the time. In that sense, the observed gaming culture is not "German" but "transnational" – which corresponds very well with current discussions about the transformation of ethnographic research fields in our globalized era (cf. Faubion & Marcus, 2009).

The game console was set up in a large living room with enough space for a screen for the video projection, several rows of chairs, and a generous playing area. Two cameras were set up in the room: one directed at the screen, and the other at the players. The first author, who was known to and invited by the festivity group, was not in the room all of the time, but was often there observing the game and checking whether the cameras were still running. The players did not take too much notice of the filming activities and the cameras after a while (and of course they consented with their participation in the research following all of the ethical principles and legislation for social-scientific research in Germany).

The console was set for "boxing" or "bowling" and linked to controllers that were held by both hands of the player(s), respectively. In this way, the player's movements were transmitted to the console and in turn converted into digital movements on the screen. For boxing (first example below), the screen was split into two fields with a boxer in each, both with their backs to the respective players. Each boxer fought his/her respective adversary in front, so that the players had their avatar in front of them without a mirror reversal. The console simulated the sounds of punches as well as the noise of a crowd. Every unblocked punch was accompanied by a ping. For bowling (second example below), the screen opened the view on the bowling alley and the bowler, with its back to the respective player, so that the player sees his/her avatar in front of him/her without a mirror reversal. The console simulated the sounds of rolling balls as well as the noise of a crowd.

First example: shadow boxing and virtual opponents

The first video sequence, which we would like to analyze here, is a boxing game from the Wii-Sports set, containing five different sport simulations:

> The two "opponents" find themselves, after the completion of two bouts, in a wild fight at the beginning of the third round. Both players strike each other with punches. It is worth noting that the youngest player (8 years old) operates at a very high tempo and without trying to block punches, while the oldest player (16 years old), operates more in the style of a real boxer, uses his fists to protect his head and places his punches in a more considered way. In the course of the fight, it is not possible to make out any feints, which must be due to the technical requirements, which as a result of the rate of punches cannot be assimilated as a strategic factor in the representation. On the other hand, the turning of the upper body with arms angled forward, as an evasive maneuver, offers a kind of reaction to the flurry of punches (see Figure 3.1). Both opponents used this evasion many times during the fight.
>
> When, as the fight develops, one of the avatar boxers – in this case the one of the older boy – falls to the ground and is counted by the referee, he bends his arms in hectic movements towards his upper body and brings them down

Figure 3.1 Evasive maneuver

again to a right angle. After the referee has counted to eight, the player relaxes and gets back into position – the avatar stands up (again). In the meantime, his rival waits in front of the screen and scratches his face with his hand. As the fight restarts with a ring of the bell, the older player takes up a defensive position, leans forward with his upper body and once again receives several punches from his opponent. After only a few seconds, however, the latter's avatar also goes to the ground and must gather his forces via arm movements – which means try to stand up.

Meanwhile, his opponent waits, as he had himself a few seconds earlier, by breathing in deeply and smoothing out his shirt while shifting his weight from one foot to the other. As the fight starts again, he punches the air three times, but after a short period he lands on the floor again, and is counted out. This brings the official part of the fight to a close. The number ten finally signifies the conclusion of the fight. It is also the reason for his adversary's jubilation, which is expressed in a gesture of triumph: the younger boxer stretches both arms vertically into the air. The loser, on the other hand, turns away from the screen with his hands knocking against his legs and immediately gives the controller to a seated viewer. At the same time, the audience starts applauding and calling out admiration (see Figure 3.2).

Figure 3.2 Jubilation

What does this scene tell about the connection between body and image? Isn't it the movement that functions as a link between the avatar on the screen and the body, isn't this the source of the circulation of the allocation of meaning? What is the relationship that occurs between the devices, the player and the image?

The data registering the location and direction of the controller is transmitted to the source of interpretation: the console. On the screen, movements are represented as significant gestures, since they demand a reaction from the human actors (cf. Mead, 1973). At least, this is suggested by the almost synchronous image playback as well as the attention of all present, since they exclusively focus on the screen, thereby promoting it to a social space. This entails the permanent circulation between the movements of the body and those on the screen through a reciprocal relation between device and body as well as from the resulting screen gestures back to the body movements.

Here, we can talk about a self-referential performative action, since off-screen symbolic operations and gestures within the image on the screen shape the constitution of meaning. The significant gestures however become visible and are defined as such through the technical devices. Only the movements converted by the console are emitted as images. However, for everyone present – audience and players – it is precisely due to the non-visible computing of the movements, that the actual cause for a hit or a successful evasive maneuver is withdrawn. Less strongly executed movements are also converted into a pre-programmed punch, which can have a no less relevant result in the context of the game. The attributes and the control of the action depend on the technical applications (hardware and software) while the player's intention is translated into another intention at the discretion of the media. A reciprocal interaction between the off-screen adversaries, who are standing next to each other, takes place only rarely. Instead, the opponent first appears on the screen, which is the place where the avatar meets its adversary.

In this constellation, the players are assigned competence by the fact that the effect (of the punch) obtains meaning through a computing process. However, resistances are also revealed: the older of the two boxers is superior to the younger in his method as well as in his strength. Through the adaptation of the game's internal rules, however, a 'badly' executed punch (in sport terms) can also be interpreted as socio-technically competent. But this can also lead to misjudging one's own (off-screen sport) abilities. Through the intersection of two overlapping fields, the game appears to be more than just an image – simultaneously also a bodily accomplishment, whereby the learning and appropriation of new patterns of movement is achieved in the shortest time possible. The feedback, which the players receive from the device, opens up an ambivalent process of evaluation, which entails potential for reflection about the relationship between the (off-screen) body and the body image (on the screen).

Second example: bowling on and off the screen

Before further discussing what kind of impact sensuous video gaming could have on formative processes, we would like to turn the reader's attention to another scene with the same video-game console but another sport simulation: bowling.

> Fred (pseudonym) is about to begin the game. The bowling alley is set. He is surrounded by the other players and one audience member, leaning on the doorframe at the back of the room. He raises the Wii remote and stops at face level, holding it in the right hand and holds this position. On the projection surface, his avatar is also standing with the virtual bowling ball at face level. Then the bowling pins are positioned – here the number of pins is seven, not 10 like in a normal bowling game. Fred begins his play by stepping forward with his left foot, and shifting his weight onto his left knee, while keeping his right foot in the starting position. Beginning at his hip, he swings the bowling ball from the backside of his body downwards and to the front. At the end of the series of gestures he poises and glances to the screen and ends his stance. One of the fellow players asks: "One can even throw it more strongly, right?" (German in original). While Fred now is standing upright, his hands on his upper legs, he sees that his throw does not knock over every pin.
>
> Another female player evokes: "Ohhh", and Fred adds: "Oh-oh, come on" (English in original). He waves his Wii remote around in front of his body, grimaces and relaxes his mimic art. He sits down on a chair behind his former position while the console arranges the rest of the pins anew. Fred rises again and elevates the Wii remote to his chin and so does his avatar and casts once again. This time, he moves the Wii remote inward and pauses. Then he turns his upper body abruptly and steps to the front with his left foot. As the bowling ball this time eliminates all pins he raises his right hand and shouts out: "Ha, ha, ha!"

While Fred is getting prepared for his next move, the presence of the technical equipment leads to a coherent reference in the direction of the projected images on the screen. The reference only changes direction in the few moments when the (off-screen) present people talk casually to each other. The content of this talk is characterized by comments or explanations about the game or its results. The socio-technical involvement of the participants is a feature of the gaming culture. The correspondence of the two reference systems (off and on the screen) – here we can talk about "actors" and "actants" – leads to a heterogeneous intermingling of the social and the technical space, which are interlinked through the human body and the Wii remote.

The performance of movements and the sensory operation of the console scanning the room can be defined as "interface", where both – the media and the players – encounter each other. In this constellation, Fred's gestures with the controller can be recognized as *intermediation*: in synchronization with the movements of the avatar, Fred starts his game both times by lifting the Wii remote up his chin. It seems that the sporting model of "real" bowling represents an orientation for the corporal and graphic movements alike. However, who is the model in this given situation: the avatar or the "human" body? "Fred" (off-screen as well as "Fred", the avatar, i.e., the image on the screen) casts the ball in the bowling alley in a concrete, directed way. The interconnection defines the direction of the ball and also the success of knocking down the on-screen pins as suggested by the synchronous execution of Fred's off-screen throw and the avatar's throw on the screen.

How the console processes the recorded data is neither of importance nor open to the public. The impact of this data processing is visible only in reference to Fred's off-screen actions and responses to the screened effects. In Fred's verbal and gestural expression of dissatisfaction ("Come on", "waving his Wii remote") after his first cast this is revealed. Nevertheless the comments are not definite in their relation to an action. "Come on" could be directed at his own performance, the execution of his avatar, or even for the unpredictability of the computation. In every case, we see how seriously the players perceive the situation. The variation of style Fred tries out in his second throw is interesting, since we can see that he tries to improve his first attempt by using a distinct set of micro-gestures in contrast to the first throw. His hand's position and his general stance lead to the assumption that he wants to influence the ball's direction after he rolled it into the bowling alley by correcting his rather poor first try.

Paraphrasing Jean Piaget, it can be emphasized here that: "the subject feels ownership over something that actually belongs to another or to the material/technological world", i.e., there is

> confusion between the self and the external world. Numerous cases are easily found in which the imitative sympathy is accompanied by a complementary attitude which consists in trying to affect the external world by some action on one's own body.
>
> (1991, p. 162)

The situations that we explore here are of course quite different from Piaget's experiments, because the "object" does not have a material, but rather a virtual status: the materiality of the images consists of the console and its algorithmic computation. The circular self-causation and self-determination of the actants – that is, Wii controller and "human" player thought of as interrelated – therefore results in the point of contact between the hand and the controller, i.e., in the virtual body, which in this sense, can be conceived of as a networked actor.

Instead of an epilogue: body and imagination in hybrid constellations

The technography of new digital cultures points to the connection of technically generated images and the "human" body (cf. Beyes, Schipper & Leeker, 2016). Most of the time, the action is free from verbal elements and concentrates on the gestures. In this collaboration the interface is the point of intersection of the "human" body and the Wii controller, while at the same time it refers to a gap between the two. Werner Rammert proposes the term "socio-technical interactivity" to describe this phenomenon (2003). The mentioned gap can be understood, if we think of George Herbert Mead's reciprocal approach to gestural communication. According to Mead, gestures have a social origin and therefore become significant only when they are received and reacted upon (1973). In the above-explored scenes, the socio-technical interactivity between images and players enables the interpretation of the gestures in and out of the media during a reciprocal attribution of meaning. The helix of constant production of images out of the sensory scan of body movements leads to the transformation of gestures to images and vice versa, as the "human" part of the network constantly allocates significance to the virtual scene on the screen. The implicit knowledge in this situation cannot be attributed to either of the parts – "humans" or "media", because they are not able to draw on knowledge if they are isolated from each other. To determine,

> what is meant by *the multiple, mediated* and *distributed* nature of agency: actions are composed of many elements, and performing those actions is a process distributed across several acts and actors. In this light, we can call the idea of an individual and autonomous actor an illusion when all agency is attributed to only one human actor. [. . .] The performance of actions is not restricted to human bodies but also involves material mechanisms and symbolic media. Even if nearly all elementary acts are performed by advanced technologies as agents showing features of intelligent, situated and self-regulated action, the projects of autonomous technical action can be defined as illusions as well when they disregard the multi-mediated character of technical action and neglect the imaginative, interactive and intentional part of human agency.
>
> (Rammert, 2012, p. 90)

Expanding on the literature and debates that we briefly reviewed in the introduction above (Apperley, 2010; Fuller, 2005; Gee, 2003; etc.), the question that poses itself is what kind of effects such hybrid constellations have on "humans". Imagination plays a key role for "humans" to develop their relatedness to and positioning in the world. The "human" body is the entity that performatively generates inner images by incorporating the outer images through mimetic processes (Gebauer & Wulf, 1998; Huppauf & Wulf, 2009b). Through its actions, the "human" body develops typical attributes and ways of interpreting the world; moreover it develops ways of interpreting these interpretations, which *constitute* culture as well as *are constituted by* culture at the same time. Central here is the link between imagination and image production: the German translation of imagination as "Einbildungskraft" (cf. Mattenklott, 2009) contains the word "Bild", i.e., "image":

> This anthropological view is to be found in Kant's definition of the faculty of imagination (*Einbildungskraft*) as the capacity to "re-present" (*vorstellen*) an object in the intuition (*Anschauung*) without its being present. According to

this view, which still remains relevant today, the faculty of imagination is tied to what has been perceived by the senses.

(Huppauf & Wulf, 2009a, p. 21, italics by authors)

In regard to the previous examples, imagination is nowadays to be understood in the context of complex social-technical interactions:

> The imagination invested and exchanged within a social network creates the basis for a symbolic order of things [. . .]. Thus, the imaginative interaction does not only involve human actors, but things as well, since they condition the visibility of what appears, as, for example, the cinematographic dispositive or the vacuum pump in experimental science. Whether we see a film or a vacuum depends not only on us, but on things radiating imagination, on intersubjective coordination and on bodily investment by the subject.
>
> (Schwarte, 2009, p. 66)

The mimetic reference to media images within newer sensuous video-gaming cultures indicates a form of mirror imaging due to the reciprocity of the media with the bodily gestures. Thereby the "human" actor has the possibility of recognizing as well as misrecognizing his/her own skills, since s/he is "playing" with his/her images. The playfully acquired media competence as recognition – attributed by oneself or others – of the ability to use the technology in question, can be best described as a formative process (*Bildung*), which is experienced through the constant self-referentiality of the circulation of meaning between the image and the body. This, in turn, produces new orientations and opens imaginary spaces for personal as well as for shared interpretations to emerge, and thus offers new sources for learning and "human" development. Indeed, by irritating and expanding the interpretation of one's world- *and* self-views, the newer sensuous video games create spaces where one encounters oneself in a quite distinctive way.

References

Apperley, T. (2010). *Gaming rhythms: Play and counterplay from the situated to the global*. Amsterdam: Institute of Network Cultures.

Apperley, T. H. & Jayemane, D. (2012). Game studies' material turn. *Westminster Papers in Communication and Culture*, 9(1), 5–25.

Beavis, C., & O'Mara, J. (2016). Shifting practices and frames: Literacy, learning and computer games. In G. Johnson & N. Dempster (Eds.), *Leadership in diverse learning contexts* (pp. 239–253). Cham: Springer.

Beyes, T., Schipper, I., & Leeker, M. (Eds.). (2016). Performing the digital: Performance studies and performances in digital cultures. Bielefeld: Transcript.

Bilstein, J. (2004). Die Hochschule als Ort ästhetischer Bildung. In Deutscher Bühnenverein (Ed.), *Zukunft durch ästhetische Bildung* (pp. 42–52). Essen: Kulturwissenschaftliches Institut Essen.

Faubion, J. D., & Marcus, G. E. (2009). *Fieldwork is not what it used to be: Learning anthropology's method in a time of transition*. Ithaca: Cornell University Press.

Ferrin, N. (2013). Selbstkultur und mediale Körper: Zur Pädagogik und Anthropologie neuer Medienpraxen. Bielefeld: Transcript.

Fields, D. A., & Kafai, Y. B. (2009). A connective ethnography of peer knowledge sharing and diffusion in a tween virtual world. *Computer-Supported Collaborative Learning*, 4(1), 47–68.

Fuller, M. (2005). *Media ecologies: Materialist energies in art and technoculture.* Cambridge: MIT Press.

Gebauer, G., & Wulf, C. (1998). *Spiel, Ritual, Geste: Mimetisches Handeln in der sozialen Welt.* Reinbek bei Hamburg: Rowohlt.

Gee, J. P. (2003). *What video games have to teach us about learning and literacy.* New York: Palgrave MacMillan.

Huppauf, B., & Wulf, C. (2009a). Imagination, fantasy and creativity: Introduction. In B. Huppauf & C. Wulf (Eds.), *Dynamics and performativity of imagination: The image between the visible and the invisible* (pp. 21–24). New York: Routledge.

Huppauf, B., & Wulf, C. (Eds.). (2009b). *Dynamics and performativity of imagination: The image between the visible and the invisible.* New York: Routledge.

Jansen, K., & Vellema, S. (2011). What is technography? *NJAS -Wageningen Journal of Life Sciences*, 57, 169–177.

Jewitt, C., Domingo, M., Flewitt, R., Price, S., & Sakr, M. (Eds.). (2017). *Digital research methods: A multimodal approach.* London and New York: Routledge.

Kien, G. (2008). Technography = technology + ethnography: An introduction. *Qualitative Inquiry*, 14(7), 1101–1109.

Kontopodis, M., & Niewöhner, J. (Eds.). (2011). *Das Selbst als Netzwerk: Zum Einsatz von Körpern und Dingen im Alltag.* Bielefeld: Transcript.

Kontopodis, M., & Perret-Clermont, A.-N. (2015). Educational settings as interwoven socio-material orderings: An introduction. *European Journal of Psychology of Education*, 30(4), 1–12.

Kontopodis, M., Varvantakis, C., & Wulf, C. (2017). Exploring global youth in digital trajectories. In M. Kontopodis, C. Varvantakis, & C. Wulf (Eds.), *Global youth in digital trajectories.* London: Routledge.

Latour, B. (1993). *We have never been modern.* Cambridge: Harvard University Press.

Latour, B. (1996). On actor-network theory: A few clarifications. *Soziale Welt*, 47, 369–381.

Latour, B. (2004). How to talk about the body? The normative dimension of science studies. *Body & Society*, 10(2–3), 205–229.

Leander, K. (2008). Toward a connective ethnography of online/offline literacy networks. In J. Coiro, M. Knobel, C. Lankshear, & D. Leu (Eds.), *Handbook of research on new literacies* (pp. 33–65). London and New York: Routledge.

Leonardi, P., Nardi, B., & Kallinikos, J. (Eds.). (2012). *Materiality and organizing: Social interaction in a technological world.* Oxford: Oxford University Press.

Mattenklott, G. (2009). Imagination. In B. Huppauf & C. Wulf (Eds.), *Dynamics and performativity of imagination: The image between the visible and the invisible* (pp. 25–41). New York: Routledge.

Mead, G.-H. (1973). Geist, Identität und Gesellschaft aus der Sicht des Sozialbehaviourismus. Frankfurt am Main: Suhrkamp.

Nintendo. (2014). *Wii remote plus.* Retrieved from http://www.nintendo.com/wiimini/what-is-wii-mini/#/controls (date of access: 20/07/2016).

Parmentier, M. (2001). Der Bildungswert der Dinge oder: Die Chancen des Museum. *Zeitschrift für Erziehungswissenschaft*, 4(1), 39–50.

Piaget, J. (1991). *The child's conception of the world.* London: Routledge & Paul.

Rammert, W. (2003). *Technik in Aktion: Verteiltes Handeln in soziotechnischen Konstellationen*. Berlin: TUTS – Working Papers. Retrieved from http://nbn-resolving.de/urn:nbn:de:0168-ssoar-11573 (date of access: 20/07/2016).

Rammert, W. (2007). *Technografie trifft Theorie: Forschungsperspektiven einer Soziologie der Technik*. Berlin: TUTS – Working Papers. Retrieved from http://nbn-resolving.de/urn:nbn:de:0168-ssoar-12091 (date of access: 20/07/2016).

Rammert, W. (2012). Distributed agency and advanced technology – Or: How to analyse constellations of collective inter-agency. In J.-H. Passoth, B. Peuker, & M. Schillmeier (Eds.), *Agency without actors? New approaches to collective action* (pp. 89–112). New York: Routledge.

Rilke, R. (2010). Apollo's archaic torso (Sarah Stutt, Trans.). *The Guardian*, 15–11–2010. Retrieved from http://www.theguardian.com/books/booksblog/2010/nov/15/apollos-archaic-torso-sarah-stutt (date of access: 14/07/2014).

Schuster, J. (2011). *Umkehr der Räume: Rainer Maria Rilkes Poetik der Bewegung*. Freiburg: Rombach.

Schwarte, L. (2009). Intuition and imagination: How to see something that is not there. In B. Huppauf & C. Wulf (Eds.), *Dynamics and performativity of imagination: The image between the visible and the invisible* (pp. 65–75). New York: Routledge.

Wulf, C. (2013). *Anthropology: A continental perspective*. Chicago: University of Chicago Press.

4 Digital filmmaking as a means for the development of reflection

A case study of a disabled university student in Moscow

Olga Rubtsova and Natalya Ulanova

Introduction: new perspectives in digital media studies

The ever-growing influence of digital media technologies and their rapid penetration into different spheres of human activity in the last few decades has resulted in a boom of research on digital media particularly in the context of upbringing and education. Digital media are claimed to have already caused a revolutionary transformation of teaching and learning practices worldwide. Not only have they expanded the traditional borders of the schooling environment, but they have also reshaped the very concept of "learning", which has moved far beyond the isolated classroom and the single teacher. Therefore it is not surprising that scholars and research groups who focus on current educational practices operate such terms as digital literacy, interactivity, multiliteracy, and multimodality, creating a totally novel perspective of learning (Alper, 2012; Bezemer & Kress, 2017; Christensen, Johnson & Horn, 2008; Cope & Kalantzis, 2009; Jenkins, Purushotma, Clinton, Weigel & Robison, 2006; Kontopodis, Varvantakis & Wulf, 2017).

However, through highlighting the global impact of digital technologies, many of the recent studies seem to pay insufficient attention to the psychological and developmental aspects of digital media usage. Most of the studies aim at answering the questions "how?", "why?", and "for what purpose?" digital technologies are used in the learning process, while the issue of their psychological implications remains almost untouched. So far there has been very scarce research devoted to the influence of digital technologies on various aspects of development, in particular regarding the development of higher psychological functions (memory, attention, etc.). From our standpoint, this situation could be explained by the dominating perception of digital media technologies as instruments, or tools, which are applied for solving concrete learning tasks. A deeper understanding of this phenomenon can be achieved by investigation through the lens of cultural-historical theory and in particular by paying attention to the essential distinctions between:

1) cultural *tools* and *signs*;
2) mediated and mediating activity.

According to L.S. Vygotsky, the substantial difference of *sign* from *tool* resides in the different purpose of the one and the other:

> The tool serves for conveying man's activity to the object of his activity, it is directed outward, it must result in one change or another in the object, it is the means for man's external activity directed toward subjugating nature. The sign changes nothing in the object of the psychological operation, it is a means of psychological action on behavior, one's own or another's, a means of internal activity directed toward mastering man himself; the sign is directed inward. These activities are so different that even the nature of the devices used cannot be one and the same in both cases.
>
> (Vygotsky, 1997, p. 62)

According to this distinction, tools are directed outward and applied to external objects, while cultural signs represent a means of internal activity directed toward the psychological functions and the relations between the functions. The employment of a tool always results in a change of activity, as well as the employment of a sign does. However, in contrast with *tools* that remain external mediators, *signs* are internalized. Thus, the use of *tools* and the use of *signs* refer to different kinds of activity. Tools refer to mediat**ed** activity (*oposredovannaya* in Russian), while signs refer to mediat**ing** activity (*oposreduyushaya* in Russian). Nikolai N. Veresov accentuates the difference between the two:

> Mediated activity is already mediated by mediators, which were given or established, i.e. are created before. [. . .] It is therefore, related to the fruits of development. Mediating activity, in contrast, is an activity that is not mediated, but mediates the whole process; it is an activity of mediating, not of mediation.
>
> (Veresov, 2010, p. 86)

This distinction is crucial for understanding the difference between digital media technologies as tools and digital media technologies as cultural signs. While answering the question "how" and "for what purpose" digital media are used in educational practices, the researcher usually regards them as tools by which the learning process is mediated. One can analyze the changes that emerged in the learning activity with their appearance, and one can also compare them to the previous mediators (for example, traditional paper textbooks or writing boards). In this case, the researcher obviously perceives learning as a mediated activity, which is easy to see in many works devoted to the study of impact of digital media technologies.

However, in order to investigate the impact of digital media on developmental processes, a totally different standpoint is needed. Since cultural-historical theory understands signs from a developmental perspective, it is extremely important to keep in mind that "the sign (or system of signs) originally exists as an external tool, as a kind of cultural material [. . .] and later it becomes a tool of internal mediating activity" (Veresov, 2010, p. 87). This means that not only shall we study cultural signs (e.g., digital media) as the result or the final product, but also trace the very process of their becoming a sign.

In this context the following questions emerge:

- What is the difference between using digital media technologies as *tools* and as *signs*?
- How are digital media technologies transformed from *tools* into *signs*?
- How can digital media technologies affect higher psychological functions and cognitive processes (such as reflection)?

To target these issues, the multidisciplinary research project "Understanding Digital Media" was launched at the Moscow State University of Psychology and Education (MSUPE) in 2011. The participants of the project set the goal of tracing the influence of digital media and technological devices on the development of students from various target groups, particularly on students with disabilities. As the data collected by our research group in 2011–2013 is rather extensive, in this chapter we would like to focus on a longitudinal case study undertaken with Arthur Kazakov – a 23-year-old student facing severe physical disabilities. Arthur voluntarily agreed to participate in the project and gave the permission to use his name in the research work without any changes.

Research context and case description

Learning environment

The International Classification of Functioning, Disability, and Health defines disability not solely in terms of health, but as the interaction between mental and physical conditions and personal and environmental factors (World Health Organization, 2001). Children with disabilities are often at the forefront of new media practices (Hartz, 2000). Moreover, they regularly drive the demand for technological development and challenge policy (Verlager, 2009) and push ahead the able-bodied population in their understanding of the media changes happening around (Jenkins, 2008, p. 33). This phenomenon is relatively easy to explain. Digital media deeply affect the lives of disabled students:

> [W]ithout access to the proper materials and technologies for communication, expression, and independence, the gap widens between a person's abilities and the sociocultural perception of their disabilities.
> (Alper, 2012, p. 243)

Not only do they contribute to reducing the "participation gap" by providing access to various opportunities, experiences, skills and knowledge (cf. Jenkins, Purushotma, Clinton, Weigel & Robinson, 2006), but they also transform the very process of interaction between the students and the surrounding environment.

Thus there is a strong demand for a deeper theoretical understanding of the potential of technology usage and media literacy in the context of various disabilities (Buckingham, 2004; Burne, Knafelc, Melonis & Heyn, 2011; Floyd, Canter, Jeffs & Judge, 2008).

The research was conducted in the context of the Department of Informational Technologies of MSUPE. Founded in 2001, for over 16 years already this department has specialized in the education of students with disabilities (particularly with visual and locomotive impairments). According to the common requirements for learning results, teaching students with disabilities is performed inclusively in mixed groups with regular students. The inclusion of students with disabilities usually demands an extensive period of adaptation. Thus a comprehensive support program was elaborated for disabled students entering the IT Department. The program includes:

1) *Pedagogical support*: The idea of pedagogical support underlies the whole educational process and presupposes a close cooperation between each student's educational supervisor and department staff including lecturers, professors, support specialists as well as administrators and students' family members (particularly parents). Altogether they perform control over attendance, thesis presentations, interim and final examinations. Periodically, briefings and seminars are held for lecturers concerning various challenges of working with disabled students. Systematic consultations are also provided concerning the physical and emotional condition of students.

2) *Technological and practical support*: This implies primarily providing students with various learning aids. Most of the educational materials are available in video-audio and digital form. Tutors and volunteers carry out extensive work as to help students in mastering computer skills to compensate for visual impairments and locomotive deficiencies. One of the key features of the educational process at the IT Department is practice-oriented learning. Learning is performed through various forms of work, which presupposes that all research and graduation works including semester projects and graduate thesis projects are practice-based. The main emphasis is put on providing an individual educational program for each student. Thus, the duration of study of certain subjects or topics may vary, an individual schedule is created for consultations with professors and supervisors, as well as specific learning or practical tasks of the curriculum are replaced with equivalent ones which are available for students due to his/her health conditions.

3) *Psychosocial support*: The lives of students with disabilities often involve many hardships on the social level. To overcome these difficulties, joint patronage is organized by social workers, city and municipal authorities. Disabled students get informed about possible benefits and financial aids. High-achieving students or students actively engaged in the university life are granted special scholarships.

The support system requires collaboration between the university and partner organizations to assist disabled students with household and transportation problems, as well as with providing medication supplies and legal consultations. Students are also assisted in inclusion into student government, amateur talent activities, research, recreation, summer vacations, cultural events, etc. Psychological support presupposes individual counseling, correction of personality distortions, motivational work, and career guidance.

Based upon 16 years' experience, the IT Department staff mention a number of factors which are the most challenging for students with disabilities, particularly: weak social orientation, knowledge deficiencies, communication skills deficit, self-indulgence, problems with regulation of behavior, lack of skills to assess adequately one's own abilities and one's own limitations, etc. Many of these challenges are closely linked with various aspects of reflection. Thus there is a strong demand for developing reflection and various reflective skills in students with disabilities.

Data collection

Arthur entered MSUPE after graduating from a boarding school. Since his childhood he has suffered from cerebral palsy. Due to a dysfunctional family background (poverty and alcohol abuse by parents), he didn't receive the necessary medical care in time. According to his own words, it was his sister who supported him the most, since she managed to organize a series of surgeries due to which he stood up from the wheel chair. Now Arthur is walking with the help of crutches.

Arthur learned about MSUPE while he was taking part in a preparatory course organized in his school by the university. He got interested in programs offered by the IT Department. During the interviews with our research group, Arthur constantly pointed out that as a teenager he had many difficulties in studying. Because of his family's background, he started attending the boarding school only at the age of 11 and needed to catch up with his classmates. However, according to his words, from the very beginning of the preparatory classes he could feel empathy and support from the administration, university staff, and professors, which to a large extent helped him to compensate for the gaps in his secondary education and succeed the entrance exams.

As far as Arthur wanted to have a creative profession, he decided to apply for the MSUPE program "Directing and Production in Cinema and Television", which attracts many disabled students every year. The curriculum includes courses in directing and production for multimedia projects, multimedia software and hardware, computer graphics and animation, computer music technologies, design and composition of multimedia programs. The educational process involves the implementation of diverse practical tasks: photo and video sessions, photo script, theatrical pieces based on modern and classical literature, video reports, photo and video montage, creating computer graphics and animation. Besides the traditional forms of work such as lectures and seminars, other learning activities like practical workshops, group brainstorming, and round tables are widely used (and special forms of support are provided as mentioned above). The professional skills of the program's graduates include production of documentary films, animation, TV commercials, design of educational DVDs, websites, etc.

The research group accompanied Arthur during the last semester of his studies (December 2012–July 2013), which was devoted to accomplishing his graduation project. The main goal of the project consisted in shooting a short film using various digital media and computer software (see Kazakov et al., 2014). In December 2012 the research group elaborated preliminary schedule of data collection, which included:

1) gathering information about the IT Department and support program for disabled students (Research activities 2, 3, 4, 5 in Table 4.1);
2) gathering information about the student and other participants of the filmmaking process (Research activities 1, 2 in Table 4.1);
3) gathering information about video-editing technologies and software used in the filmmaking process (Research activities 2, 4 in Table 4.1);
4) interviewing and video recording the student on different stages of the filmmaking process (Research activities 2, 6 in Table 4.1).

The schedule was discussed with Arthur and the department staff, and later adjusted according to the logics of the research. The final version of the schedule is given in Table 4.1.

Fragments of the filmmaking process and interviews were video-recorded, transcribed, and put on various storage devices. Thus the participants of the research group were provided access to all the materials for individual work and analysis. Later on, videos and transcripts were collectively studied and discussed by the researchers. A solid volume of the data collected during the semester provided a

Table 4.1 Data collection schedule

Research activity	Time period/duration	Means of data collection
1. First meeting with the student, project introduction, coordinating the work plan	December 2012, 120 min	Interviewing/note taking
2. Meeting with the student, his group mates, tutors and supervisors during the filmmaking process	February 2013, 120 min March 2013, 120 min	Participant observation/note taking/interviewing/video recording
3. Meeting with the department administration and staff, gathering information about the educational system	March 2013, 60 min May 2013, 60 min	Interviewing/note taking
4. Meeting with supervisors and tutors on film production	April 2013, 120 min	Interviewing/note taking
5. Participation in diploma defense	June 2013, 120 min	Observation, interviewing/note taking
6. Postproduction meeting with the student	July 2013, 180 min	Interviewing/video recording

deep and multi-facet perspective of the filmmaking process as well as of each participant's background. In the course of data analysis, our group focused on those materials which were relevant for targeting the main goals of the research, that is:

1) tracing the process of the evolution of video-editing media-tools into media-signs;
2) investigating the impact of the video-editing media on the development of reflection of the disabled student.

Video-editing media and development of reflection: data analysis

The foundation for understanding reflection in the framework of cultural-historical theory was laid by L.S. Vygotsky, who perceived this phenomenon as the image of one's own inner processes in one's consciousness. From Vygotsky's standpoint, reflection is an extremely important mechanism, since it always underlies new types of connections between the psychological functions as well as a new correlation of the psychological functions (Vygotsky, 1997). By analogy with other higher mental functions, reflection originally emerges in social interaction – that is, *between* people. Investigating it from a developmental perspective can be done by means of the genetic research method, which is based on the "experimental unfolding of higher mental process into the drama, which happened between the people" (Vygotsky, 1982a, p. 145). The concept of *drama* here implies a collision that is an emotionally colored moment of social interaction, where the mental process first appears as a social relation and later is internalized. Taking this idea as the starting point for the data analysis, our research group set the goal of tracing the stages of the filmmaking process with the aim of indicating the moment of drama.

Careful analysis of the collected data permitted identifying the following five stages: *Preparation – Shooting – Discussion – Reflective communication – Reconsideration*. It is important to highlight that the process of filmmaking was not linear – the stages did not follow each other in a clear step-by-step way. On the contrary, the students could simultaneously prepare or shoot a particular fragment of the film, while the other fragment was already at the stage of discussion. Thus each of the stages did not occur only once or twice in the course of filmmaking, but repeated many times. Due to the constant alternation of stages, roles and positions of the participants were also changing many times in the course of film shooting, which made the process very dynamic and interactive.

Let us have a closer look at each of the stages.

1) Preparation

The stage of preparation embraced the following activities:

a) choosing the topic of the film;
b) writing preliminary scenario for the film;
c) building up a filmmaking team (film crew).

At this stage the student was to decide which topic his short film would touch upon. He was free to choose any topic and any kind of genre (documentary, feature, educational, or even animated cartoon). From the very start, Arthur wanted to shoot a documentary. Originally he was thinking of making a film about carting which used to be his hobby for a few years. He shared the idea with one of his professors. The professor told him that carting was a nice topic; however, he said that he couldn't feel Arthur's enthusiasm about it – more precisely "he didn't see fire in his eyes".[1] And he asked Arthur: "Why don't you shoot a film about your wife? You always have fire in your eyes when you speak about her". This moment is crucial for understanding the context of the following semester's work and interaction. First, the professor pointed out that the main criteria in choosing the topic of the film should be the student's enthusiasm, emotional involvement, his "perezhivanie". Second, he warned against a formal approach to the film as to a graduation project, setting the pitch of the future interaction. Thus the professor's advice reshaped Arthur's attitude to the film as to a formal, alienated-from-life learning task, into a meaningful project about himself, his own life, and his "important others".

Since the final decision about the filmmaking is always made by the student, Arthur was totally free to stick with his original idea. However, he preferred to follow his professor's advice. The importance of this moment was highlighted by Arthur himself in the postproduction interview with our research group. Moreover Arthur retells this episode at the beginning of the film, which testifies that this conversation was indeed a turning point in the filmmaking process. After the choice of the topic was made, Arthur was supposed to come up with a preliminary scenario for the film. At this stage of filmmaking the student found himself in the position of the author, who was free to choose and to experiment with versions and ideas. In this creative process, Arthur was mostly interacting with the supervisor and professors – the main challenge consisted in shaping the plot and designing the main episodes. It turned out that the original version of the scenario underwent numerous changes in the course of the semester. In parallel with writing of the scenario, the filmmaking team was formed. According to the department's tradition, all the students of the group are involved in each other's work on the graduation project. Thus the film crew consisted of Arthur's group mates including other disabled students. Officially they were mostly responsible for operative work and film cutting; however from the very beginning they were so involved in the project that their attitude was totally informal. Arthur's group mates accompanied him to the film sets, took part in long-hour discussions about the film, as well as participated in his daily life problems and activities. "We perceive and treat each other like friends, rather than colleagues", – these words were repeated by Arthur and his group mates on different stages of filmmaking throughout the year. As Arthur later highlighted in his interviews, the process of filmmaking, which was originally launched as a graduation project, quickly evolved into a meaningful collaboration and even close friendship between the participants.

Arthur says:

> Despite the fact that originally I was just a stranger to them, all the guys got so deeply involved in my situation, that they participated in film production, postponing their personal plans (Все ребята, несмотря на то, что я изначально был никто, так прониклись моей историей, что участвовали в подготовке фильма, откладывая свои дела).
>
> (Postproduction interview, 04:02)

2) Shooting and film content

Film shooting was not organized according to a strict plan. Arthur's preliminary scenario and the original vision of the film kept changing throughout the semester. Thus the final version of "I Love" includes the materials from Arthur's personal archive (photos and video records of his wedding), as well as Arthur's earlier works (his first-year university film: "The Parting"). Other episodes were shot in the course of Arthur's life (bathing in the ice hole on the day of Epiphany, isolation ward, etc.). Some videos about the filmmaking process were used for the film's final version (a "film about the film"), as well as fragments of film discussions by Arthur, his group mates, and his supervisor. Thus the film, shot by Arthur and his group mates, is a true documentary, which means that the characters are not acting in any of the episodes.

The film's opening scene represents traditional ice-hole bathing on the day of Epiphany. With the help of acolytes, Arthur, the director and at the same time the protagonist of the film, performs traditional ablution in an ice hole, which for Orthodox Christians signifies purification from sins. As all the other episodes of the film, this one is a documentary – Arthur is not acting, the film crew is recording what is actually happening with the protagonist. After the opening title "I Love", the spectators are shown fragments of Arthur's personal archives about his hobby – carting. Arthur starts speaking about his work on the graduation project and how the choice of the topic was made. The story is accompanied by pieces of Arthur's interview taken by his group mates in the university, as well as by snaps of the film shooting. When Arthur talks about choosing his love story to become the main topic of the film, family photos from his smartphone appear on the screen.

In the next fragment we see an episode from Arthur's life – visiting his wife in an isolation ward. The operator – Arthur's fellow student – explains to the people around that they are making a film for their friend whose wife is in the isolation ward. At that moment Arthur tells the spectators that his wife is under arrest. Snapshots from Arthur's family archive appear on the screen, while he is explaining that their son was born in prison. The following story of their love is accompanied by scenes from Arthur's first-year project, a film called "The Parting", in which a young man (Arthur) is walking towards a girl (Arthur's wife). Scenes from the film are interlaced with snapshots from Arthur's interview, where we see Arthur's college classmates. Views of Arthur's legs and crutches constantly accompany the story. Snapshots from the carting club interlace with snapshots from the isolation ward and in the following episode we see Arthur picking up his wife's personal belongings. Arthur continues telling the story of their love which is accompanied by pictures from their family archive and snapshots from the interview.

In the next episode we see the walls of the prison where Arthur's wife is, and a church nearby. In the following scenes from the interview Arthur talks about the event that led to his wife's imprisonment. We see scenes from "The Parting" and snapshots of Arthur walking along the prison walls. When the story comes to the most tragic part – the midnight arrest – we see Arthur crossing a busy street. On the photo from the family archive Arthur's wife appears and later a fragment of the video of their marriage emerges. The story of the court session is accompanied with the scenes of a suburban train and snapshots of the municipal court building where the sentence to Arthur's wife was announced. In the next moment we see Arthur in an Orthodox church and by the monastery walls; in the voiceover he describes the circumstances which led to his wife's imprisonment. She was accused of beating her sister's baby during a quarrel, which she kept denying and which, according to Arthur's words, was extremely hard for the judge and jury to believe. The situation was complicated by the fact that there were no witnesses to testify for her upon the trial.

In the following scenes of the interview, as Arthur talks about his wife's sentence and arrest, his voice breaks. In the video from the family archive, we see the spouses' Orthodox wedding ceremony, which took place in prison, as well as a few photos of the moment when Arthur saw his baby for the first time. Next, the spectators see Arthur visiting his wife in prison and a few minutes later – carrying gifts in a railroad station. The episode of his visit to prison is accompanied with a bardic song.[2] At the end of the film the monastery walls appear on the screen once again. The closing scene brings the spectators back to bathing on the day of Epiphany and Arthur walking towards the church, which produces the feeling of a circle composition. Generally the film is shot in black and white; only the scenes of the bathing on the day of Epiphany and the final shots in the church are performed in color. The spectators see many scenes as if looking through a barred window or through a glass covered with raindrops. The film's musical score is minimal: there are church bells, a church choir singing, a bardic song, and a piece of instrumental music and city sounds.

In the production of the film, the following multimedia were used: two Sony HD semi-professional video cameras, two consumer-grade video cameras (HD and DV), a Sennheiser EW audio system, a studio microphone. The montage was made with Adobe Premiere Pro for Mac and Final Cut Pro software. It is necessary to highlight that at the stage of shooting we observed the students involved in direct operations with media. Cameras and other digital devices were used as tools for targeting a concrete objective recording various moments of reality. Thus, at this point they represented *external mediators*, and the filmmaking process itself could be perceived as the activity *mediated by digital media*.

3) General discussion among the filmmaking team and the supervisor

The shooting of episodes was followed by a preview discussion. At this stage Arthur, his supervisor, and all the members of the filmmaking team gathered together to assess the results of the latest work. It is important to stress the informal character of these meetings. They were held in the university, or sometimes in the flats of the participants in a friendly atmosphere and could take long hours. At this stage a few important changes took place. First, in the situation of discussion, the students changed their position from the participants of the shooting process to the film's exterior spectators. Their standpoint shifted from "inside" to "outside", which was especially visible in Arthur's case. Though he had already performed in two different roles – as the author of the scenario and the protagonist of the film – these roles gave him an inward perspective, while the position of a discussant immediately turned him to an "outside observer". Secondly, at this stage various digital media underwent a transformation from instruments of film shooting into an image, a mirror, which was the first step in their evolution from means of external activity into means of internal activity – in other words, from tools to signs. Consequently at this point, the mediated activity of filmmaking started to give way to *the mediating activity of reflective communication*, which we decided to single out as a particular stage of the filmmaking process.

4) Reflective communication

Apparently it is very difficult to draw the line between the stage of discussion and the stage of reflective communication, since the latter gradually emerged from the previous one. This stage was characterized by a conflict – a dramatic collision of the participants' standpoints and opinions. This moment is crucial for our research, since "the dramatic event is the form in which the higher mental function appears first as a social relation before it becomes an internal higher mental function" (Veresov, 2010, p. 83–90). At this point the participants of the discussion came to realize that each of them had a different perception of the "ideal film". These different perceptions became the source of the argument that started between discussants concerning the plot, the episodes, the acting, and other aspects of the film shooting. The participants did not agree on the means of conveying Arthur's message to the spectators – some of them claimed that his words and his way of expression were not convincing enough. Thus, we may say that *this is the point where reflection appeared as a social relation between the participants of the dramatic event*. This moment may be illustrated by a fragment of the film:

Peter: I don't believe and that's it. (Петр: Все равно, не верю. Вот не верю – и всё.)

Nikita: Arthur, eat the watermelon. (Никита: Арбуз, Артур. Съешь арбуз.)

Max:	Why don't you believe? Arthur speaks the truth. (Макс: Почему ты не веришь? Артур говорит правду.)
Peter:	He doesn't seem to speak it in the right way . . . (Петр: Ну, он как-то не так рассказывает . . .)
Supervisor:	We have Stanislavsky among us! (Научный руководитель: Здесь в наших рядах есть Станиславский!)
Peter:	I don't deny that Arthur speaks honestly. But from your words it seems that you're talking about yourself in the first place, you are anxious that your life may become hollow, and only after that you start talking about your wife. (Петр: Нет, я не отрицаю, что Артур искренне говорит. Ты как бы о себе говоришь в первую очередь, чтобы твоя жизнь не была пуста, но только потом, во вторую очередь о своей жене.)
Supervisor:	What shall we film so that you believe? (Научный руководитель: Вот что надо снять такое, чтобы вы поверили?)

(Documentary "I Love", 20:50–21:15)

5) *Reconsideration*

The stage of reconsideration included reevaluation of the previous work according to the outcome of the reflective communication and making of the corresponding changes in the film. Arthur always made the final decision. As he later stated in one of the interviews, "the film was changing together with himself and his group mates".

From Arthur's words, the most important source of self-reevaluation for him was connected with the change of positions that he experienced while working on the project. According to data analysis, throughout the filmmaking process Arthur performed at least in three different positions:

1) the author of the text
2) the protagonist of the film
3) the discussant of the film

In the first two positions he shared the inner perspective of the film crew, while in the process of discussion he was evaluating his own work from the standpoint of an external spectator. Since each of the stages did not occur only once or twice in the course of filmmaking, but repeated many times, Arthur was constantly taking on new positions and continually changing his perspective. *Together with the dramatic collision of opinions, this continuous process of role-alternation can be perceived as an important source of reflection development* that emerged as the result of the mediating activity.

Concrete references illustrating the development of Arthur's reflection may be found in various fragments of the data, collected by our research group throughout the year. The major shift in the student's attitude to himself and his own life can be traced by comparing certain episodes of his interviews and particularly the moments which concern his state of mind at the beginning and in the end of the filmmaking process. Thus, while describing his feelings at the preparative stage of the graduation project, Arthur says:

> This entire situation (*the incident that led to Arthur's wife's arrest*) happened on the fourth year of my studies and I was terribly depressed . . . I was absolutely unable to share this with anybody, and my scientific supervisor noticed it and asked me, what was going on . . . (Вся эта ситуация *(инцидент, приведший к заключению жены Артура – прим. авторов)* случилась на четвертом курсе и у меня была жуткая депрессия . . . я просто был не в состоянии ни с кем поделиться случившимся, и научный руководитель сама заметила это и спросила, что случилось).
> (Postproduction interview, 03:02–03:06)

Arthur continues depicting his feelings at the very beginning of the year:

> Yes, it was extremely hard for me to show it to everyone . . . to the unknown guys, to open my soul to them . . . but I think that I had no other way out, if only that could help me, my wife, and my family to overcome this situation and the difficulties that we had (Да, мне было безумно тяжело было показать это все всем . . . чужим мне ребятам, открыть перед ними всю душу . . . но, я считаю, что у меня не было другого выхода, если только это могло как-то помочь мне, моей жене и моей семье пережить эту ситуацию и преодолеть трудности, которые у нас есть).
> (Postproduction interview, 137:40–138:12)

And finally this is what he says about the meaning of this project shortly after the defense:

> This film has become more than just a graduation work . . . It is a chance for me to help my wife and my son (Этот фильм стал для меня больше, чем просто дипломная работа . . . Он для меня – шанс помочь своей жене и сыну).
> (Postproduction interview, 11:42–11:50)

> The most important thing for me in this film is that this film is about our love . . ., without which there is no way to live, due to which I want to live, due to which I want to exist (Из всего фильма самое важное для меня то, что этот фильм о нашей любви . . . без которой нельзя жить, с которой хочется жить, хочется существовать).
> (Postproduction interview, 147:15–148:50)

These are just a few illustrations that help to trace Arthur's way from being depressed and closed, to being ready to live and love further.

One of the main questions which emerged after the data analysis is whether the same effect could possibly be achieved without the use of digital media – e.g., if Arthur and his group mates performed the same story in the form of a dramatic play. A theatrical production would definitely have given the students the opportunity of experiencing various roles and positions. It could also provide the chance of role-alternation and emotional involvement in the process of interaction. However without the use of digital filming technologies, the perspective of the participants would probably have remained "in-ward" – the process of the interaction could not be easily recorded and become the object of further discussion and analysis. Video-editing technologies permitted Arthur and his group mates to go through the same situation in the position of spectators, to comment on it and to assess each other's words and actions. Thus, digital media allowed to capture the exact moment of "perezhivanie" and created quite a unique opportunity of "re-experiencing the experience".

Conclusions and challenges

The departing point for the case study undertaken by our research group was the basic distinction that cultural-historical theory makes between cultural tools and signs in human activity. From our point of view, digital media technologies serve for different purposes as *tools* and as *signs*. Digital media technologies-tools are directed outward; they represent a means of external activity which is directed toward an external object and results in one change or another concerning this object. Digital media technologies-signs are directed inward; they represent a means of internal activity which is directed toward human functions and relationships. Thus, it is only possible to study the influence of digital media technologies on cognitive processes (in our case on reflection) when they are used and perceived as cultural signs.

The use of *digital media technologies-tools* and the use of *digital media technologies-signs* refer to different kinds of activity. Tools refer to mediated activity (*oposredovannaya deyatelnost*), while signs refer to mediating activity (*oposreduyushaya deyatelnost*). Thus, in the course of the activities, digital media-tools remain external mediators, while digital media-signs are internalized. Originally, digital media technologies exist as external tools, as a kind of cultural material. However, they might evolve into signs in the processes of interaction between humans and between humans and tools.

In the undertaken case study our research group set the goal of tracing:

a) the process of transformation of video-editing digital media technologies into digital media-signs;
b) the influence of video-editing digital technologies on the development of reflection of a disabled student.

In order to explore these issues, our group focused on film shooting in which the disabled student and his group mates were involved. The filmmaking process was divided into five stages and a detailed analysis of each stage was carried out. Data analysis permitted to formulate the following conclusions:

1) In the first two stages (preparation and film shooting), video-editing media were used as tools, necessary for recording. Their function consisted in

capturing concrete moments of reality. At this point they represented *external mediators*, and the filmmaking process itself could be perceived as the activity, *mediated by digital media.*

2) At the stage of discussion digital filming underwent a transformation from instruments of film shooting into an image, a mirror, which meant that they could no longer be perceived as external *tools*, but as *signs*, oriented toward internal functions and processes. Consequently at this point the mediated activity of filmmaking gave way to *the mediating activity of reflective communication*, which immediately resulted in the change of Arthur's (and other participants') perspective.

3) Throughout the filmmaking process Arthur performed at least in three different positions:

   1) the author of the scenario;
   2) the protagonist of the film;
   3) the discussant of the film.

The first and the second positions granted him the perspective of the internal participant. At the stage of discussion he turned into one of the film's exterior spectators and his standpoint shifted from "in-side" to "out-side". Thus, due to the constant alternation of roles and positions, in the undertaken case study video-editing media provided quite a unique opportunity of "re-experiencing the experience". We hope that this study can be regarded as a first step into understanding the impact of digital media on development. Further research should address the issue of using digital media as cultural signs that could stimulate not only the development of reflection, but of other higher psychological functions, such as memory and attention.

Acknowledgements

The research group would like to thank the Rector of the Moscow State University of Psychology and Education Prof. Vitaly Rubtsov and the Dean of the IT Faculty Prof. Lev Kuravsky for help and assistance. Our deepest gratitude to Arthur Kazakov and his family, Victoria Fomina and all other students, who participated in the film production and our research project.

Notes

1 All fragments are translated from Russian by the authors.
2 Relating to Russian bards' poetry.

References

Alper, M. (2012). Promoting emerging new media literacies among young children with blindness and visual impairments. *Digital Culture & Education*, 4(3), 243–256.
Bezemer, J., & Kress, G. (2017). Young people, Facebook, and pedagogy: Recognizing contemporary forms of multimodal text making. In M. Kontopodis, C. Varvantakis, & C. Wulf (Eds.), *Global youth in digital trajectories*. London: Routledge.

Buckingham, D. (2004). *The media literacy of children and young people*. London: Centre for the Study of Children Youth and Media, Institute of Education, University of London.

Burne, B., Knafelc, V., Melonis, M., & Heyn, P. C. (2011). The use and application of assistive technology to promote literacy in early childhood: A systematic review. *Disability and Rehabilitation: Assistive Technology*, 6, 207–213.

Christensen, C. M., Johnson, C. W., & Horn, M. B. (2008). *Disrupting class: How disruptive innovation will change the way the world learns*. New York: McGraw-Hill.

Cope, B., & Kalantzis, M. (2009). Multiliteracies: New literacies, new learning. *Pedagogies: An International Journal*, 4, 164–195.

Floyd, K. K., Canter, L. L. S., Jeffs, T., & Judge, S. A. (2008). Assistive technology and emergent literacy for preschoolers: A literature review. *Assistive Technology Outcomes and Benefits*, 5, 92–102. Retrieved from http://www.atia.org/i4a/pages/index.cfm?pageid=3305 (Date of access: 20/08/2014).

Hartz, D. (2000). Literacy leaps as blind students embrace technology. *The English Journal*, 90(2), 52–59.

Jenkins, H. (2008). Media literacy: Who needs it? In T. Willoughby & E. Wood (Eds.), *Children's learning in a digital world* (pp. 16–39). Oxford: Blackwell.

Jenkins, H., Purushotma, R., Clinton, K., Weigel, M., & Robison, A. J. (2006). *Confronting the challenges of participatory culture: Media education for the 21st century*. Chicago: The John D. & Catherine T. McArthur Foundation.

Kazakov, A., Orehov, M., Roshin, N., Kuznetsova, K., Kirilkina, A., Troitskaya, S., Sapkovsky, N., Belyaev, P., Prilukova, D., Abdullaev, E., Samorocsky, I., & Fomina, V. (2014). *Documentary "I love"*. Retrieved from http://vimeo.com/76526895 (Date of access: 20/08/2014).

Kontopodis, M., Varvantakis, C., & Wulf, C. (2017). Exploring global youth in digital trajectories. In M. Kontopodis, C. Varvantakis, & C. Wulf (Eds.), *Global youth in digital trajectories*. London: Routledge.

Veresov, N. N. (2010). Introducing cultural historical theory: Main concepts and principles of genetic research methodology. *Cultural-Historical Psychology*, 4, 83–90.

Verlager, A. K. (2009). Literacy as process: The multiple literacies of blind readers. *Journal of Media Literacy Education*, 55(1 & 2). Retrieved from http://www.journalofmedialiteracy.org/index.php/past-issues/2-cultural-diversity-v55-n1a2/23-literacy-as-process-the-multiple-literacies-of-blind-readers (date of access: 20/08/2014).

Vygotsky, L. S. (1982a). *Sobranie sochinenii, Tom tretii. Problemy razvitiya psikhiki* [Collected works, Vol. 3: Problems in the development of mind]. Moscow: Izdatel'stvo Pedagogika.

Vygotsky, L. S. (1997). *Collected works: The history of the development of higher mental functions*. New York: Plenum Press.

World Health Organization. (2001). Agenda item 13.9: International classification of functioning, disability, and health. Resolution of the Fifty-Fourth World Health Assembly. Geneva: WHO.

5 Youth tubing the Greek crisis
A cultural-historical perspective

Manolis Dafermos, Sofia Triliva, and Christos Varvantakis

Introduction: youth cultures and crises in Greece

Social crises have been perceived by researchers as "natural experiments" (Elder, 1974) or real-life experiments. The complex crises that have taken hold in Greece in the past four years have been dubbed "a failed experiment on the people" (McKee, Karanikolos, Belcher & Stuckler, 2012, p. 346), "humanitarian crisis" (Dalakoglou, 2013), "healthconomic crisis" (Williams & Maruthappu, 2013), and as yielding a "lost generation" (Malkoutzis, 2011), or a "sacrificed generation" (Castellani, 2012). The "experimental protocol" included the manipulation of the following variables: fiscal austerity, economic shock, and the withdrawal of social protection (Karanikolos et al., 2013). The outcomes and social ramifications of the experimentation have been documented as:

> The young generation sacrificed: social, economic and political implications of the financial crisis [. . .] the young generation in Europe is disproportionally hit by unemployment, underemployment, poverty and exclusion. This is nothing less than a tragedy in the making. If no tangible improvements are made, Europe risks not only producing a 'lost generation' of disillusioned young people, but also undermining its political stability and social cohesion, justice and peace, as well as its long-term competitiveness and development prospects in the global context.
> (Council of Europe, 2012, Resolution 1885)

Undeniably and obviously, no matter how it is described there is lots of experimentation taking place across Europe and particularly in Greece. The country has become a crisis-ridden nation and the younger generation has been gravely impacted.

The extreme austerity measures that have been implemented in Greece have changed youths' lives, their dreams, and their prospects greatly (Triliva, Varvantakis & Dafermos, 2015). Over fifty percent of youth in Greece are unemployed (EUROSTAT, 2015). Greece has among the highest rates of young people *not* in Education, Employment, or Training (NEETs) within the EU. The term NEETs describes a country's young population, aged 15–24 years, who are not in education, training, and employment; in essence they are unemployed and excluded from the care of the welfare state and are, subsequently, prolonging their dependence on the older generation (parents and extended family). Gouglas (2013) identifies this generation as the "young precariat", a new social "class" of people who confront the developmental challenges of the labor market, employment and representation insecurity, and who have not acquired a collective voice. In order to juxtapose these abysmal figures to youth's lives and to contextualize their world(s), it is important to explore what experiences social scientists describe as defining of this particular social, economic, and historical situation, and hence the lives, of this generation.

In December 2008, Greek youth reacted massively and violently to the killing of Alexandros Grigoropoulos, a 15-year-old high school student, by the police. Both what transpired on December 6 and the forcefulness of the public response culminated in an amalgamation of vexation, dissatisfaction, and discontent and catalyzed social science dialogue. Youth demonstrated both peacefully and violently for days and their immediate and forceful reactions intrigued social scientists who tried to make sense of the "social crisis" through their analyses. Some characterized the events that ensued as "the revolt of December" and explained that the changing urban and economic landscape in Athens alienated and oppressed specific groups, including youth, and both the context and its young inhabitants were transformed "into the terrain of insurrectionary praxis" (Dalakoglou, 2013, p. 33).

Andronikidou and Kovras (2012) describe the December 6 uprising as "cultures of rioting" that have been abetted by sympathy toward protesting and related to the culture of resistance to authority, which has been vibrant in Greece since the resistance to the military dictatorship in the 70s. According to Andronikidou and Kovras (2012), a rioting culture has developed in Greece because of the endemic social duty to resist authority, youth's acquisition of independent agency and subjectivity through such acts, and the disenfranchisement brought about by the economic crisis. Sotiris (2010) argues that the "youth social movements" expressed opposition to the neoliberal restrictive policies that have resulted in greater unemployment, insecurity, precarity, and economic hardship. For Sotiris (2010), youth's mobilization was indicative and parallel to the sense of peril that they faced in their everyday lives. Unemployment, the privatization of social goods such as health-care and education, and the violence of the "disciplinary and restrictive" neoliberal agenda posed grave challenges for their everyday existence. Sakellaropoulos (2012) also emphasizes youth's plight, highlighting exploitation, migration, growing mistrust, and repression. The "policies that kill our dreams" united youth and some analysts believed that perhaps a "new identity" or social movement (Psimitis, 2011) or the molding of a radical political subject (Mentinis, 2010) was taking place.

According to the analyses cited thus far, a great deal of interpretation and conjecture regarding youth's lives, subjectivities, and political leanings developed in academic and other spheres. Youth were in the limelight and many social scientists tried to "understand them" although from afar. In Memos's (2010) analysis:

> The traditional roles and values that used to be necessary for the social cohesion of capitalist societies are undergoing a tremendous crisis. Neoliberal

values are increasingly losing their strength and the vitality that allowed the processes of social integration and identification to be carried out. More and more young people realize that they cannot find human motives and a positive meaning of life in neoliberalism. More and more they react against isolation, humiliation and the poverty of everyday life. Hence the revolt represented above all a struggle for dignity, a struggle regarding the meaning of human existence, a struggle against emptiness, oppression, mental anguish and the neoliberal deceit.

(pp. 214–215)

It is possible that this is what was going on with youth and in some ways youth "expressed" themselves and "had spoken". The analyses, however, were mostly from the perspectives of social scientists that tried to "read", "make sense of", and interpret all that youth were expressing. Some of these erudite commentators used youth's words. Panayotakis (2009) writes about youths' "need for communication, solidarity, and for genuine participation in the decisions that affect one's life. As one of the slogans written on a wall in Athens put it: 'We live as long as we change the world. As long as others change it, we die'" (Panayotakis, 2009, p. 100).

Astrinaki (2009) echoes similar sentiments in her argument regarding what youth were expressing in the December 2008 protests. She argues that in the neoliberal landscape youth did not see a way out of an oppressive, uncreative, and dissolution-rife reality, hence, they revolted. Youth used social media, cell phones, blogs, and other social network means to organize their revolt and to resist the discourses which "labeled and categorized" them in mainstream media that depicted them as "hooded wild youth" and, more importantly, to speak for themselves (Panourgia, 2011). New "networked publics" (boyd, 2014) were created, new ways of communicating evolved, and alternative media landscapes where youth "talked about", "visually presented", and developed "a cultural mindset" (boyd, 2014) emerged. These new networking spaces were decentralized, non-hierarchical, flexible, and non-dogmatically aligned with the ruling elite. Newly emerging forms of resistance, presentation, and politicization in Greek society were in the making. These "networked publics" emerged as the multitude of crises took hold in Greece from 2009 through to today. According to boyd (2014), "Networked publics are publics that are restructured by networked technologies. As such, they are simultaneously (1) the space constructed through networked technologies and (2) the imagined community that emerges as a result of the intersection of people, technology, and practice" (p. 8). Youth appear to have "moved" to these spaces because their voices and realities were not being heard, understood, or given credence.

The purpose of this paper is to examine how the current social milieu in Greece is talked about and visually presented by youth in one network public landscape: YouTube. By multimodally analyzing youth's YouTube videos from the perspective of cultural-historical theory, we will attempt to shed light on the processes and the outcomes of youth's psychological development in this crises-ridden context.

Cultural-historical insights

The digitalization of social life has challenged developmental theorists and social scientists to study the networked landscape and the new "public spheres" and "imagined communities" in which young people live, learn, and develop. Along with other paradigms previously used in understanding youths' activities, development, and learning, cultural-historical psychology has also been trying to understand how these social spaces where young people digitally gather, connect, and meet are impacting youths' everyday lives. Contrary to the empirical, descriptive methods of psychological research, cultural-historical theory focuses on investigating the process of mental development. In Vygotsky's words,

> The method we use may be called experimental-genetic method in the sense that it artificially elicits and creates a genetic process of mental development [. . .] The principal task of analysis is restoring the process to its initial stage, or, in other words, converting a thing into a process.
> (Vygotsky, 1997b, p. 68)

"Restoring the process to its initial stage" refers to the reconstruction of "the social relation as primary form in which the menial function originally exists" (Veresov, 2010b, p. 275).

Cultural-historical theory can be described as an inquiry into the origin and development of higher mental functions (Veresov, 2010b). Development is the fundamental concept in cultural-historical theory. From the perspective of cultural-historical theory, development is not a linear process or a progression from lower to higher stages, but a contradictory process. Vygotsky highlighted the contradictory character of development by noting that it is constituted by a dialectical relationship between progression and regression, although he focused mainly on the study of progressive development of higher mental functions. Vygotsky investigated not only matured psychological functions but also not fully developed functions in their embryonic state from the perspective of their further progressive development. Moreover, the processes involved in psychological regression were also included in Vygotsky's research agenda. Vygotsky in his work "Thought in Schizophrenia" analyzed the regression to earlier form of thought that is often observed in patients with schizophrenia. He argued that "disintegration of personality follows certain psychological laws" (Vygotsky, 1994c, p. 324).

Vygotsky challenged the individualization and psychologization of human development: "an individual only exists as a social being, as a member of some social group within whose context he follows the road of his historical development" (Vygotsky, 1994a, p. 175). He considered individual psychological development in the context of the historical development of society. "Already in primitive societies, which are just taking their first steps along the road of their historical development, the entire psychological makeup of individuals can be seen to depend directly on the development of technology, the degree of development of the production forces and on the structure of that social group to which the individual belongs" (Vygotsky, 1994a, p. 176). Hence, from the perspective of cultural-historical theory, young people are not viewed as unitary, isolated from their cultural milieu or context, are not innately and always rationally developing within specific "outwardly" imposed norms, and they are not always consensual beings.

Vygotsky argued that there is a close connection between the system of social relations and the structure (and development) of personality. "The various internal contradictions which are to be found in different social systems find their expression both in the type of personality and in the structure and development of human psychology in that historical period"(Vygotsky, 1994a, 176). Cultural-historical theory differs radically from theories based on the psychologization and pathologization of human development, primarily because it clearly posits that there are inexorable links between social and individual development.

In this study we apply a set of concepts derived from cultural-historical theory – *cultural sign, mediating activity, perezhivanie, crisis,* and *zone of proximal development* to develop understandings of how Greek youth represent their lives in their YouTube videos in accordance with these developmental mechanisms (Table 5.1 presents an outline and the definition of these concepts).

The Vygotskian concept of *cultural signs* refers to mediators involved in the development of higher mental functions that enable subjects to become masters of their own behavior.[1]

> The tool serves for conveying man's activity to the object of his activity, it is directed outward, it must result in one change or another in the object, it is the means for man's external activity directed toward subjugating nature. The sign changes nothing in the object of the psychological operation, it is a means of psychological action on behavior, one's own or another's, a means of internal activity directed toward mastering man himself; the sign is directed inward.
>
> (Vygotsky, 1997b, p. 62)

Table 5.1 The set of concepts of cultural-historical theory used in this study and their definitions

Cultural sign	Mediator that enables subjects to become masters of their own behavior
Mediating activity	Processes of active searching for and/or creating a sign
Perezhivanie	An indivisible unity of personal and situational characteristics
Crisis	Major shift coinciding with a transformation of the one's social situation of development
Zone of proximal development	The distance between the actual developmental level and the level of potential development

Mediation and mediating activity through the use of tools and signs is one of central concepts of cultural-historical psychology: "The central fact of our psychology is the fact of mediation" (Vygotsky, 1997a, p. 133). He argued that a reconstruction of mental processes occurs through the creation and use of signs (Vygotsky, 1987). In this endeavor, video making is the mediating activity and videos are the products of mediation.

Veresov (2010b) highlights the difference between mediated (*oposredovannaya* in Russian) activity, and mediating (*oposreduyushaya* in Russian) activity. Mediated activity is based on the use of mediators such as signs and tools that have been created before. The concept of *mediating activity* refers to the "processes of active searching and finding a sign, as well as transforming of the whole unit and *transition* from direct connection to indirect (mediated) connection"(p. 86). The Vygotskian concept of *perezhivanie* is used in capturing how young people describe and present their experiences of the social crisis in their lives. The concept of *perezhivanie* refers to an indivisible unity of personality and the social environment.

> An emotional experience [perezhivanie] is a unit where, on the one hand, in an indivisible state, the environment is represented, i.e. that which is being experienced – perezhivanie is always related to something which is found outside the person – and on the other hand, what is represented is how I, myself, am experiencing this, i.e., all the personal characteristics and all the environmental characteristics are represented in perezhivanie [. . .] So, in an emotional experience [perezhivanie] we are always dealing with an indivisible unity of personal characteristics and situational characteristics, which are represented in the emotional experience [perezhivanie].
> (Vygotsky, 1994b, p. 342)

According to Veresov and Fleer, the concept of *perezhivanie* can be understood through the analysis of the relationships between three other concepts: 1) the social world as a background source for human development; 2) the interaction of ideal (developed) and real (present) forms as specific features of mental development; and 3) the general genetic law of cultural development which describes its dramatic character as inter-psychological and intra-psychological collisions (Veresov & Fleer, 2016).

The dialectic between real and ideal form is an important dimension of the general genetic law of cultural development.

> The social environment is the source for the appearance of all specific human properties of the personality gradually acquired by the child or the source of social development of the child which is concluded in the process of actual interaction of <ideal> and present forms.
> (Vygotsky, 1998, p. 203)

The ideal form refers to the developed form that acts as a model for that which should be achieved at the end of the developmental period. Vygotsky (1998) argued that the existence of appropriate ideal forms in the child's environment is a necessary condition for his or her psychological development. The interaction and the dialectics between real and ideal forms are essential for further psychological development not only for children but also for adolescents. In the present study we analyze the interaction between real and ideal forms as they are presented in young people's videos.

The Vygotskian concept of *crisis* is used in analyzing and developing understandings of the contradictorily character of developmental transition periods such as the one from childhood to adulthood and in investigating the conflicts voiced by the adolescent creators of the videos as they depict the crisis-ravaged landscape that colored their social world and the context of their daily lives.

> During these periods, abrupt and major shifts and displacements, changes, and discontinuities in the child's personality are concentrated in a relatively short time . . . In a very short time, the child changes completely in the basic traits of his personality. Development takes on a stormy, impetuous, and sometimes catastrophic character that resembles a revolutionary course of events in both rate of the changes that are occurring and in the sense of the alterations that are made.
> (Vygotsky, 1998, p. 191)

Vygotsky argues that during a crisis the *social situation of development*, the relationships between child (or adolescent) and the social reality surrounding him or her is transformed. During "this adolescent crisis", an essential transformation of the system of relations between the adolescent and adults in his or her social world occurs. What are the challenges faced by adolescents in the process of their development in the context of a decomposing social world?

In contemporary literature, the concept of *zone of proximal development* has been used mainly in the context of teaching/learning process, somewhat isolated from the whole system of concepts of cultural-historical theory (Veresov, 2010b). In contrast to this mainstream tendency in Vygotskian perspectives, the concept of zone of proximal development refers to processes that promote development. Usually the following definition of the zone of proximal development is applied:

> [T]he distance between the actual developmental level as determined by independent problem solving and the level of potential development as determined through problem solving under adult guidance, or in collaboration with more capable peers [. . .] The zone of proximal development defines those functions that have not yet matured but are in the process of maturation, functions that will mature tomorrow but are currently in an embryonic state.

These functions could be termed the buds or flowers of development rather than the 'fruits' of development. The actual developmental level characterizes mental development retrospectively, while the zone of proximal development characterizes mental development prospectively

(Vygotsky, 1978, pp. 86–87)

In the present study the investigation focuses on the impact of the deep social crisis on the zone of proximal development of young people. Specifically, this study aims to explore how youth who are in the throes of tumultuous and complex social crises are "talking" about and presenting their and their age cohorts' everyday lives on videos from the perspective of Vygotsky's cultural-historical theory. Recapitulating the questions of this research endeavor in accordance with the theoretical underpinnings, the following queries will be addressed:

1) How are youth using video making as a developmental tool and as mediating activity?
2) How is the social world presented through the prism of the videos made by young people?
3) What are the relational potentialities that the young people have internalized and which define aspects of their development?
4) How are the characteristics of Greek adolescents' personal crises impacted by the crises in their social milieu?
5) Is it possible for young people in times of social crises to promote their own development by creating and using cultural signs?

Data collection procedures

A three-phase search on internet videos was performed, first using the key words – "crisis", "Greece", "young people" – and eventually narrowing down the diverse videos (34) by reviewing and filtering the materials yielded by the first search by applying the following criteria: video made between 2008 and 2012, created by young people, directly or metaphorically addresses the issue of the economic crisis in Greece, and is in the public domain. Thirteen videos covering a wide range of "genres", i.e., reportage-style, fictional, documentaries, and "political ideology or propaganda" were judged as adhering to the criteria. The third phase of the search short-listed the shortest five videos excluding the "ideology or propaganda genre". In this paper we will present the results of the analysis the five videos identified at the end of the three-phase processes: 1) "Young People Talk about Greece in the Throes of Crisis" (Alexiptoto, 2012); 2) "Greek Financial Crisis: Youth React" (Katsoulis, 2012); 3) "Dreams under Occupation" (Lookart, 2011); 4) "News Broadcasts Severely Harm Your Health" (Pis, 2012); and 5) "KAV 3132" (Plano, 2011). Table 5.2 provides details regarding each video's title, genre,

Table 5.2 The five videos used in the analyses, their titles and genres, dates of production, producers, and descriptions

No.	Title and genre	Date	Video maker	Video description
1	"Dreams under Occupation" (In Greek: "Όνειρα υπό κατάληψη") Genre: Education "Dramatic production"	Nov. 2011	Loukas Lelovas (YouTube name: Lelovasart)	The film shows the extreme pressure that teenagers are under in contemporary times. The pressure often leads to negative consequences in that youth are left without the space to follow their own dreams and they erupt in problematic ways.
2	"KAV 3132" (In Greek: "ΚΑΒ 3132") Genre: Film and narration	Sep. 2011	"Neaniko Plano" (In Greek: "Νεανικό Πλάνο") (The film is the result of a workshop in Konitsa.)	A youthful glance on today's reality. In the asphyxiating and anxiety-provoking context that the economic crisis has created in Greece, young people problematize and seek ways out.
3	"Young People Talk about Greece in the Throes of Crisis" (In Greek: "Η Νεολαία Μιλάει για την Ελλάδα της Κρίσης") Genre: Reportage	Apr. 2012	"Alexiptoto" (parachute)	In this video young people respond to the most pressing problems that occupy Greece in crisis. The youth who present their views are "undecided" voters from various political orientations. The creators of the video stated: "It would be a great success for us if we convince even just one citizen to change opinion and to punish with his/her vote those that have brought us to this predicament". The aim of the video is not only for youth's voices to be heard but to also provoke problematizaton in the viewers, who are invited to answer the questions posed.
4	"Greek Financial Crisis: Youth React" (Original in English) Genre: Sousveilance	May 2012	Alexandra Katsoulis	Youth React: Multimedia assignment
5	"News Broadcasts Severely Harm Your Health" (In Greek: "Τα δελτία ειδήσεων βλάπτουν σοβαρά την υγεία") Genre: Reportage	Nov. 2012	1st EPAL (technical secondary school) of Argos.	This video was created as part of an assignment for a class. It focuses on news programming and broadcasting in Greece, more specifically, the discourses and techniques applied in presenting the socioeconomic crisis as it was unfolding.

date of YouTube posting, the producers, and how the video creators describe their videos.

Data analysis

In order to derive nuanced and detailed understandings of what Greek adolescents are expressing in the videos identified, we drew on an approach derived from media studies that has been used in analyzing cultural texts such as YouTube videos in which the "text" is not the only evidence of what is being expressed, and such an approach is in line with the agenda for multimodal analysis (cf. Bezemer & Kress, 2017). What the text signifies can be used as evidence to reposition the meaning of the texts to a wider field of analysis (Saul, 2010). Using a playlist folder of the YouTube videos, two researchers viewed each text together, re-reading each one several times until concordance was reached regarding its genre. The re-reading consisted of multimodal analysis of each video. In this analysis the following components were re-read: actions; movements; and semiotic analysis of camera movement, image, written or spoken language, and visual and musical socio-cultural references. They also derived a common narrative account of the visual, auditory, and symbolic textual materials and extracted a common dialogical narrative of the meanings/connotations, interpretations, and understandings presented by the filmmakers and those of the commentators by incorporating the comments and numerical indicators of re-readings from the web concerning the text. Figure 5.1 and 5.2 depict examples of the metadata collection and analysis.

By adhering to the aforementioned procedures, including excerpts from the texts and providing evidence of how and why specific meanings were derived, the lucidity and validity of the interpretations were bolstered. Moreover, the third researcher audited the "texts-on-texts" as a means to limit or control bias and, in this manner, offering "investigator triangulation" (Denzin & Lincoln, 2008, p. 17). Finally, three discussion groups were conducted in order to further verify and triangulate the "readings" of the texts. These included a discussion with students, parents, and teachers, one with the two secondary school instructors who were the technical advisors of one of the videos identified, and one which followed the viewing of one video at a university campus.

In a previous paper we have presented the thematic analysis using processes and procedures outlined by Braun and Clarke (2006) that we applied to systematically assess and code the data, develop understandings regarding actions, process, representations, symbols, and compositional components within each protocol and between protocols (Figure 5.3 presents the coding of the cultural-historical theme).

In their videos, Greek youth describe their dreams as occupied, rendering them into a state of hypnogogia, stunting their development both socially and

Youth tubing the Greek crisis 79

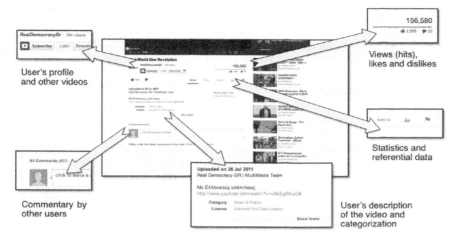

Figure 5.1 Metadata collection example

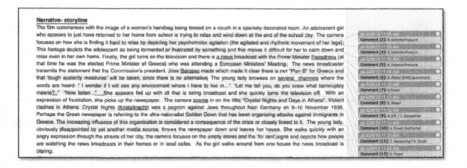

Figure 5.2 One of the five texts-on-texts

politically and consigning them to be sacrificed (Triliva, Varvantakis & Dafermos, 2015). There are three core themes analyses that we will focus on in this paper: 1) the cultural-historical elements found in the protocols, 2) the experiencing categories and codes, and 3) the interrelationships, convergence, and interaction of the themes and this from the perspective of the Vygotskian theoretical tenets previously described. Being that the researchers brought their own perspectives and ways of understanding to the endeavors of analyzing the data with multimodal analyses, we shall start with them.

Codebook categories	Sub-categories	Initial codes
OCCUPATION	o Of lived experience- life	Mass media Austerity policies Colonized by international businesses Hypnagogia Occupied lives: taken over by hopelessness, despair, insecurity Occupied lives, dreams, future, prospects, aspirations, motivations, aims Occupiers take over youths' lives Life occupied by the time in school, all day Time occupied by fears, worries Life occupied by time, all day revolves around being on time to follow lessons By the players of the chess game, when one identifies with that pawns that are being sacrificed Is there light at the end of the tunnel? By cultural, ethnic rituals aimed at homogenizing
	o Space	YouTube videos Colonized by big business Rendered unrecognizable through the infiltration of huge investments (power companies) Left without space to imagine, since dreams are occupied (2) Hypnagogia: Living in a dreamlike state – a state between being awake and sleeping Like a pawn that can only make certain moves, follow the symbolic protocol

Figure 5.3 Example of code-categorizing and processing of the cultural-historical theme of the data corpus

The researchers

In qualitative research the researchers are considered instrumental since analyses do not reside in the data alone (Glaser & Strauss, 1967) so possible researcher bias was examined. Analyses were carved out of the patterns that the researchers identified in the data, by each researcher's interpretations and conceptualizations as s/he pondered the data set, and by the dialogical interaction between the researchers as they read and re-read and reviewed the video texts and imposed their "texts" on to them. Each researcher brought his/her own unique background and point of view to this process. Sofia Triliva is an assistant professor with a background in psychology. She immigrated to the United States with her parents and was raised and educated there. She returned to Greece 25 years ago, is married and the mother of a son who grew up in Greece. Her research interests have focused on the mental health of youth, families, and communities. Christos Varvantakis works as an anthropologist and has a background in sociology and in visual anthropology.

He has undertaken research in Greece, India, and Germany, is currently working for the University of Sussex, undertaking ethnographic research with children in Athens, and has a 2-year-old son. Manolis Dafermos is an associate professor with a background in philosophy. He studied and lived in Moscow for 11 years. He has had first-hand experience with the collapse of the Soviet Union and its negative effects on people's well-being. He is married and the father of a daughter who grew up in Greece and is an adolescent. Possible biases include knowledge of familial effects of the socioeconomic crises and how it impacts one's own children; frustration with the austerity measures and effects of the crisis and the issue of migration which all three researchers have experienced and which have come to the forefront in the midst of the crises.

Our aim below is to describe what happens when young people live in circumstances where social integration breakdown occurs and to identify the effects of such social destruction on psychological development. In this instance, we are applying cultural-historical theory in a context that has been categorized as being in a state of crisis.

Video making as a developmental tool in the networked realm of youth's lives

Youth are expressing how their everyday lives have been impacted by the socioeconomic crises that have taken hold in their country in their YouTube videos. They are also interacting and communicating with each other in these "new" digital "public spaces" that are available to them, trying to arouse people's political sensibilities. Additionally, they are clearly stating that "usual" or "real" (in their words, for example, mainstream media, political parties, schools) public spaces are oppressive for them in that there is a great deal of surveillance and control by authorities (be it the police, teachers, policies, or adults in general). Youth use the videos as political tools, to beckon their cohorts to awaken, to voice their struggles, and to incite or at least call for social change.

Producing videos that are systems of cultural signs serves as a developmental tool for these young people who otherwise feel trapped in a highly oppressive and confining social milieu (Astrinaki, 2009). As boyd (2014) writes, the mainstream media narratives that constantly produce and reproduce competition, consumerism, and commercialism, as well as the surveillance and regulation by schools and parents have impinged on youth's lives and circumscribed their development. Hence, video productions allow youth to express themselves, communicate with peers, and contribute to new world-scapes. Youths' criticism of mass media serves as a stimulus for them to create and upload videos on YouTube, making their struggles visible to the world. The young people in the videos we analyzed implicate the mass media as a major source of oppression and silencing, especially for youth. They blatantly state that the mainstream media are controlled, steered into reporting in certain ways and in producing discourses that are manipulative and oppressive. A participant of the movie "Young People Talk about Greece in the Throes of Crisis", (Giannis) says: "It is foolish to convene a junta (military regime) with tanks, when there is television". Consequently, these networked teens make their struggle to be heard, to assert control, to create, and to politically engage evident in their YouTube videos.

Of the five videos we analyzed in our research, three were created and produced within school settings through collaborative learning activities. A small number of educators are encouraging and supporting their students to "create", "speak for themselves", and change the sterile and memorization-based learning that schooling has become in Greece (Astrinaki, 2009; Lazaratou, Dikeos, Anagnostopoulos & Saldatos, 2010; Sianou-Kyrgiou, 2010). In other words, creating and sharing videos can be considered as a kind of creative collaborative mediating activity for these young people. From this perspective, video making and posting is a system of signs that appears to serve as a developmental tool. Creating and using tools and signs such as videos in online landscapes such as YouTube shapes indirect-mediating forms of relating, learning, and communicating in the networked social world.

Video making as mediating activity

In contrary to the functionalistic approach to mediation which dominates media studies, Vygotsky (1987) focused on subjects mastering themselves by searching, creating, and using cultural signs. The main question is not what kind of *cultural signs* are used by subjects, but what kind of *mediating activity* subjects are engaged in and involve by using cultural signs. In his time Vygotsky analyzed artifacts such as tales, poetry, literature, and printed publications, but his approach could be expanded for the investigation of video artifacts. Of course, it is important to take into account the complex configurations of digital media and their influence on the relationship between author and public.

The creation and uploading of the videos on YouTube for the Greek adolescent creators seem to serve as a means to communicate with each other and the wider networked publics. Moreover, the young video producers share their ideas, feelings, political positions, and experiences of the crises that have shocked their communities. Creating videos and sharing them in YouTube can be considered as a kind of mediating activity. YouTube is emerging as a "dynamic experimental forum built around shared information" (Uricchio, 2009, p. 35).

Through their involvement in the new public spaces and by using the new cultural signs, Greek youth combine the old with the new and express themselves, voice their political wills, and bring about change by connecting in new ways. From the perspective of cultural-historical theory, the video with the paradoxical title "KAV3132", which presents the current Greek crisis through the eyes of adolescent girl, is a good example of how literary tools of the past are combined to communicate through video making about youths' experiences in the present. In the video, an adolescent girl who appears to just have returned to her home from school is trying to relax and wind down at the end of the school day. The adolescent is portrayed as being tormented or frustrated by something and this makes it difficult for her to calm down and relax even in her own home. The girl turns on the television and the news broadcaster transmits the statement that the Commission's President, Jose Barosso, made: there is no "Plan B" for Greece and that "tough austerity measures" will be taken, since *"there is no alternative"*.

The young girl, obviously disappointed, checks the news in a newspaper her parents bought - disappointed yet again by this other media source, she throws the newspaper down and leaves her house. She walks quickly with an angry expression through the streets of her city; the camera focuses on the empty stores and the "for rent" signs and depicts how people are watching the news broadcasts in their homes or in local cafes. Her non-verbal communication expresses anger, angst, frustration, worry, disappointment, and a sense of feeling trapped, helpless, and rudderless. The movie illustrates a dramatic collision between the young girl and adults connected with oppression and alienation. The social drama of the Greece is expressed through the personal drama of a young girl, combining new and old cultural signs.

The young protagonist walks on a path with trees, birds, and a horse. She is walking more calmly and slowly. As she walks, the chirping birds are heard and these are intermingled with the sound of running river water. In the distance there is a bridge and the young lady bends over and drinks some water from the clean and peaceful river. Suddenly, she finds a stone that has the inscription: KAV 3132. The next scene takes place in a library. The protagonist has found a book by Konstantinos Kavafi and she begins to read it. The musical accompaniment is with upbeat music as the young lady reads the words of Kavafi's poem, "In a large Greek Colony, 200 B.C.": "maybe the moment has arrived, yet, let's not is too hasty: haste is a dangerous thing. Precarious measures bring repentance. And after all, let us move forward". The protagonist expresses that she now understands what is going on in her country today.

The stone with the inscription KAV 3132 serves as a cultural sign that helps girl solve the problem that she could not solve in another way. It is worth reminding the reader that for Vygotsky, ". . . the key to controlling behavior lies in controlling stimuli. We cannot master our own behavior except through appropriate stimuli" (1997b, p. 210). Vygotsky argued that "a voluntary action begins only where one controls one's own behavior with the help of symbolic stimuli" (1987, p. 36).

In the concrete case, the young girl uses a cultural sign to find an alternative to the neoliberal one-way road of the crisis. Cultural signs can be considered as crystallizations of societal meanings. The message, the way out of the entrapment, is found in a poem of Konstantinos Kavafi that was written in the interval between 1931–1932 ("KAV 1931–1932"). Kavafi's words acquire new meaning in the social context that Greece is situated in at the moment. Reading Kavafi's poem, the young girl understands the historical and societal meaning of the current crisis in Greece. A cultural sign serves a means of the young girl for gaining control of her own behavior. The current social crisis is reframed through the mediating activity of the young girl. The epiphany-like experience of the young girl is connected with the re-contextualization of current social crisis by using traditional literary cultural signs that are imbued with collective meanings.

Greek literature (examples from the videos include the writings of Kazantzakis, Kavafi), songs (for example, "Ballad to Mr. Mentiou" by N. Xilouris), music (for example, anti-authority popular music, and music from the video game *The Matrix: Path of Neo*) and other cultural artifacts were used by young people in their videos as a means of resistance against their enslavement. Historicizing and reframing the current social crisis onto the wider cultural-historical context through creative mediating activity offers adolescents outlets for expressing themselves and opens up developmental trajectories. In all five movies, youth are urging each other to find means of resistance against oppression, the enslavement of their souls, and their potential to develop. A particular poignant example of the creative mediating activity is how the epigram from Kazantzakis's tomb is used in the video "Young People talk about Greece in the Throes of Crisis" is portrayed in the following excerpt of the "texts on texts" derived from the multimodal analysis:

> Kazantzakis's tomb with the epigram: "I do not hope for anything, I am not afraid of anything, I am free". The words chiseled on the tomb are turned into emblems with regard to freedom. This particular phrase is a message that urges one to overcome fear. In essence, freedom comes about when one's fears are overcome. The paradoxical third phrase in this inscription states that to gain freedom one needs to overcome hope also. In other words when you hope for something you become bound to it emotionally and cognitively, so one needs to go beyond thought and emotion, in order to overcome.
>
> (Text by the authors, retrieved from the data analysis)

The references and the footage in the interview that takes place on Kazantzakis's tomb is probably the most culturally affiliated message for freedom without fear and without hope. This message that seems paradoxical and anti-authority concomitantly highlights youths' predicament, their voices, their words, and their longing for change. Youth echo the existentialist message on Kazantzakis's tomb, which is profoundly philosophical, and at the same time political. It captures the subjectivity, the consciousness raising, and the social change impetus the young people portray in their videos, as it is simultaneously mediated by literary reference points and political mediating activity.

YouTube postings of an occupied social world: experiencing the crises-ridden milieu

The videos that Greek youth are posting on YouTube are used as a prism to present their social world, which they portray as ridden with economic, social, political, and humanitarian crises. These interconnected crises are described when youth use the overarching and encompassing term "occupation". In the videos, youth present their country as being occupied, colonized, and forced to adhere to the advice of "outside" institutions and the policies they put into place. Economically, the severe and relentless austerity measures have been imposed by outside forces (troika). According to the youth video creators and those speaking for themselves in the videos, the country's economy has been colonized by the globalized neoliberal dictates. In one video "Young People Talk about Greece in the Throes of Crisis", each participant depicted replies to the question: What will Greece be like in five years to come? One participant, Kostas, says: "It will be a colony, colonized and I hope it is still called Greece". Another participant, Georgos, who is featured while standing on Kazantzakis's tomb, says: "Greeks are undergoing a slow economic death, where the average Greek has been transformed to a contemporary economic slave". For the young video creators, the Greek subject has been influenced and rendered a slave without his/her volition. They categorically surmise that there is no democracy in the land where democracy was born.

Moreover, the videos depict forms of political occupation. This is substantiated by Michael Herzfeld (2002) who argues that Greece was "crypto-colonized" by the West. Meaning that it is a nation that has been rendered nominally independent and this minimal independence comes at the price of a humiliating form of economic dependence (Stewart, 2011). The young people in their productions imply that the recent debt crisis has been used by the banks, the IMF, and the European Union as a modern instrument of enslavement in the country.

With regard to the humanitarian aspects of the crisis, the videos depict the power of oppression and occupation. They illustrate how the disempowerment and economic enslavement of people destroys the prospects for development and living. The dramatic processes involved in the social disintegration trigger dramatic interpersonal collisions and personal dramas as it is evidenced by the large increases in suicidality (Economou, Madianos, Theleritis, Peppou & Stefanis, 2011; Stavrionakos et al., 2013), and declining health (Kentikelenis, Karanikolos, Reeves, McKee & Stuckler, 2014). Living within an "occupied" context where "outside" surveillance predominates everyday life, youth express that their individuality is thwarted and that there is a homogenization of their being and subjectivity. This is reflected in how they describe schooling and all aspects of everyday living. Moreover, they emphatically portray that for them these forms of subjugation nullify who they are or can be. In two of the videos this form of experience and subjectivity is depicted in scenes where the students march in unison in school, scenes of pawns being sacrificed on a chessboard and as dominoes crumbling down one by one.

The videos portray the social world as it is experienced by youth. They describe and portray a milieu that is oppressive, restrictive, and homogenizing – in other words a social situation that is inherently usurping every aspect of their freedom and limiting their development (Triliva, Varvantakis & Dafermos, 2015). These videos express young people's *perezhivanie* in the midst of turmoil. They represent how young people become aware, interpret, and emotionally and cognitively relate to the deep social crises within the surrounding cultural and social landscape. Young people's *perezhivanie* refers to personal experiencing of the social drama of Greece in the state of multiple crises. The onerous, dispiriting, unjust, and overbearing social world, as it has been emotionally and cognitively experienced by young people through their *perezhivanie*, destroys their potential and limits their zone of proximal and distant development.

Onslaught and aftermath of the crises: crumbling potentialities

The multimodal analysis of the five videos substantiated interactions of real and ideal forms in the crises-engulfed social environment and in the everyday lives of the young video creators. In the challenging reality of austerity-burdened Greece, young people confront the destruction of social institutions, the privatization of public sectors of social life, the demise of ideals such as education. As Astrinaki (2009) describes this,

> Anything public and collective (law, justice, politics, ethics, the very idea of society) is devalued by the pervasive neoliberal ideology – a degeneration of ideals from which no way out is visible.
>
> (p. 105)

Youth, in turn, talk about their lives as being taken over by hopelessness, fear, insecurity, and a sense that the values and institutions that comprised Greek society are no longer a means of support for them. They see their social world tumbling down and they are finding it hard to dream, make plans, and hope for a better future. The young people categorically state in their video productions that there is no democracy in the land where democracy was born. They explain and represent how their nation is occupied, colonized, and forced to have "outside" institutions and policies put in place for its "survival". In all the videos analyzed, there were no references or specific or clear representations of parental figures. This notable absence comes into great contrast when one considers that the "Greek family" is considered the bedrock of the culture. It seems that the young video creators hold the older generation responsible for the situation because they have voted for corrupt politicians and have through their interactions with those in power set up a system where there is no meritocracy; a system of clientelism. The young people implicate the mass media in all of this, stating that they are controlled and steered into reporting in certain ways and in (re-)producing discourses that are manipulative and oppressive.

Moreover, youth depict over and over again in their videos that they have a hard time dreaming about their futures, are self-critical with regard to how politically or socially active they are, feel depleted of hope and aspirations, call upon each other to become socially/politically active and to turn things around. For some, demonstrations are not enough. They call upon each other to wake up, to become proactive, and to be free. In one unifying voice they condemn the warped institutions, those in power, and the societal powerbrokers. In this light, youth's ideals are presented and contrasted to the experimentation that is going on in their society. By using YouTube to "circulate their struggles" (Baym & Shah, 2011) and voice their resistance (Karamichas, 2009) and using novel public networked spaces to communicate and create (boyd, 2014), new ideals and perhaps potentialities may emerge.

Education has traditionally been valued and idealized in Greek society (Sotiris, 2010), yet the adolescents present schools and schooling in very negative terms. The videos describe how youths' dreams and lives have been occupied by pointless and meaningless routines imposed by teachers and schools (the official pedagogues). The formalization and homogenization of the relationships between students and their teachers is something that is stated clearly in the five videos (cf. Figure 5.4). Teachers are represented as offering only information, not knowledge that can transform their lives. In the movie "Dreams under Occupation", a teacher says: "Are you guys serious? What will you do with your life? Are you irresponsible? You have to study, you have to get into university or else you will surmount to nothing . . ." (translated from Greek by the authors). In this way, exhorting students to follow the dictates of an oppressive society if they are to be deemed "responsible and successful".

This kind of authoritarian educational system has been characterized by Freire (1998) as "banking education" based on isolation of the learner from the process of learning. The teacher deposits information which students should mechanically receive, memorize, and reproduce. Rubtsova (2012, p. 3) argues that

> [S]chool education is still perceived exclusively as a means for transferring knowledge, skills and habits, not cultural tools, which means that children have to seek for them on their own outside the classroom.

Time and the pressures of it are present in all of the videos. Time constraints and pressures occupy young people's lives. They show clearly that their days revolve around being on time and how their entire day is under the surveillance of a "tutor" or teacher, in school and in the *frontistiria* (i.e., after-school cram lessons, cf. Sotiris, 2010). There is footage of expressionless young people in school, of school parades where the students march in unison and are dressed

Figure 5.4 Student chained to the school desk. Still from the video "Dreams under Occupation" (Lookart, 2011)

identically, and finally a young man literally tied down and chained to a school desk. The young man is trying to break away from the chairs that bind him. The schooling scenes and footage visually depict nightmarish scenarios and confining, oppressive, and homogenizing conditions. Examples of these signifiers include scenes of "parading" students and of a young man collapsing to the ground. In studies focusing on the Greek education system, there are reports of "stratification" in higher education (Sianou-Kyrgiou, 2010), social inequalities (Sianou-Kyrgiou & Tsiplakides, 2011), and the false promises of "Trojan" horse degrees (Livanos & Pouliakas, 2011). In the psychiatric literature, the negativity, the competition, and the relentless pressure have been linked to increases in self-reported suicide attempts in teens (Kokkevi, Rotsika, Arapaki & Richardson, 2011; Lazaratou, Dikeos, Anagnostopoulos & Saldatos, 2010). This, combined with the budget cuts and restructuring in social support services, has been dubbed "tragic" in that the most vulnerable groups' health and well-being are the experimental subjects (Kondilis, Giannakopoulos, Gavana, Ieorodiakonou, Waitzkin & Benos, 2013).

Youth, unconditionally, express that authority figures are experienced as oppressive and demoralizing. In their video productions, they question the legitimacy of authority and express that they do not want to identify with or emulate in any way with those holding power. A blanket condemnation of school, media, politicians, the economic powerbrokers, and the wider culture is a very poignant message (Triliva, Varvantakis & Dafermos, 2015). This, however, leaves them bereft of ideal figures or prototypes during a developmental period where such identifications are needed. This may explain their difficulties in "dreaming", in waking up and imagining other possible ways of being (Astrinaki, 2009; Triliva, Varvantakis & Dafermos, 2015). Without ideals how can one be inspired to imagine?

One of most serious aspects of the current crisis in Greece is connected with the destruction of the ability of young people to make future plans. When asked: "What are your future plans?" a young man in the video "Young People Talk about Greece in the Throes of Crisis" answers: "I have no future plans. There is no future. I cannot think of the future, there is no present, how could there be a future"? Young people feel that they have lost the control of their own life: "We do not have the rights to lead our lives". "We need to take the control of our lives in our hands". As in a song of Greek singer Vasilis Papakonstantinou: "I'm afraid for all these things that will be done for me without me". Young people's lives have been occupied by hopelessness, despair, insecurity, etc. Their dreams, future, prospects, aspirations, motivations, and aims have been occupied.

In accordance with Vygotsky's general genetic law of cultural development:

> "[E]very function in the cultural development of the child appears on the stage twice, in two planes, first, the social, then the psychological, first between the people as an intermental category, then within the child as a intramental category [...] Genetically, social relations, real relations of people, stand behind all the higher mental functions and their relations".
>
> (1997b, p. 106)

Veresov (2010b) notes that not every interaction between people becomes a source for the development of their mental functions, yet, dramatic events between them can become such sources. A social crisis can be considered as a dramatic event connected with disintegration of social relationships. Can such dramatic events lead to psychological development?

According to Rubtsova (2012), an inner role conflict representing the contradiction between the teenager's imaginary and actual role behavior underlies the adolescent crisis. This inner role conflict reveals the complex relationship between the real and the ideal form, which has been analyzed by Vygotsky (Rubtsova, 2012). On the other hand, dramatic interpersonal and intrapersonal collisions occur when a social crisis connected with the destruction of social relationships comes about. The social crises in Greece, as manifested in the videos that have been made by young people, illustrate rapid disintegration of social relationships.

Visually the crises are presented by young people in terms of a domino effect and a chessboard where the pawns are being sacrificed. They feel like pawns in a game of chess: confined by strict authorities to only make certain moves and follow symbolic protocols. In other scenes, the students are marching, a teenager is looking at himself in the mirror in apparent angst and distress, and he has large bold spots on his head. There are dominoes lined up and collapsing; if one falls, all fall together. The set of relationships that creates the zone of proximal development of young people has been destroyed, in that in their social worlds hallow protocols and procedures predominate, sacrificing their creativity and their development. The endless and repetitive activities take away their voices (only in one of the videos is there discussion and the youths' voices are heard), ability to communicate with each other, creative potential and perhaps subjectivity. This is clearly and eerily presented in Figure 5.5, from the video "Greek Financial Crisis: Youth React".

Figure 5.5 Still from the video "Greek Financial Crisis: Youth React" (Katsoulis, 2012)

The dramatic societal processes provoke dramatic intrapsychic tensions, collisions and conflicts. The social drama of contemporary Greece is carried out in a matrix of personal dramas (Dafermos, 2013). A dramatic social event such as an occupation of a country provokes a set of dramatic personal events connected with its internalization. The occupation of the social world (the occupation of Greece) led to occupation of the life world and the minds of young people. This generation of young people clearly depict how they have been sacrificed for the Euro to sail ahead. The conflict between young people's imaginary and their actual role behavior acquires dramatic (tragic) dimensions in this context. Moreover, the devaluation of ideal social forms as a result of the demise of social institutions, the individualization and fragmentation of social life creates a developmental vacuum. On the other hand, their videos allow for the unknown – perhaps somebody will hear, understand, respond, or commemorate with them.

The psychological consequences of the contemporary occupation of Greece have been presented in the videos made by young people. The video "News Broadcasts Severely Harm Your Health" – made by students in a technical school in the Greek town Argos criticize the manipulation of people by the Greek mainstream media outlets. The title is identical to the warning on cigarette containers implying that people are addicted to news programs and that both cigarettes and news programs harm one's health, the former one's psychic health the latter, one's physical health.

In the film a confrontation between colorful, blossoming flowers and the black reality reproduced through mass media is presented. Blossoming flowers in Greek culture are equated with youth and young people's ability to grow, flourish, and become what their potential allows them to be. In the context of cultural-historical theory the principle of "buds" and "flowers" has been used in order to depict the process of development of mental functions. The image of "buds" refers to functions that have not yet developed but are in the process of developing (Veresov, 2014). In this fashion, the video productions are contrasted to the social crises that stagnates their growth and taking away from their development. Mass media is equated to "a blackened" psyche and an early death by suffocation. The young students depicted in the videos state, in many ways, that they do not want this slow death and paralysis. Young people are trapped without choices or volition. They want to dream, they want to live, and they want to engage with others, hence they turn to other landscapes, new media landscapes and publics to escape an early death.

Our study focused on a multiplicity of concomitant and interwoven crises and on what happens when social crises interface with the personal crisis associated with the transition from childhood to adulthood. Youth experience mass media as manipulative; hence, they create videos for critical consciousness raising and move onto new media networks in order to create possibilities and potentialities. According to Vygotsky (1994d), adolescents' mental life is characterized by the coexistence of contradictory tendencies: conceptual thinking appears and at the same time visual thinking does not disappear. Vygotsky argues that during adolescence daydreams take up "the middle ground between a real dream and abstract thought" (1994d, p. 273). "It amounts to a creative dream vision which is conceived by the adolescent's imagination and which he experiences when awake" (1994d, p. 273).

Young people appear to be using their video creations as new tools to situate their everyday lives onto new landscapes. Through these new engagements youth are participating as young citizens and creating a "participatory culture" (Chau, 2010). YouTube videos are occupying a new landscape with great potential for youth to connect with each other and with a wider networked landscape. As Pechtelidis (2011) points out in describing how social media aided young students to react against an oppressive, contradictory, and unfair reality that had led to the death of their age cohort: "transnational network of relations" can evolve and involve

> Various agents, events, and discourses. The youth movement in Greece bears resemblances with the so-called anti-corporate globalization movement, which is currently conceptualized as the 'new, new' movement . . . The concept 'new, new' social movements illustrate a new way of thinking about active youth citizenship in the global era.
>
> (Pechtelidis, 2011, p. 451)

At that point in time, new kinds of protest emerged and as some researchers suggest, the digital media landscape facilitates active participation and communication of discontent, resistance, and defiance from the bottom-up (Papailias, 2011; Saul, 2010). Young people participate on such sites, present their lived experiences, reflect upon them, and construct new ways of relating and developing.

Outlook: escaping from the matrix of crises

Cultural-historical theory has traditionally focused on how mental functions originate and develop (Veresov, 2010a). The present study is one of the first inquiries into how a deep social crisis is impacting adolescents' development using cultural-historical theory. The analyses carried out demonstrate the contradictory nature of development as youth transverse social crises. On one hand, there are obvious tendencies towards distorted development which are reinforced by the disintegration of social relations. Youth blatantly state that their dreams have been usurped, their prospects diminished, their aspirations nullified, and ideal forms need renegotiation. In Vygotskian terms, in times of social crises the process of development from "buds" to "flowers" is blocked. On the other hand, young people actively are looking for cultural signs that may enable them to cope with the often insurmountable challenges brought to the fore. From this perspective, young people are not passive victims in the maelstrom of social crisis but active agents searching new ways to react, protest, and develop.

The socioeconomic and political crises in Greece have been dubbed dangerous social experiments where austerity measures and oppressive policies predominate. Vygotsky pointed out that, "As a result of the advance of capitalism, the development of material production simultaneously brought with it the progressive division of labor and the constantly growing distorted development of the human potential" (1994a, p. 178). Especially, in periods of crisis where physical and intellectual degradation define the capitalist system of interchange, the development of human potential is stunted.

A social crisis can be considered as a "natural experiment" (Vygotsky, 1997b, p. 227), a huge laboratory where what happens to psychological development when society is destroyed can be studied. Our findings suggest that individualization and fragmentation of social life obstructs the zone of proximal development for the generation of young people entering emerging adulthood. The social drama of the country triggers the personal dramas of young people and vice versa. However, the young people we studied through the prism of their video productions appear to be active citizens and not passive victims of the social crises that have occupied their country. The young people who created the videos attempt to find ways to escape from the matrix of social and personal crises that have dominated their lived experiences by using the sets of cultural signs available to them.

They engage in such activities away from surveillance, venturing into new territories which are remote from the oppressive rituals of their schools. Making videos and sharing them on YouTube is a creative mediating activity, and one where they venture into new networked spaces, communicate with their friends by "repurposing technology to fulfill their desires and goals" (boyd, 2014, p. 212). Using cultural signs that inspire them, young people can attempt to gain the control of their own behavior and their lives. Famous Greek literary figures such as K. P. Kavafi and N. Kazantzakis inspired the young video creators and offered them the opportunity to rethink social and personal crises in a wide cultural-historical context. Through these cultural signs and the mediated activity of creating and posting videos on networked landscapes, youth are reacting to injustices and are actively contesting what they consider to be an "occupation" of their lives, dreams, and futures by severe austerity, restrictive measures, inequalities, and injustices. As Theocharis's (2011) research highlights, young people seek new forms of "collective" political engagement.

Young people by means of their mediating activity are looking for cultural signs that will allow them to understand their current situation and transform the onerous, disheartening, and despotic conditions that have taken hold in their country. From being slaves within their environment, young people become "masters of their own behavior" (Vygotsky, 1978) looking for ways to resist enslavement.

Note

1 Regarding the difference between tool and sign cf. Rubtsova and Ulanova, 2017.

References

Alexiptoto. (2012, April 29). *Η νεολαία μιλάει για την Ελλάδα της κρίσης (Young people talk about Greece in the throes of crisis)*. Retrieved from https://www.youtube.com/watch?v=SX-hAHQQfD4 (date of access: 10/07/2013).

Andronikidou, A., & Kovras, I. (2012). Cultures of rioting and anti-systemic politics in Southern Europe. *West European Politics*, 35(4), 707–735.

Astrinaki, R. (2009). (Un)hooding a rebellion: The December 2008 events in Athens. *Social Text*, 27(4), 97–107.

Baym, G., & Shah, C. (2011). Circulating struggle. *Information, Communication and Society*, 14(7), 1017–1038.

Bezemer, J., & Kress, G. (2017). Young people, Facebook, and pedagogy: Recognizing contemporary forms of multimodal text making. In M. Kontopodis, C. Varvantakis, & C. Wulf (Eds.), *Global youth in digital trajectories*. London: Routledge.

boyd, d. (2014). *It's complicated: the social lives of networked teens*. New Haven: Yale University Press.

Braun, V., & Clarke, V. (2006). Using thematic analysis in psychology. *Qualitative Research in Psychology*, 3(2), 77–101.

Castellani, M. (2012). *Young people in Europe: Φrom "lost generation" to "sacrificed generation"?* Retrieved from http://www.theeuros.eu/Young-people-in-Europe-from-lost,5686.html?lang=fr (date of access: 10/07/2016).

Chau, C. (2010). YouTube as a participatory culture. *New Directions for Youth Development*, 128, 65–74.

Council of Europe, Parliamentary Assembly. (2012). *Resolution 1885. The young generation sacrificed: Social, economic and political implications of the financial crisis*. Retrieved from http://assembly.coe.int/ASP/XRef/X2H-DW-XSL.asp?fileid=18918&lang=en (date of access: 30/05/2012).

Dafermos, M. (2013). The social drama of Greece in times of economic crisis: The role of psychological therapies. *European Journal of Psychotherapy & Counselling*, 15(4), 401–411.

Dalakoglou, D. (2013). The crisis before "The Crisis": Violence and urban neoliberalization in Athens. *Social Justice*, 39(1), 24–42.

Denzin, N. K., & Lincoln, Y. S. (2008). Introduction: The discipline and practice of qualitative research. In N. K. Denzin & Y. S. Lincoln (Eds.), *Strategies of qualitative inquiry* (pp. 1–43).Thousand Oaks: Sage.

Economou, M., Madianos, M., Theleritis, C., Peppou, L. E., & Stefanis, C. N. (2011). Increased suicidality amid economic crisis in Greece. *Lancet*, 378(9801), 1459.

Elder, G. (1974). *Children of the great depression: Social change in life experience*. Chicago: University of Chicago Press.

Freire, P. (1998). *Pedagogy of the oppressed*. New York: Continuum.

Glaser, B. G., & Strauss, A. L. (1967). *The discovery of grounded theory: Strategies for qualitative research*. Chicago: Aldine.

Gouglas, A. (2013). The young precariat in Greece: What happened to "Generation 700 Euros?" *Journal on European Perspectives of the Western Balkans*, 5(1), 30–49.

Herzfeld, M. (2002). The absent presence: Discourses of crypto-colonialism. *South Atlantic Quarterly*, 101(4), 899–926.

Karamichas, J. (2009). The December 2008 riots in Greece. *Social Movement Studies*, 8(3), 289–293.

Karanikolos, M., Mladovsky, P., Cylus, J., Thomson, S., Basu, S., Stuckler, D., Mackenbach, J. P., & McKee, M. (2013). Financial crisis, austerity, and health in Europe. *Lancet*, 381(9874), 1323–1331.

Katsoulis, A. (2012, May 15). *Greek financial crisis: Youth react*. Retrieved from http://www.youtube.com/watch?v=hWi4SI66sf0 (date of access: 10/07/2013).

Kentikelenis, A., Karanikolos, M., Reeves, A., McKee, M., & Stuckler, D. (2014). Greece's health crisis: From austerity to denialism. *The Lancet*, 383, 748–753.

Kokkevi, A., Rotsika, V., Arapaki, A., & Richardson, C. (2011). Increasing self-reported suicide attempts by adolescents in Greece between 1984 and 2007. *Social Psychiatry and Psychiatric Epidemiology*, 46(3), 231–237.

Kondilis, E., Giannakopoulos, S., Gavana, M., Ieorodiakonou, I., Waitzkin, H., & Benos, A. (2013). Economic crisis, restrictive policies, and the population's health and health care: The Greek case. *American Journal of Public Health*, 103(5), 973-979.

Lazaratou, H., Dikeos, D. G., Anagnostopoulos, D. C., & Saldatos, C. R. (2010). Depressive symptomatology in high school students: The role of age, gender and academic pressure. *Community Mental Health Journal*, 46(3), 289–295.

Livanos, I., & Pouliakas, K. (2011). Wage returns to university disciplines in Greece: Are Greek higher education degrees Trojan Horses? *Education Economics*, 19(4), 411–445.

Lookart. (2011, November 28). *Όνειρα υπό κατάληψη (Dreams under occupation)*. Retrieved from http://www.youtube.com/watch?v=sl7QMkddZI=0 (date of access: 10/07/2013).

Malkoutzis, N. (2011). Young Greeks and the crisis: The danger of losing a generation. *International Policy Analysis*. Friedrich-Ebert Stiftung. Retrieved from http://library.fes.de/pdf-files/id/ipa/08465.pdf (date of access: 30/05/2012).

McKee, M., Karanikolos, M., Belcher, P., & Stuckler, D. (2012). Austerity: A failed experiment on the people of Europe. *Clinical Medicine*, 12(4), 346–350.

Memos, C. (2010). Neoliberalism, identification process and the dialectics of crisis. *International Journal Urban and Regional Research*, 34(1), 210–216.

Mentinis, M. (2010). Remember, Remember the 6th of December . . . A rebellion or the constituting moment of a radical morphoma? *International Journal of Urban and Regional Research*, 34(1), 197–202.

Neaniko Plano. (2011, September 28). *KAB3132 (KAV3132)*. Retrieved from https://www.youtube.com/watch?v=1E3WJ2Ln2w8 (date of access: 10/07/2013).

Panayotakis, C. (2009). Reflections of the Greek uprising. *Capitalism, Nature, Socialism*, 20(2), 97–101.

Panourgia, N. (2011). The squared constitution of dissent. In hot spots: Beyond the "Greek crisis": Histories, rhetorics, politics. *Cultural Anthropology*, 10. Retrieved from http://www.culanth.org/fieldsights/243-beyond-the-greek-crisis-histories-rhetorics-politics (date of access: 30/05/2012).

Papailias, P. (2011). Beyond the "Greek Crisis": Histories, rhetorics, politics. *Cultural Anthropology*, 10. Retrieved from http://www.culanth.org/fieldsights/243-beyond-the-greek-crisis-histories-rhetorics-politics (date of access: 30/05/2012).

Pechtelidis, Y. (2011). December uprising 2008: Universality and particularity in young people's discourse. *Journal of Youth Studies*, 14(4), 449–462.

Pis, Nik. (2012, November 15). *Τα δελτία ειδήσεων βλάπτουν σοβαρά την υγεία (News broadcasts severely harm your health)*. Retrieved from https://www.youtube.com/watch?v=h4CLe9pWcY0 (date of access: 10/07/2013).

Psimitis, M. (2011, April). The protest cycle of spring 2010 in Greece. *Social Movement Studies*, 10, 191–197.

Rubtsova, O. (2012). Adolescent crisis and the problem of role identity. *Cultural-Historical Psychology*, 1, 1–7.

Rubtsova, O., & Ulanova, N. (2017). Digital filmmaking as a means for the development of reflection: A case study of a disabled university student in Moscow. In M. Kontopodis, C. Varvantakis, & C. Wulf (Eds.), *Global youth in digital trajectories*. London: Routledge.

Sakellaropoulos, S. (2012). On the causes and significance of the December 2008 social explosion in Greece. *Science & Society*, 76, 340–364.

Saul, R. (2010). KevJumba and the adolescence of YouTube. *Educational Studies*, 46, 457–477.

Sianou-Kyrgiou, E. (2010). Stratification in higher education, choice and social inequalities in Greece. *Higher Education Quarterly*, 64(1), 22–40.

Sianou-Kyrgiou, E., & Tsiplakides, I. (2011). Similar performance, but different choices: Social class and higher education in Greece. *Studies in Higher Education*, 36, 89–102.

Sotiris, P. (2010). Rebels with a cause: The December 2008 Greek Youth Movement as a condensation of deeper social and political condensations. *International Journal of Urban and Regional Research*, 34(1), 203–209.

Stavrionakos, K., Pachi, A., Paplos, K., Nikoviokis, D., Fanouraki, E., Tselebis, A., Lekka, D., Karakasidou, E., Kontaxakis, V., & Moussas, G. (2013, January). Suicide before and during the financial crisis in Greece. *European Psychiatry*, 28(1), 1.

Stewart, C. (2011). Colonizing the Greek mind? Indigenous and Exogenous Psychotherapeutics. Paper presented at the conference *Colonizing the Greek mind: The reception of western psychotherapeutics in Greece*, Athens. The American College of Greece. Retrieved from http://www.ucl.ac.uk/anthropology/people/academic_staff/c_stewart/Stewart-Introduction.pdf (date of access: 30/05/2012).

Theocharis, Y. (2011). Young people, political participation and online postmaterialism in Greece. *New Media Society*, 13(2), 203–223.

Triliva, S., Varvantakis, C., & Dafermos, M. (2015). YouTube, young people and the socioeconomic crises in Greece. *Information, Communication and Society*, 18(4), 407–423.

Uricchio, W. (2009). The future of a medium once known as television. In P. Snickars & P. Vonderau (Eds.), *YouTube reader* (pp. 24–39). Stockholm: National Library of Sweden.

Veresov, N. (2010a). Introducing cultural historical theory: Main concepts and principles of genetic research methodology. *Cultural- Historical Psychology*, 4, 83–90.

Veresov, N. (2010b). Forgotten methodology: Vygotsky's case. In A. Toomela & J. Valsiner (Eds.), *Methodological thinking in psychology: 60 years gone astray* (pp. 267–295). Charlotte: IAP Publishers.

Veresov, N. (2014). Refocusing the lens on development: Towards genetic research methodology. In M. Fleer & A. Ridgway (Eds.), *Visual methodologies and digital tools for researching with young children transforming visuality* (pp. 129–149). London: Springer.

Veresov, N., & Fleer, M. (2016). Perezhivanie as a theoretical concept for researching young children's development. *Mind, Culture & Activity*. 23(4), 325-335.

Vygotsky, L. (1978). *Mind in society: The development of higher psychological processes*. Cambridge: Harvard University Press.

Vygotsky, L. (1987). Tool and sign in the development of child. In R. Rieber & J. Wolloc (Eds.), *The collected works of L.S. Vygotsky* (Vol. 6, pp. 1–70). New York and London: Plenum Press.

Vygotsky, L. S. (1994a). The socialist alteration of man. In R. Van Der Veer & J. Valsiner (Eds.), *The Vygotsky reader* (pp. 175–184). Oxford: Blackwell.

Vygotsky, L. S. (1994b). The problem of the environment. In R. Van Der Veer & J. Valsiner (Eds.), *The Vygotsky reader* (pp. 338–344). Oxford: Blackwell.

Vygotsky, L. S. (1994c). Thought in schizophrenia. In R. Van Veer & J. Valsiner (Eds.), *The Vygotsky reader* (pp. 313–326). Oxford: Blackwell.

Vygotsky, L. S. (1994d). Imagination and creativity of the adolescent. In R. Van Veer & J. Valsiner (Eds.), *The Vygotsky reader* (pp. 266–288). Oxford: Blackwell.

Vygotsky, L. S. (1997a). The problem of consciousness. In R. Rieber & J. Wolloc (Eds.), *The collected works of L.S. Vygotsky* (Vol. 3, pp. 129–138). New York and London: Plenum Press.

Vygotsky, L. S. (1997b). The history of the development of higher mental functions. In R. Rieber & J. Wolloc (Eds.), *The collected works of L.S. Vygotsky* (Vol. 4, pp. 1–252). New York and London: Plenum Press.

Vygotsky, L. S. (1998). The problem of age. In R. Rieber & J. Wolloc (Eds.), *The collected works of L.S. Vygotsky* (Vol. 5, pp. 187–205). New York and London: Plenum Press.

Williams, C., & Maruthappu, M. (2013). "Healthconomic crises": Public health and neoliberal economic crises. *American Journal of Public Health*, 103(1), 7–9.

6 Dove YouTube campaign "the pressure on young girls and women to fit an artificial body ideal"

A sequential analysis

Alexios Brailas, Giorgos Alexias, and Konstantinos Koskinas

Introduction

Despite the increasing popularity of the YouTube platform, little empirical research accounts for the opinions that users express regarding a popular uploaded video. Users' opinions are manifested through the ongoing interaction between them and through the interexchange of comments within the virtual discussion space that is reserved for each YouTube video. Social media in general facilitate comment postings and exchange of opinions giving rise to potential consensus or conflict. Suitable research methods are needed to further develop the research in virtual spaces, virtual communities, and computer mediated environments that facilitate asynchronous threaded discussions. A key methodological framework suitable for analyzing artifacts employing multiple presentation modes is multimodal analysis (Kress, 2010; Bezemer & Kress, 2017).

Some other key methodological frameworks that can be successfully applied to the analysis of websites, blogs, social media, and other virtual environments are semiotics, genre, narrative, discourse, and content analysis (Fernandez-Luque, Grajales III & Elahi, 2009; Keelan, Pavri-Garcia, Tomlinson & Wilson, 2007; Pace, 2008). Content analysis is often used in virtual environments for studying the content of communication between users (Lange, 2007; Milliken, Gibson & O'Donnell, 2008). Content analysts examine text, digital media, and artifacts or data of any possible form in order to interpret their meaning in a given context (Krippendorff, 2004). YouTube videos are often at the focus of content analysis research in order to understand their impact, what they mean to people and in what ways they stimulate them to act (Hussin, Frazier & Thompson, 2011; Kim, Paek & Lynn, 2010; Waters & Jones, 2011; Yoo & Kim, 2012).

However, traditional approaches to content analysis do not offer a sequential view on the interaction between individuals. An important question is how each comment sequence is related to and evokes consequent patterns of responses, moving on the overall discourse towards a specific direction. In other words, traditional content analysis techniques focus on the meaning of isolated utterances and not on the systematic interaction between them. Examining comment sequences might be crucial in understanding the evolving dynamics of a discussion in a specific virtual setting. This analysis can be used to estimate the probability of a particular answer to follow a previous posted comment. The focus of this paper is on demonstrating the application of sequential analysis method (as introduced by Bakeman & Gottman, 1997) to study the dynamics of an online discussion. The steps followed are presented in detail in order to help other researchers to utilize this method in similar or different discussion spaces or adapt it to meet their own research pursuits.

Dialogism as theoretical background for sequential analysis

Dialogism, the theory developed by Michael Bakhtin, offers a suitable theoretical background for analyzing comments in their context, as instrumental parts of a progressive discussion:

> Dialogism argues that all meaning is relative in the sense that it comes about only as a result of the relation between two bodies occupying simultaneous but different space, where bodies may be thought of as ranging from the immediacy of our physical bodies, to political bodies and to bodies of ideas in general (ideologies).
>
> (Holquist, 2002, p. 19)

Bakeman and Gottman, in their introduction to sequential analysis (Bakeman & Gottman, 1997) do not attempt to make any connection between Bakhtin's dialogism and their method. However, we think dialogism, due to its emphasis on dialogue, offers a strong theoretical background to the rationale of sequential analysis. According to Bakhtin, no utterance is generated from nothing and no utterance could be understood isolated from its dialogic context. The meaning of a posted comment is relative as it comes about only as a result of its relation to the previous comments and to the comments that are anticipated to follow.

Bakhtin argues that we cannot choose not to be in a dialogue, not only with other persons, but also with the cultural settings around us (Holquist, 2002). In line with Bakhtinian theoretical tradition, every posted text comment in an online discussion is ultimately involved in an ongoing dialogue not only with all the other user comments but also with the very media artifact, the YouTube video and the virtual audience of the discussion, either participating actively or lurking behind the main discussion stage. This argument raises the importance of studying the responses that follow a video or a comment in a *systematic sequential way*. For Bakhtin the relation between a center and a not-center is what integrates them into a unique triad of meaning:

> Dialogue is a manifold phenomenon, but for schematic purposes it can be reduced to a minimum of three constituents, having a structure very much

like the triadic construction of the linguistic sign: a dialogue is composed of an utterance, a reply, and a relation between the two.

(Holquist, 2002, p. 36)

A relation is always under a constant negotiation, always in the process of being made or unmade (Holquist, 2002). Social context is accorded so much importance in dialogism that, according to Holquist, it almost begins to verge on determinism. Previous comments can determine probabilities of subsequent comment sequences:

... an utterance is never in itself originary: an utterance is always an answer to another utterance that precedes it, and is therefore always conditioned by, and in turn qualifies, the prior utterance to a greater or lesser degree.

(Holquist, 2002, p. 58)

Every single comment can be understood solely on the base of its relation to all the other neighboring comments in a specific discussion. A Bakhtinian a priori is that nothing is anything in itself: an utterance is void until the generation of a response (Holquist, 2002). Based on the assumptions of the Bakhtinian theory as a theoretical background for sequential analysis, this study focuses not only on the analysis of the isolated comments (nonsequential view) but also on the relations and the transitions between these comments (sequential view) on the YouTube video's discussion.

Sequential analysis vs. nonsequential analysis

Content analysis can be used for analyzing the content of a discussion: what is it at stake, what arguments are articulated, the concepts that emerge, even how the individuals may be experiencing their own active participation. But this important evaluation of the comments in a discussion does not tell us much about how the actual interaction evolves. What has been stated before determines the responses that are following and the arguments that are going to be articulated. Nonsequential evaluation of the content of a discussion does not help us to understand how an argument or an opinion resonates with the previous ones or with those expected to follow later on. In a focus-group discussion, in a family therapy session, in a school class activity, or in any virtual discussion space where two or more persons are actively participating in an ongoing dialogue by posting comments, in order to evaluate the discussion dynamics, in order to understand the way persons are relating to each other and experiencing their encounter, a sequential view is essential (Bakeman & Gottman, 1997).

A systematic observation of what is virtually occurring in the discussion space is a prerequisite before analyzing the interaction pattern. The aim of systematic observation is to identify various forms of behavior and construct a set of possible behaviors that can be used later as a coding scheme (Bakeman & Gottman, 1997). In the case of a YouTube discussion space and under the prism of Bakhtin's theory for dialogism, this coding scheme contains a set of categories that can be used to represent the different positions, arguments, opinions, or judgments in relation to the content of the video. This set is used by the researcher to code every single utterance in the discussion page. A general coding scheme paradigm based on an extensive content analysis of more than 66,000 user comments on YouTube videos was developed to aid researchers in their analysis (Madden, Ruthven & McMenemy, 2013). However, a coding scheme to be used does not need to be predefined; the researcher can construct the set based on the peculiarities of the particular research data (Bakeman & Gottman, 1997).

Several different coding schemes can be used to highlight different aspects of a discussion (Bakeman & Gottman, 1997). Revisions of the coding scheme are quite often during the coding process as the researcher gains deeper knowledge of the empirical data. Adaptations are usually needed to match a different context, like a different artifact uploaded on a different social media platform that triggers the initiation of a discussion between online viewers. In any case, just coding every unique comment in isolation and not in its discussion context does not tell us the entire story. It does not tell us much about how specific opinions might be sequenced in the stream of the discussion:

> Sequential analysis can provide an additional level of information about whatever behavior we are observing, a level that is not accessible to nonsequential analysis.
>
> (Bakeman & Gottman, 1997, p. 7)

Nonsequential analysis can tell us what the user attitudes toward a specific video are. Sequential analysis of the observed data can give answers to questions like: what happens to a person who is expressing an opinion opposite to the mainstream opinion in a cyber-discussion space? In what way is a personal point of view treated by other participants?

Case study: Dove's Onslaught campaign on YouTube

The ideal of beauty today, at least as many women perceive it via the advertisements and the mass media productions, is considered to be unnatural, unhealthy, and unrealistic (Dye, 2009). The film *Onslaught* produced in 2007 for the Dove beauty products company and directed by Tim Piper is meant to show the pressures on young girls and women to fit an artificial body ideal, the pressure to be "perfect" no matter the cost paid. The video features a young girl being bombarded by images of impossible-to-obtain beauty. The video ends with the message: "talk to your daughter before the beauty industry does". This viral video and the text comments made by users can be accessed on YouTube platform under the title *Beauty Pressure* at: *http://www.youtube.com/watch?v=Ei6JvK0W60I* (accessed on May 5, 2014). For the purposes of the present study, the first 600 comments posted were retrieved and consequently analyzed.

Dove YouTube campaign 101

Constructing coding schemes

Initially, the coding scheme was constructed from the tentative analysis of the 600 retrieved text comments. The main unit of analysis for the formation of the coding scheme categories was the position of a comment in relation to the video's central message (considered to be: beauty industry pressure on young girls). Thirteen coding scheme categories were identified as listed in Table 6.1. Subsequently, applying a content analysis approach, each comment was categorized and coded, according to this categorization. A few comments not in English were omitted because it was not possible to analyze them. Some composite comments were coded in more than one category (for example a comment stating agreement with the video message and praise for the girl-actor simultaneously).

After the initial coding phase, sequences of comments and responses were identified. YouTube's discussion space allows technically for a comment to be posted as a response to the video or to the previous discourse in general or as a

Table 6.1 Coding scheme categories and relative observed frequencies

Code	Explanation
U1	A comment in sheer agreement with the central manifest message of the video (beauty industry pressure on young girls)
U2	A comment in partial agreement with the central message of the video (explicitly citing some objections).
U3	A comment in sheer disagreement with the central message of the video.
U4	A comment in partial disagreement with the central message of the video (explicitly citing some objections).
U5	An insulting comment against someone who previously expressed an agreement with the video's message.
U6	An insulting comment against someone who previously expressed a disagreement with the video's message.
U7	A comment implying that the central video message is not the manifest (not about the beauty industry pressure on young girls) but something else.
U8	A comment expressing praise for the nice artistic and technical work done by the filmmakers.
U9	A comment expressing praise for the appearance and the performance of the little girl (the main film actor).
U10	A comment about the music theme of the video (expressing praise, asking for extra info or where to find it).
U11	A comment posting a link to another web resource (usually to another similar YouTube video).
U12	A comment without clear meaning (using inapprehensible words, grammar, syntax, words, so that it cannot be interpreted).
U13	Other comment not in the above categories (sometimes users are posting comments possibly irrelevant to the main discourse, like spam).

Note: Categories U1 to U7 are comments explicitly or implicitly expressing a position in relation to the central video message. Categories U8 to U10 are concerning characteristics of the specific media product (actor, music, director), while categories U11 to U13 do not relate to the previous groups.

102 *Brailas, Alexias, and Koskinas*

response to a particular comment, forming hierarchically organized interaction threads. Every hierarchical interaction thread was recorded in relation to the initial comment that fired the chained response. In some cases it was obvious that a comment was initiated as a response to a previous one, even though it was not hierarchically organized in a strict technical manner, that is visually indented (for example by explicitly using the nickname of a previously participating user at the beginning of a comment). These comment-response sequences were also taken into account. A total of 219 comment-response pairs were identified.

Nonsequential results: youth in agreement with Dove's campaign?

Systematic coding using coding scheme categories resulted in 593 coded comments (it was not possible to code some comments not in English). The relative (%) frequencies of comment occurrences according to the proposed categorization are listed in Chart 6.1. Computing such frequencies is a nonsequential use of data, but it does allow us to determine whether some utterances are more common than others or which specific positions are more popular (Bakeman & Gottman, 1997). Most of the comments (226 or 38.45%) have expressed sheer agreement to the central video message (beauty industry pressure on young girls) and approval to the production of the video by Dove. Another 12.31% (73) of the user comments were in partial agreement with the video message by clearly stating what

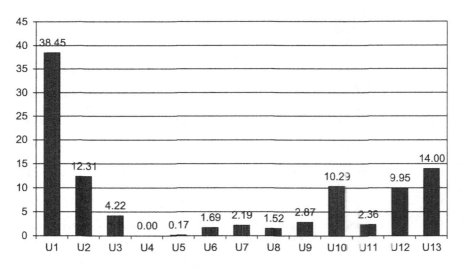

Chart 6.1 Coding scheme categories and relative observed frequencies

Note: U1 = agreement; U2 = partial agreement; U3 = disagreement; U4 = partial disagreement; U5 = insult to agreement; U6 = insult to disagreement; U7 = "the point is other..."; U8 = praise for the art/technical work; U9 = praise for the little girl performance; U10 = music theme; U11 = providing external link; U12 = incomprehensible; U13 = other – spam

Dove YouTube campaign 103

they considered as a paradox; Dove is a member of the same industry which is responsible for bombarding young girls with unnatural and unhealthy images about beauty. For example a user commented:

> Dove's parent company, Unilever, produces Axe shower gel – how's that for a positive female image. Even worse, Unilever India produces skin lightening creams under the names 'Fair and Lovely' and 'Fair and Handsome'. The commercials for these products depicted darker-skinned Indians as unsuccessful at courting members of the opposite sex. Positive self-image, eh?

Another 4.22% (25) of the comments were categorized as U3 (expressing opposition to the main message of the video campaign). For example, a user commented:

> two things: ugly people are ugly people, don't try thinking its ok to be ugly. Second ugly people are hard to look at.

The percentage of disagreement comments (U3) is relatively small (4.22%) in comparison to the total comments of sheer or partial agreement (U1 and U2 in total: 50.76%), indicating that the prevailing public opinion is in consonance with the message that the beauty industry is bombarding children with vicious stereotypes. This observation will be helpful in a later stage, during sequential analysis in order to find out what responses were provoked by those comments categorized as opposite to the prevailing opinion (U3).

None of the 593 coded comments were coded as partial disagreement (U4). However, this code category was included in the coding scheme set in order to be employed in a future analysis of other campaign YouTube videos. Maybe the domination of agreement comments (U1+U2) forced users in partial disagreement (U4) to be polarized behind sheer disagreement (U3), but this is a hypothesis that cannot be addressed by the present analysis. Only 11 of the 593 coded comments were categorized as insulting, either against those in agreement with the video (only one) or against those in disagreement (10 comments). These facts indicate that the overall debate between users was in a climate of respect for each other's opinions on this particular video. Sequential analysis will show later what (if anything) has provoked the insulting comments.

A few comments (2.19%) were coded as U7, considering the central question is something else (not whether the beauty industry is bombarding girls or not). For example a user posted the comment:

> This campaign could only exist in such a decadent society as ours. All the other countries in the world where people don't have to worry about being fat because they're STARVING TO DEATH.

Very few comments (1.52%) expressed praise for the nice technical work (U8), congratulating the video director. The young girl's acting performance was praised in 2.87% of the comments (U9). There were many comments (10.29%) about the music theme of the video, asking or giving information about the performer or expressing praise. In 2.36% of the comments, users were posting links to other internet resources (U11), usually to other official videos by Dove or parodies of these videos. Some comments (9.95%) were totally incomprehensible or spam (coded as U12). Another group of comments (14%) were irrelevant or it was not possible to categorize them in other existing coding scheme categories and so they were coded as U13.

Applying sequential analysis: consensus or polarization?

When utterances are recorded sequentially, we can answer to a different set of questions (Bakeman & Gottman, 1997). For example, we can go on to ask: what happens after a user praises Dove's campaign or after a user criticizes Dove? In order to catch the sequential dimension, after the initial coding of each separated utterance according to the coding scheme, every comment-response sequence was coded jointly as a pair. Table 6.2 shows the absolute occurrences of all the recorded 219 two-comment sequences. Based on Table 6.2, the transitional probabilities between comments and responding comments were calculated and are shown in Table 6.3. The conditional probability P(Ux|Uy) is the probability that Ux occurs given that event Uy occurred (Asimow & Maxwell 2010). Transitional probability is one special application of conditional probability, when a time lag is involved (Bakeman & Gottman, 1997; Yoder & Symons, 2010). The transitional probability $P_{tr}(Ux|Uy)$ can be defined as the probability of a comment coded as Ux to follow an antecedent comment coded as Uy, thus indicating the probability of a "transition" from Uy to Ux.

Table 6.2 Absolute frequencies of observed coding scheme categories

	U1	U2	U3	U4	U5	U6	U7	U8	U9	U10	U11	U12	U13
U1	10	10	6				1				2		8
U2	29	17						1	1			1	
U3	27		4		10								7
U4													
U5						1							
U6			1		1								
U7	2						7						
U8								1					
U9									2				
U10	1									29			1
U11											1		
U22												10	1
U13	1										1		25

Note: U1 = agreement; U2 = partial agreement; U3 = disagreement; U4 = partial disagreement; U5 = insult to agreement; U6 = insult to disagreement; U7 = "the point is other...."; U8 = praise for the art/technical work; U9 = praise for the little girl performance; U10 = music theme; U11 = providing external link; U12 = incomprehensible; U13 = other – spam

Dove YouTube campaign 105

Table 6.3 Transitional probabilities of observed coding scheme categories

	U1	U2	U3	U4	U5	U6	U7	U8	U9	U10	U11	U12	U13
U1	,27	,27	,16	,00	,00	,00	,03	,00	,00	,00	,05	,00	,22
U2	,59	,35	,00	,00	,00	,00	,00	,02	,02	,00	,00	,02	,00
U3	,56	,00	,08	,00	,00	,21	,00	,00	,00	,00	,00	,00	,15
U4	,00	,00	,00	,00	,00	,00	,00	,00	,00	,00	,00	,00	,00
U5	,00	,00	,00	,00	,00	1,00	,00	,00	,00	,00	,00	,00	,00
U6	,00	,00	,50	,00	,50	,00	,00	,00	,00	,00	,00	,00	,00
U7	,22	,00	,00	,00	,00	,00	,78	,00	,00	,00	,00	,00	,00
U8	,00	,00	,00	,00	,00	,00	,00	1,00	,00	,00	,00	,00	,00
U9	,00	,00	,00	,00	,00	,00	,00	,00	1,00	,00	,00	,00	,00
U10	,03	,00	,00	,00	,00	,00	,00	,00	,00	,94	,00	,00	,03
U11	,00	,00	,00	,00	,00	,00	,00	,00	,00	,00	1,00	,00	,00
U22	,00	,00	,00	,00	,00	,00	,00	,00	,00	,00	,00	,91	,09
U13	,04	,00	,00	,00	,00	,00	,00	,00	,00	,00	,04	,00	,93

Note: U1 = agreement; U2 = partial agreement; U3 = disagreement; U4 = partial disagreement; U5 = insult to agreement; U6 = insult to disagreement; U7 = "the point is other ..."; U8 = praise for the art/technical work; U9 = praise for the little girl performance; U10 = music theme; U11 = providing external link; U12 = incomprehensible; U13 = other – spam

In each cell of the matrix in Table 6.3, the calculated transitional probabilities for each possible two-comment sequence are listed. For example, a posted comment coded as U3 (expressing opposition to the prevailing stance) was followed 56% of the time by a U1 comment (sheer agreement), 00% of the time by a U2 comment (partial agreement), 8% of the time by another U3 comment, 21% of the time by a U6 comment (insulting comment against someone who disagrees) and so on. So the transitional probability $P_{tr}(U6|U3) = 0.21$, that is the probability of transition from a U3 comment to U6 comment is 0.21 (in 21% of the observed cases an opinion against the prevailing one was followed by an insulting comment).

What we want to know is whether certain transitions are especially characteristic of this particular discussion space. By observing Table 6.2 and Table 6.3 we can see that most of the comments are posted in the area defined by the intersection of the first three rows and the first three columns, that is comment combinations of U1, U2, or U3. Actually 103 of the total 219 coded comment-response sequences were pairs of U1, U2, or U3 comments. Comments in sheer agreement with the video's message (U1) were followed in 27% of the cases by comments of identical position (U1) and in 27% of the cases were followed by comments of partial agreement (U2). This is indicating the existence of a discussion polarization on the side of U1 and U2 comments. Only in 16% of the cases, sheer agreement comments were followed by sheer disagreement (U3). The existence of a symphony between comments expressing sheer agreement and partial agreement is evident in the second row of Table 6.3. U2 comments were followed in 59% of the cases by U1 comments. So the probability of having a U2, U1 sequence was almost double in comparison to the probability of a U1, U2 sequence. This might be interpreted as some users were feeling the need to defend the production of this video, no matter potential flaws. For example, a user commented:

> dove = the beauty industry, dove says talk to your daughter before the beauty industry does, so by listening to them and talking to her you are obeying the beauty industry, becoming a total hypocrite and continuing the process they are trying to 'stop'. Whoever thought of this xxxxxx is an absolute GENIUS. kudos!!

to receive the answer:

> I don't think it matters who is bringing the issue up, it's just great that its being discussed.

Comments of partial agreement (U2) were followed in 35% of the cases by similar position comments (U2) showing there is a significant consensus about partial agreement.

Comments in sheer disagreement with the video's message (U3) were followed in 56% of the cases by comments of sheer agreement and never by comments of partial agreement. This is indicating that the debate between agreement and disagreement comments may be causing a polarization of opinions and a shift from partial agreement positions to sheer agreement. Comments of disagreement were followed by same comments only in 8% of the cases. But in 21% of the cases were followed by insulting comments (U6) something that did not happen in the case of agreement comments (either sheer or partial, U1 or U2). It turns out that expressing a position against the prevalent one often results in conflicts and insults.

Reflection and discussion

Central in sequential analysis is the construction of coding categories (Bakeman & Gottman, 1997). Bakhtin argues that:

> we can make sense of the world only by reducing the number of its meanings (which are potentially infinite) to a restricted set.
>
> (Holquist, 2002, p. 46)

This is the role of the coding scheme in the present study. The way the coding scheme is constructed determines the level and the focus of analysis. In this study what was analyzed and investigated were mainly the positions of the users in relation to what was regarded to be the central video message. Also some other categories of comments were analyzed that proved to be prevalent in the discussion space, like the music theme used in the video or the performing of the little girl-actor. The specific coding scheme can be adapted and expanded to include more categories of comments, or radically altered in order to be utilized in the analysis of other user discussions in different contexts. Coding scheme categories depend on the research questions, if these research questions are set before. On the other hand, coding scheme categories can emerge from empirical data, if a more grounded approach is adopted and totally unknown patterns of comment interactions need to be discovered. In the latter case, a pilot analysis is needed to determine the tentative coding scheme categories.

The point of this study is that, given a sequential view, coupled with simple probabilities calculation, we were able to understand some extra, important aspects of the way users interact in a virtual discussion space. By applying sequential analysis we identified significant patterns in the exchange of comments in this particular video discussion space. Interaction patterns of most interest were those associated with the opposition against the prevailing public opinion. For example, comments categorized according to the coding scheme as "in disagreement to the central video message" were followed in 21% of the cases by insulting responses, while agreement comments were never followed by a direct insult. Going against the public opinion maybe is a risky business that can escalate to a conflict in a virtual discussion setting.

This research is preliminary and bounded to the particular context analyzed. The above conclusions have to be regarded as tentative until other studies support the results with further data. Although we suppose that most comments were posted by young people, a key limitation of this research is that it was not possible to collect any demographic data about the users. YouTube users are not obliged to give their full credentials during registration. In addition to this, a user can declare, for example, the opposite sex and practically nobody, under normal conditions, will check it. Also, YouTube users can have their profiles set not to be displayed in public, so even "what you declare to be info" cannot be retrieved. Another key limitation present in many virtual discussion spaces is that the data collected are skewed. For example, lurkers, users that simply read the discussion and do not post comments, are not represented in the data set (Gaffney & Puschmann, 2014). As Golder and Macy note:

> As a discipline devoted to explaining patterns of human behavior and social interaction, sociologists often have to choose whether to rely on direct real-time observation of very small numbers of non-representative individuals (e.g., in field observation or in the laboratory) or to rely on indirect retrospective accounts obtained through survey responses from large representative samples. Social media offers us the opportunity for the first time to both observe human behavior and interaction in real time *and* on a global scale.
> (2012)

However, inferences about the population at large are not possible without demographic data and the usefulness of this research from the sociological perspective is limited (Gaffney & Puschmann, 2014).

Despite the above limitations, the research findings in this study strongly highlight that sequential analysis can be a quite useful research method for understanding the dynamics of user interactions in social media discussions, given that a way for collecting enough metadata (like demographic information) will be available in the future. In the present study, sequential view was utilized to analyze the dialogue dynamics in a discussion initiated in the YouTube comments space on the Dove's *Onslaught* video campaign. Discussion spaces with similar properties are quite common in cyberspace. The continued use of the sequential analysis method could be instrumental in analyzing comments exchange in other YouTube videos (of the same or different type) or in different social media platforms, where threaded virtual interactions are thriving. In this direction, sequential analysis can be used as a building block to the development of a methodological research toolkit for understanding virtual social interactions. We hope that the added sequential view layer will offer a useful additional analysis tool towards this new methodological toolkit for advancing empirical research in virtual environments.

References

Asimow, L. A., & Maxwell, M. M. (2010). *Probability and statistics with applications: A problem solving text*. Winsted: ACTEX Publications.

Bakeman, R., & Gottman, J. M. (1997). *Observing interaction: An introduction to sequential analysis*. Cambridge: Cambridge University Press.

Bezemer, J., & Kress, G. (2017). Young people, Facebook, and pedagogy: Recognizing contemporary forms of multimodal text making. In M. Kontopodis, C. Varvantakis, & C. Wulf (Eds.), *Global youth in digital trajectories*. London: Routledge.

Dye, L. (2009). Consuming constructions: A critique of Dove's campaign for real beauty. *Canadian Journal of Media Studies*, 5(1), 114–126.

Fernandez-Luque, L., Grajales, F. J. III, & Elahi, N. (2009). An analysis of personal medical information disclosed in YouTube videos created by patients with multiple sclerosis. In K. P. Adlassnig (Ed.), *Medical Informatics in a United and Healthy Europe* (pp. 292–297). Amsterdam: IOS Press.

Gaffney, D., & Puschmann, C. (2014). Data collection on twitter. In K. Weller, A. Bruns, J. Burgess, M. Mahrt, & C. Puschmann (Eds.), *Twitter and society* (pp. 55–68). New York: Peter Lang.

Golder, S., & Macy, M. (2012). Social science with social media. *ASA Footnotes*, 40(1), 7.

Holquist, M. (2002). *Dialogism: Bakhtin and his world*. New York: Routledge.

Hussin, M., Frazier, S., & Thompson, J. K. (2011). Fat stigmatization on YouTube: A content analysis. *Body Image*, 8(1), 90–92.

Keelan, J., Pavri-Garcia, V., Tomlinson, G., & Wilson, K. (2007). YouTube as a source of information on immunization: A content analysis. *JAMA*, 298(21), 2481–2484.

Kim, K., Paek, H.-J., & Lynn, J. (2010). A content analysis of smoking fetish videos on YouTube: Regulatory implications for tobacco control. *Health Communication*, 25(2), 97–106.

Kress, G. (2010). *Multimodality: A social semiotic approach to contemporary communication*. Abingdon: Routledge.

Krippendorff, K. (2004). *Content analysis: An introduction to its methodology*. New York: Sage.

Lange, P. G. (2007). Commenting on comments: Investigating responses to antagonism on YouTube. Presented at the annual conference of the *Society for applied anthropology*,

Florida. Retrieved from http://sfaapodcasts.files.wordpress.com/2007/04/update-apr-17-lange-sfaa-paper-2007.pdf.

Madden, A., Ruthven, I., & McMenemy, D. (2013). A classification scheme for content analyses of YouTube video comments. *Journal of Documentation*, 69(5), 693–714.

Milliken, M., Gibson, K., & O'Donnell, S. (2008). User-generated video and the online public sphere : Will YouTube facilitate digital freedom of expression in Atlantic Canada? *American Communication Journal*, 10(3), 1–14.

Pace, S. (2008). YouTube: An opportunity for consumer narrative analysis? *Qualitative Market Research: An International Journal*, 11(2), 213–226.

Waters, R. D., & Jones, P. M. (2011). Using video to build an organization's identity and brand: A content analysis of nonprofit organizations' YouTube videos. *Journal of Nonprofit & Public Sector Marketing*, 23(3), 248–268.

Yoder, P., & Symons, F. (2010). *Observational measurement of behavior*. New York: Springer.

Yoo, J. H., & Kim, J. (2012). Obesity in the new media: A content analysis of obesity videos on YouTube. *Health Communication*, 27(1), 86–97.

7 Youth, Facebook, and mediated protest in India
A cross-media exploration

Supriya Chotani

Introduction

Internet use has grown phenomenally across the world in the last two decades. However, access to it continues to be marked by a digital divide, which overlaps, albeit not neatly, along contours of gender, class, geography, and other structural asymmetries (Stern, Adams & Elsasser, 2009). For instance, India is one of the fastest growing internet markets and has the third largest number of users in the world, next to United States and China.[1] However, it still has the lowest broadband penetration, about 11 percent, among the top 10 countries in internet usage. This enormous digital divide is largely skewed in favor of young, urban, middle class users.[2] Notwithstanding this unequal spread and use, the web is now indispensable for a large volume of civic communication and business operations. Within it, social media websites such as Facebook and Twitter have particularly become popular for exchange, discussion, and debate.

Since its early days, the web also shaped as a critical space for expression of protest. Movement activists have used a repertoire of online tools to connect, plan, and report on protests, as also for public advocacy (Bennett, 2006; McCaughey & Ayers, 2003; Porta, Andretta, Mosca & Reiter, 2006). In recent years, social networking platforms have been talking points for facilitating mobilization in the many pro-democracy protests in countries of Asia and North Africa, including the green movement in Iran in 2009, the Arab Spring in Tunisia and Egypt in 2011 (Howard & Hussain, 2011; Khamis & Vaughan, 2011; Wojcieszak & Smith, 2013), as well as the anti-capitalist Occupy protests in 2011–12, which began in New York and spread across many cities in the world (Penney & Dadas, 2013). These protest potentials of social media have alarmed regimes all over the world, and they are thus tightening their grip on this media (Casilli & Tubaro, 2012; Christensen, 2011; Dick, 2012; Morozov, 2011; Wojcieszak & Smith, 2013).

In India also, social media networking sites have found a growing number of followers, and are used for a variety of expressions, including for dissent (Chattopadhyay, 2011; Hussain, 2010).[3] Among these sites, Facebook has found the most followers, with almost 97 percent of the social media users accessing it (IAMAI, 2013). This makes India the third largest Facebook market after United States and Brazil. Given this scenario of growing Facebook use, the paper is concerned with if and how this social media site is emerging as a space of protest in India. The central mode of inquiry here is the interplay between Facebook and television news, as two representative sites of protest. It asks, if and how television news has an influence on which issues of protest become dominant on social media.

The interplay between these two spaces is critical to explore because of the massive, concurrent growth in private television and internet in India, as propelled by the liberalization of the economy in 1991. The interplay is also important to probe in the context of the proliferating debate on the use and potentials of social media for mobilization of protest, which, to put it simply, is split between two sets of views, one that is keenly optimistic of social media use, captured in narratives such as 'Facebook Revolution' or 'Twitter Revolution', and one that is skeptical of such assessments. Scholars who express skepticism emphasize the importance of analyzing the larger socio-political context and role of traditional political work in the eruption, mobilization, and impact of protests (Howard & Hussain, 2011; Morozov, 2011; Porta, Andretta, Mosca & Reiter, 2006; Sreberny & Khiabany, 2010; Wojcieszak & Smith, 2013; Wolfsfeld, Segev & Sheafer, 2013). Importantly, many of them also underline the continuing flows between social media and the mainstream news media, highlighting the critical role of the latter in framing and disseminating information of protests at scale (Bakardjieva, 2012; Rahimi, 2011) or even point to the similarities in the discourses of web and mass media (Gerhards & Schäfer, 2010; Poell & Borra, 2012). This paper hopes to contribute to this ongoing inquiry on flows between older and newer media, within the larger rubric of mediated politics. The question of interplay, as posed, is addressed here by noting the correspondence of protest representation on television news and Facebook. The sections below elaborate the methods chosen for the same and data analysis.

Methodology

There are numerous protests, campaigns, and movements that are present or are represented both on television news and on Facebook. In order to examine which protests find dominant presence on both these spaces, and the nature of correspondence between them, if any, I drew up a purposive sample of six different protests, across issue and region, which are listed below in the box. I monitored two national English TV channels for a one year period (April 2011–March 2012), namely *NDTV 24 x 7* and *Headlines Today* to note the total number of news stories on the protests, as this quantitative measure is one of the most important, if not the only, indicator of how dominant a protest is in the news media.[4] The monitoring of channels was done by a daily scan of their web portals, which have an archive of all the aired news stories. It is important to note, however, that the focus was less on analyzing inter-channel differences, and more on assessing a general pattern of protest representation within TV news media. Alongside I also relied on the media monitoring data on specific issues by the Centre for Media Studies in Delhi.

To map the respective presence of these protests on Facebook, I used its search engine to map both the number of pages that were related to these protests, including the official page of the campaign/movement, if any, as well as the respective likes/followers on each of these pages.[5] The search keywords that were used are listed in brackets in the sample of protests below.[6]

The research sample included:

- Anti-POSCO movement, Orissa: The anti-POSCO movement under the banner of POSCO Pratirodh Sangram Samiti (PPSS) has been ongoing since 2005, when the Orissa government signed an agreement with the Pohang Steel Company (POSCO) of South Korea, promising a supply of 12 million tons of steel and captive iron ore. The movement has stood against land acquisition and human rights violations, destruction of forests and natural resources. Through a series of protests it had managed to block government acquisition of vast tracts of land till 2012. (Posco).
- Movement against Koodankulam Nuclear Plant, Tamil Nadu: The anti-Koodankulam movement has been ongoing since 1987 and opposes the construction of a nuclear plant at the site owing to its potential destruction of natural resources as well as safety hazards. The movement saw continuous, high intensity protests in 2011. (Koodankulam).
- Ghar Bachao, Ghar Banao Andolan, Mumbai: This campaign, which translates as 'save homes, make homes' has been ongoing since 2009 in Mumbai against slum demolitions and against corporate interests in slum development. In May 2011, campaign activist Medha Patkar led an indefinite fast on this issue in an area called Golibar when a slum community was illegally and forcefully demolished by the corporation, Shivalik Builders. (Ghar Bachao, Ghar Banao).
- Jan Sansad in Delhi (People's Assembly): In March 2012, a Jan Sansad or a people's assembly was organized by the National Alliance of People's Movement (NAPM) in Delhi to demand a pro-people budget from the government. It brought together campaigns and movements from across the country, variously challenging corporate control of land, water, forest, minerals, and other resources. As part of it, a protest rally was held on March 23, 2012 in which about 3,000 people participated. (Jan Sansad, NAPM).
- India Against Corruption: The Anti-Corruption Campaign was launched in 2010 demanding civil society involvement in the drafting and passage of a Lokpal Bill in order to put in place an ombudsman to tackle growing corruption in the country. Some of its key protests happened in 2011–12, including an indefinite fast under the leadership of activist Anna Hazare on April 5–9, 2011; June 8, 2011; and August 21–27, 2011 in Delhi; December 10, 2011 in Mumbai; and March 25, 2012 at Jantar Mantar, Delhi. (India Against Corruption).
- All India Trade Unions Strike: The All India Trade Union strike was jointly organized on February 28, 2012 by trade unions affiliated to large political parties, and backed by seven bank unions and 5,000 small trade unions including of transport and postal workers and state run phone companies. (Trade Union Strike and India).

Television news and Facebook: mediations

The following two tables present the monitoring data and answer the question on which protests in the sample claim dominant space on the news media and Facebook respectively. The first table lists the number of news capsules on these protests in two TV channels in one year. The second table lists the number of Facebook pages related to these protests and approximate total followers, arrived after summing up the likes/followers on each of the pages.

The two tables reveal the nature of correspondence between television news and Facebook on protest representation.[7] The protest claiming the highest number of stories in television (more than 800), which is the India Against Corruption (IAC) campaign, also has the highest number of followers on its official page (about a million).[8] Among the other protests, POSCO and Koodankulam, which have a somewhat higher focus on television, compared to protests related to Jan Sansad, Ghar Bachao, Ghar Banao, or the All India Trade Union Strike, correspondingly have more pages and followers on Facebook.[9]

The television news coverage of the IAC campaign is not only exceptionally high, but also unprecedented. As mentioned before, the IAC campaign emerged in response to a series of high profile corruption cases or scams that came to public notice in 2010. In 2010, under the leadership of activist Arvind Khejriwal, the campaign team organized a few protests, but later, in order to claim a larger public acceptance, they invited Anna Hazare, a veteran Gandhian activist to lead them.

Table 7.1 News capsules on protests in two channels (April 2011–March 2012)

S No.	Issue	NDTV 24 x 7	Headlines Today
1	POSCO	15	10
2	Koodankulam	29	25
3	India Against Corruption	821	827
4	Jan Sansad/NAPM	0	0
5	Ghar Bachao, Ghar Banao	1	0
6	All India Trade Union strike	5	2

Table 7.2 Pages and followers of protests on Facebook (accessed on June 10, 2013)

S No.	Issue	Number of Facebook pages	Total online followers (approx.)
1	POSCO	3	5,000
2	Koodankulam	3	3,000
3	India Against Corruption	1	10,00,000
4	Jan Sansad/NAPM	1	1,500
5	Ghar Bachao, Ghar Banao	1	15
6	All India Trade Union strike	0	0

The strategy worked well, as when Hazare sat on an indefinite fast in Delhi on April 5, 2011, many channels covered it live (Ananth, 2011). Later, as more fasts were organized through the year, these were covered as 'big, breaking and live' events by almost all national news channels, especially the longest stretch of fast in August, 2011.

The scale of coverage can be gauged from the monitoring data by the research organization Centre for Media Studies (CMS) in Delhi. It carried out a study of the prime-time coverage of IAC in four news channels, namely *NDTV 24 x 7*, *CNN-IBN*, *AajTak*, and *Star News*, which revealed that these channels devoted 68–98 minutes of prime time per day on a fast held in April, and 151–161 minutes on the August fast (CMS, 2011). The study also looked at trends in prime-time coverage of over a longer, six year period (2005–2011) in six television news channels, which showed more than an 11 times increase in the percentage of time given for stories on corruption in 2011 compared to that in 2005 (CMS, 2011).

As a result of the live news coverage, thousands of people joined the protests on the streets. Media coverage also transformed what D'Arcus (2006) refers to as the "geographic scale" of the campaign, for soon protests spread from Delhi to other cities and towns. The sustained news coverage fueled support for the campaign not only on the streets, but also online, including on Facebook. This is demonstrated by the large number of pages on corruption opened in 2011, independent of, yet concomitant to the campaign (see Table 7.3). The following is an indicative list.[10]

The question is why the IAC campaign found such a phenomenal support both on television news and on Facebook as compared to others. One can relate this perhaps to the pan-Indian appeal of corruption as an issue, and equally to the time and resources spent by the campaign on its publicity. But more importantly, this can be understood by noting that the audience demographic of national news media and internet is largely the same, i.e., largely urban and middle class.[11] While the IAC campaign attracted a cross-section of people across cities, it was within the urban middle classes that it had the widest appeal and drew massive participation from (Kumar, 2011; Sitapati, 2011). Their participation can chiefly be understood by bringing into view the discursive construction of corruption

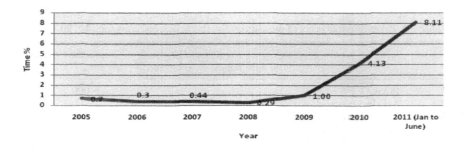

Figure 7.1 Trends in corruption coverage (2005–2011) in six news channels (CMS, 2011)

Table 7.3 User created Facebook pages on corruption in India

S No.	Title of Facebook page	Date of opening
1	Make India Corruption Free	Oct 16, 2010
2	Stop Corruption!!! Lead India	March 19, 2011
3	India's Corruption	June 8, 2011
4	India fights Against Corruption	June 11, 2011
5	India Fights Corruption	June 14, 2011
6	Stop Corruption. . . . . . Save India	June 29, 2011
7	Young Guns of India Against Corruption	July 6, 2011
8	India against corruption (Bharatiya ki awaaz)	August 7, 2011
9	India A Corruption	Sept 23, 2011
10	India Corruption	Sept 23, 2011
11	Corruption Free India	Oct 9, 2011
12	India "corruption free"	Dec 17, 2011
13	Action Committee Against Corruption in India (ACACI)	Jan 16, 2012
14	India Anti-Corruption	Oct 23, 2012
15	Corruption in INDIA	May 15, 2013

both by the campaign team and the news media, which was able to 'interpellate' middle classes as subjects.[12] To begin with, the daily context and experiences of urban middle classes were recounted at length in the framing of the problem. One of the key themes was bribery, and while all classes negotiate with bribery, the urban middle classes' experience with bribery was prominently articulated in both activist speeches and media reporting, where they were shown mainly as victims, rather than actors or participants (Muralidharan, 2011).

Secondly, while the bill brought under scrutiny the political class, including law makers and law enforcers, it curiously and conspicuously excluded the corporations, which were equally indicted in the scams that unfolded before; the discourse also separated corruption from the political economic context of neoliberalism, which is the backdrop for the evolving state-market nexus (Banerjee, 2011; Kaur, 2011; Navlakha, 2011). Such an exclusivist construction appealed to these classes, who in many ways heartily support the neoliberal agenda (Fernandes, 2006; Giri, 2011). Additionally, like all other classes, the middle classes have very real exasperations with political systems, and they were able to vent that by supporting this campaign (Bhaduri, 2011).

The political economy of news media explains why other issues of protest concerning the urban and rural poor comparatively had marginal number of news stories. As such, the missing picture on the news screens of rural India and its distresses has been studied at length (Chakroborti, 2005/2006; Fernandes, 2011; Sainath, 2003). It is also corroborated in the longitudinal study of television news by CMS. Their news monitoring of six news channels in the period 2008–2012 revealed that issues related to rural India were not more than one percent of the total coverage in all the channels (CMS, 2012).[13] Overall, as the above data reveals, when it comes to protest representation, there is a positive correlation between

116 *Chotani*

television news and Facebook such that protests that get a relatively dominant space in the news media also find a sizeable support on Facebook, as compared to others.[14] Social media activity reflects thus the hegemonic influence of television news in shaping public opinion and discourses. Television's influence in galvanizing larger public support for certain protests is not only online, but also on the streets. This is further substantiated if we look at the protests against the Delhi Gang Rape in Delhi between December 2012 and January 2013.

Anti-rape campaign

On December 16, 2012, a young girl named Jyoti Singh Pandey was gang raped in a public bus in Delhi, in which she was travelling with a male friend. While gang rape in Delhi and elsewhere in India is not new, this incident provoked mass anger, and this was mostly to do with how the national television news picked up this story in a campaign mode. Private news media not only broadcast live updates about the girl who was battling for her life at a hospital, and later died, but also, much like in the case of the IAC campaign, gave live coverage to a few protests that took place on the incident. Additionally, news channels organized a number of debates and discussions on the issue of violence against women. According to a study by the Centre for Media Studies, almost no other gender-related issue in recent past compares with the kind of media attention that this incident got (CMS, 2013).[15]

The scale of media coverage furthered mass protests across Delhi and other cities. Supporters of this campaign, especially young people, actively used Facebook to express their anger against this incident, as well on the larger issues involved. The use of Facebook during this time can be seen in Table 7.4, which puts together a list of 37 pages on the issue, which individual users opened in the brief period between December 16, 2012 and January 2013, the time that this issue remained in prime-time focus on television news. What is important to note is that unlike the IAC campaign, which was coordinated by a campaign team, and whose online support consolidated on its official Facebook page, the anti-rape protests had no single organization steering it. Facebook support to the campaign was therefore spread across personal pages as well as public pages such as those listed in the following indicative list below (Table 7.5).[16]

Table 7.4 Total prime-time (7–11 PM) coverage of gang rape cases and related issues (Dec 17–31, 2012)

Channel	News stories	Time (mins)	Specials	Time (mins)	Total time (mins)
AajTak	33	200	41	904	1104
DD News	78	709	20	499	1208
Star News	225	300	31	626	926
Zee News	89	418	46	857	1275
CNN-IBN	72	353	23	687	1040
NDTV 24 x 7	49	559	33	1439	1998
Total	546	2539	194	5012	7551

Source: CMS Media Lab Analysis (2013)

Table 7.5 Facebook pages opened after December 16, 2012

S.No.	Title of Facebook page	Date of opening	Likes/members
1	Delhi Gang-Rape Case Dec 2012	Dec 16, 2012	82
2	Protest against Delhi Gang Rapes	Dec 17, 2012	390
3	Stop Sexual Violence in India	Dec 19, 2012	150
4	Protests against Delhi Gang Rape. We Want Justice	Dec 19, 2012	4963
5	Indian Men against Sexual Violence	Dec 20, 2012	51
6	Gang Raped in Delhi	Dec 20, 2012	7288
7	Delhi Gang-Rape Incident	Dec 20, 2012	986
8	Another Girl Gang Raped in Delhi – Can We Stop It?	Dec 20, 2012	318
9	Protest against Gang-Rape Incident in Delhi	Dec 20, 2012	1097
10	Join Fight against Delhi Gang Rape	Dec 20, 2012	2301
11	Woman Gang Raped in Delhi Bus, Battles for Life	Dec 21, 2012	805
12	Delhi Gang Rape; Handover Trial of Heinous Crimes to Military Courts	Dec 21, 2012	301
13	Swift Justice in Delhi Gang-Rape Case	Dec 21, 2012	290
14	The Protest against Delhi Bus Gang Rape	Dec 21, 2012	302
15	I Protest for 'Damini Gang Rape'	Dec 22, 2012	3702
16	Kerala-Protests against Delhi Gang Rape. We Want Justice	Dec 22, 2012	107
17	Gang-Rape Horror in Delhi: Girl Fights for Life	Dec 22, 2012	516
18	Delhi Gang-Rape Protest by Youth	Dec 22, 2012	1513
19	Delhi Gang Rape	Dec 23, 2012	2310
20	India against Rape, Rapists, and Rapism	Dec 23, 2012	1466
21	India against Violence on Women	Dec 23, 2012	1442
22	Delhi against Gang Rape	Dec 23, 2012	179
23	Delhi Gang Rape: Spare a Thought for Our Police	Dec 24, 2012	283
24	Delhi Gang-Rape Protest	Dec 25, 2012	325
25	Protests against Delhi Gang Rape. We Want Justice	Dec 25, 2012	29
26	Rip Damini – Delhi Gang-Raped Girl	Dec 29, 2012	6249
27	Stop Violence against Women	Dec 29, 2012	66
28	We Are against Female Discrimination	Dec 29, 2012	572
29	Demanding Justice for "Delhi Gang Rape"	Dec 29, 2012	59
30	Delhi Gang Rape Hit 1 Like, 1 Bullet to Rapist	Dec 30, 2012	65
31	Delhi Gang Rape (group)	Dec 31, 2012	322
32	Swift Justice in Delhi Gang-Rape Case	Dec 31, 2012	290
33	Massive Protests over Delhi Gang Rape (group)	Jan 2013	380
34	India against Women Violence	Jan 1, 2013	284
35	Delhi Gang Rape Bandh (group)	Jan 2, 2013	416
36	PIL on Delhi Gang Rape towards Safety for Women	Jan 27, 2013	614
37	STOP Violence against Women India	Feb 7, 2013	39

TV news media's support to this campaign and the visible response on streets and social media helped foreground, and forcefully so, the increasing incidents of rape and sexual assaults on women. As Shakil (2013) notes, this is the first time young students, both men and women, came out demanding women's rights. Earlier, protests on rape, dowry or similar issues largely had women participants. Media not only prompted a new cultural turn within the women's movement by mobilizing new mass of supporters to its issues, but also expanded somewhat the discourse on gender violence, by bringing into spotlight sexual assault on Dalit women, on women in custody or in conflict situations (Roy, 2013). These issues were mainly articulated by women's groups and activists, who found space in many media debates. The momentum of protests had a political impact in how the government was forced to set up a committee under the chairpersonship of Justice J. S. Verma to review the existing rape legislation. The committee invited public suggestions on amendments, and received thousands of submissions by January 5, 2013. According to Philipose (2013):

> the unusual longevity accorded to the gang-rape incident in terms of the news cycle – where generally news breaks die by the minute – provided significant opportunities for expression that were grasped by activists and academics alike. The exceptional articulation of women activists, whose long years of work on the central issue of violence against women had never been given the attention it deserved, got play whether through newspaper columns, television studio discussions or personal blogs for arguably the first time in the history of the Indian media, which had traditionally deemed "women's issues" as "soft news". The fact that the Justice Verma Committee received over 60,000 responses on reforming the criminal justice system testifies to that unprecedented engagement.
>
> (p. 21)

Following the many recommendations by the Verma Committee, in the same year, the Criminal Law (Amendment) Bill, 2013 was enacted as law by the Parliament, which, while not "comprehensive", significantly "transformed the way legal redress for sexual offences have been framed in the law" (Mehra, 2013). Media thus played an important role in facilitating this political trajectory, albeit not without a downside.[17]

As such, gender is a visible category if we see the protests and campaigns that private television news picked up pro-actively in the past. One of the first such campaigns was in 2006 to reopen the investigation of the murder of Jessica Lall.[18] In the following years the media campaigned on many other cases of legal justice for women such as Priyadarshini Mattoo, Ruchika Girhotra, and Aarushi Talwar, most of who belonged to different strata of the urban middle class. This can be related to the media's preference for this demographic, as explained earlier. Jyoti Singh Pandey, the victim of the brutal gang rape in Delhi in December 2012, whose story and related protests was perhaps most widely covered, many would argue, was not yet middle class, given the abject conditions she and her family actually lived in.[19] But I would argue that while on parameters of income, she may have been at the very lower end of middle class, but if we bring in view the fact of her enrollment in an institution of higher education for becoming a medical practitioner (physiotherapist), we can pose that she and the family were close to the ladder of becoming middle class, a category which is now very heterogeneous. On the evening of the incident, like any other college-going, urban middle class girl, Jyoti was on her way home after having watched a film in a multiplex with a friend. And therefore her story, like that of Jessica Lall, was one that a cross-section of urban middle classes could relate to, including students and working women, who struggle and negotiate with these very potentially unsafe environs.[20] Jyoti's story, thus, "emerged as a metaphor for the whole middle class's abject vulnerability" (Sachdev, 2013, online).

News media's focus on middle class women, and the relative lack of focus therein on urban working class or rural women on similar question of violence and injustice, has been noted by both scholars and media professionals. Recounting her experience as a television journalist and commenting on the nature of media coverage on gender issues, Trivedi (2006) poses a question:

> Why is it that reams of newspaper and hours of television programming are devoted to a Jessica Lall, but no one wants to invest the same energy in reporting the stories of Shahnaz, Medina and Zohrabibi? Jessica's case was an outrage, but is her tragedy any less than these other women? Or is it that it requires a beautiful, glamorous woman (made for television and color supplements) to be gunned down in a page three party for the media to wake up to the reality of hostile witnesses and a justice system that is horribly skewed in favor of the rich and powerful? What about the fact that ninety-nine percent of the Dalit women who are raped and tortured get no justice from any court, and why does nobody petition the President or take up their cases with the same ferocity?
>
> (p. 43)

Chakroborti (2006) also underscores this argument and says that while media celebrates beauty pageants, it lends no space to the achievements of women from rural India and the caste, class, and gender violence they face. On a similar note, writing after the protests on the gang rape in Delhi, Teltumbde (2013, p. 10) makes a similar observation and asks: "why all those candle bearers did not shed a single tear over the rape and murder of Surekha and Priyanka Bhotmange that was committed in a festive mode by Khairlanji villagers"? Further, focusing on the selective nature of media coverage on rape, a crime that has increased over the years, he states:

> If we do not know many such cases it is not because they were less brutal but simply because they were never highlighted in the media . . . the fact remains that like in any other issue that flared up in public in recent times, the media played a big role in making an exception of the case.
>
> (Teltumbe, p. 11)

Perhaps the issue here is not that women from marginalized sections are not represented at all, for that is not the case, but that these stories never become an object of media-generated campaigns or find mass support both on the streets and on social media in the way that some other stories do.

Conclusion

This paper brought into focus Facebook as a protest space in India in its interplay with television news. It sought to understand which protests claim dominant space in these two media and why, and the nature of correspondence between them. As was seen, television news gave dominant space to those protests, which have a potential resonance with middle class contexts, as compared to those which are more deeply embedded with lives of rural or urban poor; this preference can be read in relation to news media's political economy. The protests that television news covers at length do galvanize a larger public discourse and participation on the concerned issue, which is visible not only in mounting protest activity on the street, but also on Facebook. As the data reveals, the two campaigns that the news media gave a sustained coverage in the past three years, namely the IAC campaign and the anti-rape protests, found a corresponding high response on Facebook, in the shape of pages and followers, which had significant political implications. Television news has thus a hegemonic presence on social media. This does not of course undermine the fact that social media sites such as Facebook are as such a storehouse of diverse discourses, manifest in the variety of movements and campaigns having presence on it, including a large number of those which might be completely absent from media gaze.

How do we then read Facebook as a protest space, in its relationship with television news media in India? Such a reading needs to be made, I argue, in reference to the ongoing debate on protest potentials of social media, as mentioned earlier. This debate is itself situated in a larger discussion between scholars who positively evaluate the web and see it in proximity to the ideal, and those who contest such a theorization, pointing to persistent digital divides and controls of this sphere by the state and/or the market.

There are however scholars who take a more cautiously optimistic view of the political potentials of internet and social media. Here I quote Milioni (2009), who particularly evaluates the web in relation to mass media. He suggests that the idea of the public sphere is still a useful concept to qualify online spaces, provided one acknowledges the multiplicity and diversity of publics and public spheres, both hegemonic and counter-hegemonic. He says that the internet is a sign of multiplicity of public spheres and has broken in some ways the influence of mass media such that "the general public sphere today cannot be defined univocally by the informational and symbolic content of the mass media". However, mass media "still exert strong influence on agenda-setting as well as the conditions under which discussion is conducted and opinion is formed. For these reasons, the space occupied by the mass media has the character of a dominant or 'hegemonic' public sphere, which is associated with the production, circulation and reproduction of the dominant public opinion" (Milioni, pp. 410–11). My findings concur with such a theoretical position. While the social media in India is alive and diverse, the deafening loudness of television news still influences which protest issues become relatively dominant on social media and draw larger publics, especially of the young.

Notes

1 Internet use in India is periodically documented by trade bodies and industry associations pertaining to the sector. According to a study carried out by the Internet and Mobile Association of India (IAMAI), India crossed the 100-million mark of internet users in September 2011 (IAMAI, 2012). The portal, Internetworldstats.com, which also compiles internet use data from international and national bodies, highlights that by June 2012, India had approximately 137 million internet users.
2 According to the research report, 'Internet in Rural India' published by IAMAI in September 2012, the penetration of internet in rural India in 2012 was only 4.6 percent (IAMAI, 2012). In terms of the gender and age profile of internet users, a study carried out by the Internet Analytics Firm, ComScore, for the Indian industry body, Assocham, showed that in 2012, women accounted for 40 percent of the users, indicating an almost equal gender distribution. The study also showed that the younger lot who were most connected and active on the web, including children below 18 years of age. About 75 percent of online audience was between the age-group 15–34 years, making "India one of the youngest demographic online globally" (ComScore, 2012, p. 4).
3 This has necessarily alerted the Indian government, which has over the last few years augmented its efforts to survey and censor the web at large (Prakash, 2011); (Vij, 2012).
4 Both channels were launched in 2003. While *NDTV 24 x 7* belongs to the production house New Delhi Television Limited, *Headlines Today* belongs to the group India Today.
5 The website *socialbrakers.com* compiles likes or followers of different Facebook pages and ranks top 100 pages in a few categories such as Brands, Media, Politics, Celebrities, and Sports. It does not however have any category on movements or campaigns. The top 100 pages on Politics, as monitored on June 13, 2013, also did not include any movements.
6 These include protests that occurred one time or recurred through the year, and were either part of campaigns, or social movements, or a network or alliance of such movements. Here I use the term 'protests' to include all these forms of collective action.
7 The paper presents Facebook data as noted in 2013. As we will see below, the difference in time period from television monitoring does not bear on the difference in proportion of news coverage and Facebook followers on different protest issues. A limitation here is that I have looked at only pages created in English. As such, while Facebook is used in other languages, i.e., often people write posts in their native languages, its interface is largely English.
8 Along with the official page, there were numerous pages of campaign branches that opened in the country and outside.
9 There were three pages on the movement against the nuclear plant at Koodankulam, among which two pages were started in 2011, namely "Anti-Kudankulam Atomic Power Project Protesters" and "People's Movement Against Koodankulam Nuclear Power Project" and these had 985 and 70 likes respectively. Another page "No Nuke Power in India | Stop Koodankulam", which opened in March 2012, had 720 likes. The anti-POSCO movement had three separate pages (groups), of which the highest followers were on page titled "Resist POSCO" with 2766 members; while

groups "TISS anti posco student action committee" had 349 members and "Solidarity for posco pratirosh movement" had 1009 members respectively. The Ghar Bachao, Ghar Banaho page founded in March 11, 2013 had only 15 likes and NAPM page which opened on 13 October 2011 had 1413 likes. Data was accessed on June 13, 2013.

10 These pages were searched through keywords India *and* Corruption, and were accessed on June 14, 2013.

11 A range of scholars studying the political economy of Indian news media have noted how TV news channels are largely concentrated with a select group of corporate media houses, and run and make profit through sponsorship. The ways in which ownership of a channel bears on content cannot always be directly established, but content practices can be seen more clearly linked to the influence of sponsorship, especially since there is now a blurring of functional boundaries between departments of advertising, management, and editorial (Batabyal, 2012; Chaudhuri, 2005). As sponsors gain influence, they push for, if not wholly determine, the nature of news content, such that it is increasingly tuned to the needs and desires of the middle classes, who potentially buy the goods advertised (Thussu, 2007).

12 Althusser's (1984) concept of 'interpellation' illustrates how viewers are made to identify with the 'ideal subject' offered by texts, which occurs through means of 'ideological recognition'.

13 The CMS Media Lab Analysis of prime-time news (7–11 PM) was done for six national news channels, namely *AajTak, CNN-IBN, DD News, NDTV 24 × 7, Star News* and *Zee News*.

14 The dominant presence of a campaign on the news screen, the streets and in the social media spaces has political consequences too. As seen in the IAC campaign, the fasts in 2011 created pressure on the Parliament to bring the Lokpal Bill under lengthy discussion. Further, one of the leading architects of the campaign, Arvind Khejriwal, later translated the mass support to form a political party by the name of Aam Aadmi Party (Common man's party). The party contested its first elections for the Delhi State Assembly in December 2013 and won substantial seats, allowing it to form a government in the state.

15 The study shows that almost 252 hours of news coverage, special bulletins, and talk shows were covered in four news channels in this time period, against the 46 minutes devoted to all rape cases in March 2012 and 17 minutes to cases of molestation.

16 These pages were searched through keywords Delhi Gang Rape and accessed on July 31, 2013.

17 The downside is to do with media's search for short, quick fix solutions to social problems, here seen in the anti-rape protests. According to Agnes (2013, p. 12), instead of discussing complexities of the issues involved, TV channels suggested retributive justice measures such as the death penalty, public hanging, castration or instant 'justice'. Similar observations are made by Teltumbde (2013), who writes: ". . . the discourse on capital punishment and chemical castration for all rapists that emerged almost immediately after the incident . . . was first raised in television studios before finding easy acceptance among the protestors. Once voiced in the street, it was taken by television anchors (not so much by newspaper commentators) as evidence of a social consensus on the issue. This seamlessly circular flow of information was so overwhelming in its emotional appeal that even the government was forced into stating that it was looking at the capital punishment option for rapists" (p. 12). Media's fervent support to 'death penalty' also translated in practice, as Agnes (2013) points out, in the application of maxim of "rape and murder" and the "rarest of rare" within the Rape Law. At the same time, such discourses were predominant in the discussions within Facebook pages opened by users (Table 7.6).

18 Jessica Lall was a model cum bartender, who was shot dead in 1999 by the influential son of a former member of Parliament, following her refusal to serve him a drink. Despite much reporting in the media at the time, the accused was acquitted by the Delhi High Court in February 2006. At that point, the English Channel,

NDTV 24 x 7 launched a campaign called 'Justice for Jessica Lall', which was soon picked up by other channels. The news channels campaigned to reopen the case and in this process asked its audience to support it both through SMS, as well as through street protests in various cities. Hundreds of mostly young middle class men and women joined in these various protest gatherings with candles and placards such as in Delhi (Chaudhury, 2007); Pandey, 2006). As a result of the campaign, within a few weeks, the case was reopened, and the accused, who underwent another trial, was sentenced to life imprisonment. This was the first time television channels had been able to mobilize activism of its young, middle class audience on an issue of gender justice.

19 At the time, her father worked as a porter at Delhi's International Airport. The family lives in a small house in a poorer settlement in Delhi (North, 2013).

20 Delhi has been noted for its high rate of crime against women not only in India but the world. A study on safety of public spaces in Delhi from a gendered perspective was carried out in 2007 by Jagori, an organization working on women's rights. The study revealed "women face tremendous vulnerabilities in negotiating public spaces. In addition, there are other factors which compound this vulnerability – such as age, class and others" (Vishwanath & Mehrotra, 2007, p. 1548).

References

Agnes, F. (2013). No shortcuts on rape make the legal system work. *Economic & Political Weekly*, xlviii(2), 12–15.

Althusser, L. (1984). *Ideology and ideological state apparatus*. London: Verso.

Ananth, V. K. (2011). Lokpal bill campaign: Democratic and constitutional. *Economic & Political Weekly*, xlvl(16), 20–22.

Bakardjieva, M. (2012). Reconfiguring the mediapolis: New media and civic agency. *New Media & Society*, 14(1), 63–79.

Banerjee, S. (2011). Anna Hazare, civil society and the state. *Economic & Political Weekly*, xlvi(36), 12–14.

Batabyal, S. (2012). The story of nandigram. *Journal of Media & Cultural Studies*, 26(2), 261–273.

Bennett, W. L. (2006). Communicating global activism: Strengths and vulnerabilities of networked politics. In W. v. d. Donk, B. D. Loader, & P. G. Nixon (Eds.), *Cyberprotest: New media, citizens and social movements* (pp. 109–128). London: Routledge.

Bhaduri, A. (2011). Corruption and representative democracy. *Economic & Political Weekly*, xlvi(36), 15–17.

Casilli, A. A., & Tubaro, P. (2012). Social media censorship in times of political unrest – a social simulation experiment with the UK Riots. *Bulletin of Sociological Methodology/ Bulletin de Méthodologie Sociologique*, 115(1), 5–20.

Chakroborti, U. (2005/2006). State, market and freedom of expression: Women and electronic media. In B. Bernard (Ed.), *Communication processes: Media and mediations* (Vol. 1, pp. 295–314). New Delhi: Sage.

Chattopadhyay, S. (2011). Online activism for a heterogeneous time: The pink chaddi campaign and the social media in India. *Proteus*, 27(1), 63–67.

Chaudhuri, M. (2005). A question of choice: Advertisements, media and democracy. In B. Bernar (Ed.), *Communication processes: Media and mediations* (Vol. 1, pp. 199–226). New Delhi: Sage.

Chaudhury, S. (2007, January 13). Is this only protest theatre. *Tehelka*. Retrieved from http://archive.tehelka.com/story_main25.asp?filename=essay01132007_p14–17PF.asp (date of access: 09/12/2014).

Christensen, C. (2011). Twitter revolutions? Addressing social media and dissent. *The Communication Review*, 14(3), 155–157.

CMS. (2011). *Table: Trend in corruption coverage 2005–2010*. New Delhi: Centre for Media Studies Media Lab.

CMS. (2012). *Table: TV news trends 2008–12*. New Delhi: Centre for Media Studies Media Lab.

CMS. (2013). Table: Total prime-time (7–11 PM) coverage of gang rape case and related issues (17–31 Dec 2012). New Delhi: Centre for Media Studies Media Lab.

ComScore (2012). State of e-commerce in India: A research report by ComScore for Assocham India. New Delhi: ComScore.

D'Arcus, B. (2006). *Boundaries of dissent: Protest and state power in the media age*. New York: Routledge.

Dick, A. L. (2012). Established democracies, internet censorship and the social media test. *Information Development*, 28(4), 259–260.

Fernandes, L. (2006). *India's new middle class, democratic politics in an era of economic reform*. Minneapolis: University of Minnesota Press.

Fernandes, N. (2011). The uncomfortable truth behind the corporate media's imagination of India. In S. Batabyal, A. Chowdhry, M. Gaur, & M. Pohjonen (Eds.), *Indian mass media and the politics of change* (pp. 208–217). London & New York: Routledge.

Gerhards, J., & Schäfer, M. S. (2010). Is the internet a better public sphere? Comparing old and new media in the USA and Germany. *New Media & Society*, 12(1), 143–160.

Giri, S. (2011). The anticorruption movement and its false divides. *Economic & Political Weekly*, xlvi(26 & 27), 14–16.

Howard, P. N., & Hussain, M. M. (2011). The upheavals in Egypt and Tunisia: The role of digital media. *Journal of Democracy*, 22(3), 35–50.

Hussain, A. (2010, August 27). *Facebook, YouTube used as weapons in Kashmir fight*. Retrieved from http://www.salon.com/2010/08/27/as_kashmir_internet_war/ (date of access: 09/12/2014).

IAMAI. (2012). *I-Cube report on internet in rural India*. Internet and Mobile Association of India (IAMAI). Retrieved from http://www.iamai.in/upload/research/11720111091101/icube_3nov11_56.pdf. (date of access: 09/12/2014).

IAMAI. (2013). *Social media in India – 2012*. Delhi: Internet and Mobile Association of India (IAMAI).

Kaur, R. (2011). India Inc. and its moral discontents. *Economic & Political Weekly*, xlvii(20), 40–45.

Khamis, S., & Vaughan, K. (2011). Cyberactivism in the Egyptian revolution. *Arab Media & Society*, 13, 1–37.

Kumar, K. (2011). Cleansing the state. *Economic & Political Weekly*, xlvi(48), 14–17.

McCaughey, M., & Ayers, M. (Eds.). (2003). *Cyberactivism: Online activism in theory and practice*. Lanham: Rowman & Littlefield.

Mehra, M. (2013, May 5). Taking stock of the new anti-rape law. *Kafila*. Retrieved from kafila.org/2013/05/05/taking-stock-of-the-new-anti-rape-law-madhu-mehra/ (date of access: 09/12/2014).

Milioni, D. L. (2009). Probing the online counterpublic sphere: The case of indymedia Athens. *Media, Culture & Society*, 31(3), 409–431.

Morozov, E. (2011). *The net delusion: How not to liberate the world*. London: Penguin.

Muralidharan, S. (2011). Media as echo chamber: Cluttering the public discourse on corruption. *Economic & Political Weekly*, xlvi(37), 19–22.

Navlakha, G. (2011). Lokpal movement: Unanswered questions. *Economic & Political Weekly*, xlvl(44 & 45), 19–21.

North, A. (2013, January 21). *Tragedy of Delhi rape victim seeking better life*. Retrieved from http://www.bbc.co.uk/news/world-asia-india-21121412 (date of access: 09/12/2014).

Pandey, G. (2006, March 9). India campaign for murdered Delhi model. *BBC News*. Retrieved from http://news.bbc.co.uk/2/hi/south_asia/4783394.stm (date of access: 09/12/2014).

Penney, J., & Dadas, C. (2013). (Re)Tweeting in the service of protest: Digital composition and circulation in the Occupy Wall Street movement. *New Media & Society*, 16(1), 174–190.

Philipose, P. (2013). Anxieties in the republic media metamorphosis and popular protest. *Economic & Political Weekly*, xlviii(6), 20–22.

Poell, T., & Borra, E. (2012). Twitter, YouTube, and Flickr as platforms of alternative journalism: The social media account of the 2010 Toronto G20 protests. *Journalism*, 13(6), 695–713.

Porta, D. d., Andretta, M., Mosca, L., & Reiter, H. (2006). *Globalization from below: Transnational activists and protest networks*. Minneapolis: University of Minnesota.

Prakash, P. (2011, December 15). *Invisible censorship – How India censors without being seen*. The Centre for Internet and Society. Retrieved from http://cis-india.org/internet-governance/invisible-censorship (date of access: 09/12/2014).

Rahimi, B. (2011). The agonistic social media: Cyberspace in the formation of dissent and consolidation of state power in postelection Iran. *The Communication Review*, 14(3), 158–178.

Roy, R. (2013). Men and their lakshmanrekha. *Economic & Political Weekly*, xlviii(8), 24–26.

Sachdev, R. (2013). When rape claims prime time. *The Hoot*. Retrieved from http://thehoot.org/web/Whenrapeclaimsprimetime/6552-1-1-9-true.html (date of access: 09/12/2014).

Sainath, P. (2003). The globalisation of inequality. *Seminar*, 533. Retrieved from http://www.india-seminar.com/2004/533/533%20p.%20sainath.htm (date of access: 09/12/2014).

Shakil, A. (2013). Protests, the Justice Verma Committee and the government ordinance. *Economic & Political Weekly*, xlviii(6). Retrieved from http://www.epw.in/web-exclusives/protests-justice-verma-committee-and-government-ordinance.html (date of access: 09/12/2014).

Sitapati, V. (2011). What Anna Hazare's movement and India's new middle classes say about each other. *Economic & Political Weekly*, xlvi(30), 39–44.

SN, V. (2012, May 30). Anonymous defaces more Indian websites. *Medianama*. Retrieved from http://www.medianama.com/2012/05/223-anonymous-defaces-more-indian-websites/.

Sreberny, A., & Khiabany, G. (2010). *Blogistan: The internet and politics in Iran*. London: I.B. Tauris.

Stern, M. J., Adams, A. E., & Elsasser, S. (2009). Digital inequality and place: The effects of technological diffusion on internet proficiency and usage across rural, suburban, and urban countries. *Sociological Inquiry*, 79(4), 391–417.

Teltumbde, A. (2013). Delhi gang rape case: Some uncomfortable questions. *Economic & Political Weekly*, xlviii(6), 10–11.

Thussu, D. K. (2007). The "Murdochization" of news? The case of Star TV in India. *Media, Culture & Society*, 29(4), 593–611.

Trivedi, S. (2006). Forays into the heartland. *Seminar*, 561, 41–43.

Vij, S. (2012, May 1). Unpacking India's internet censorship debate. *Kafila*. Retrieved from http://kafila.org/2012/05/01/unpacking-indias-internet-censorship-debate/ (date of access: 09/12/2014).

Vishwanath, K., & Mehrotra, S. T. (2007). Shall we go out? Women's safety in public spaces in Delhi. *Economic & Political Weekly*, 42(17), 1542–1543.

Wojcieszak, M., & Smith, B. (2013). Will politics be tweeted? New media use by Iranian youth in 2011. *New Media & Society*, 16(9), 191–109.

Wolfsfeld, G., Segev, E., & Sheafer, T. (2013). Social media and the Arab spring: Politics comes first. *The International Journal of Press/Politics*, 18(2), 115–137.

8 Enhancing multimedia use in state secondary schools in São Paulo

A critical collaborative perspective

Fernanda Liberali, Maria Cecília Magalhães, Maria Cristina Meaney, Camila Santiago, Maurício Canuto, Feliciana Amaral, Bruna Cababe, and Jéssica Aline Almeida Dos Santos

Introduction

The accelerated rate at which communication technology has developed in the last decades has created, on the one side, a wide variety of artifacts that are able to convey information and produce new modes of interaction and, on the other side, a legion of near illiterate citizens struggling to learn how to use new tools and adapt to never-ending changes. In the middle of this crisis, at a much lower pace, schools debate whether these changes should affect their life-long programs and their reliable practices. In Brazil, in spite of the investments being made towards the use of multimedia in classrooms (see CGI report[1]), their use is still timid and has not significantly changed school routines and relations among teachers and students.

Schools draw on a limited range of modes of representation and communication to introduce and dispose their subjects to students and many teachers, unlike their students, have little contact with media apart from the most obvious and basic uses. Brown (2010, p. 6) states that new media use "raises important issues about traditional learner-teacher relationships, ownership of lecture content, and of control over the dialogue in a classroom." He prompts that the roles of learner and teacher would not be fixed and learning would be far more collaborative, distributed, and personalized if new media were broadly used in classrooms.

This chapter will describe and analyze the actions organized by our research group – Language in Activities in School Contexts (LACE) – in 2013 while discussing the use of multimedia in a classroom with students, educators, and school managers from public schools in São Paulo. The analysis will illustrate the production of a creative chain (Liberali, 2009), in which actions are intentionally put forward so that meanings on teaching and learning are produced and carried out from one context to another. The ultimate purpose of the project has been to jointly produce critical collaborative curricular proposals through reflection afforded by the use of multiple media in the process of planning, developing, and discussing curricula. This is in conformance with the multiliteracy perspective supported by the New London Group (1996/2000), which stresses that meaning conventions vary according to context and culture and have specific cognitive, cultural, and social effects. Besides, it also implies that multiple modes to convey meaning become resources that users recreate to achieve contextualized purposes. Participation of all in the production of curricular proposals enables learning and engagement in critical and collaborative practices that will be resignified in ever-expanding cycles of creation of meanings in multiple environments.

Critical collaboration and argumentation in creative chains

In examining collaboration in contexts of media use, researchers such as Hillman (2014) and Warwick and Mercer (2011) focus on the concept of collaboration among children and/or children and teachers in collective activities. Warwick and Mercer (2011) understand collaboration as a procedure to consider options, plan actions, and make joint decisions. Based on the concept of scaffolding, they understand collaboration as related to talking productively in groups to enable children to co-regulate their learning. Similarly, Hillman (2014) understands collaboration as "shared understandings produced through interactions" in a task directed by the teacher, in which teacher and students hold traditional roles (p. 172).

Expanding the concept of collaboration, McCormick (2004) discusses the challenge for information and communication technology (ICT) in educational settings to promote students' creative development in a collaborative process. Collaborating is not only working together towards a common goal but also purposely sharing decision making and evaluating outcomes. In this direction, Rosales (2013) discusses the participatory culture at the Echo Park Film Center that combines activism with education through filmmaking for the community, which creates a collaborative, social, and participatory context to teaching-learning about media. The concept of collaboration is understood as students' and teachers' joint work to share ideas and critically reflect on social-cultural-historical and political issues of society, as well as on their opinions and judgments.

Our concept of critical collaboration goes to a similar direction. Based on Vygotsky's discussions (1930/1978), we assume that we learn and develop by interacting with others through dialectical relations that are embedded in social-cultural-historical practices and situated in the contexts of our daily experiences (cf. Dafermos, Triliva & Varvantakis, 2017). Collaborating in this perspective is a continuous process of developing one's own self with others. In collaboration, people deliberately make joint decisions, evaluate outcomes through discourse, critically reflect on social-cultural-historical and political issues, and interweave the collective and the individual through language.

To foster these relationships in critical collaboration, it is essential to take into account the role of argumentation. According to Mosca (2004), argumentation is situated within intersubjective relations that involve dialogue among subjects. Emmel, Resch and Tenney (1996) consider that there are always conflicts and differences that give rise to different positions with values to be considered. In a pre-teacher education project, Ogan-Bekiroglu and Aydeniz (2013) viewed argumentation as a pedagogical tool that can help students engage in meaningful learning. According to the authors, argumentation is "the process of proposing, supporting, criticizing, evaluating, and competing ideas using evidence, critical thinking and rationality" (p. 233). Argumentation is seen as a process that encourages students to engage in learning at a higher cognitive level as they are constantly engaged in questioning, justifying, substantiating, and evaluating their and their peers' claims, rationality, and knowledge.

Furthermore, argumentation is seen as the foundation for an active and intense participation of each individual in the constitution of the group (Liberali, 2013). It occurs through the opposition, interrelationship, and combination of ideas during an argumentative clash. This generates an approximation of shared ideas that strengthen the power of acting of each participant and allows the development of individual and collective capacities. Through argumentation, temporary stabilizations of meanings are made possible through joint decision making. Argumentation allows for positions to be stated, contrasted, supported, deepened, contested, rejected, combined, negotiated, or accorded. When this is achieved, each one becomes an agent in the construction of the group identity and of its activities.

Argumentation, however, is not seen here as exclusively verbal. It is essential, in a critical collaborative context, that each person realizes that multiple modes may be used for expressing, contrasting, and supporting a position which will contribute to the expansion of the general understanding about the topics in discussion. This implies that knowledge may be represented in multiple modes in order to make sense of reality. Such a multimodal argumentation can be afforded, for example, by improvisational theatrical performances in which participants are invited to assume new roles. By acting out these new roles, participants are compelled to go beyond their own immediate reality in order to experiment with new possibilities. By doing so, they can invest their emotions and knowledge to create new ways of being. In our research group, this strategy to foment argumentation provides a locus for the gathering of multiple modes of signifying and their multiple meaning. The basis for it is the constitution of a *creative chain*.

As stated by Liberali (2009), a *creative chain* is achieved in partnered activities in which meanings are produced and intentionally transported to other subsequent contexts and activities. An object which is collaboratively constructed in the first activity leaves marks in the participants, such as the appropriation of new instruments. These are then used as base for the construction of following activities in which these participants deliberately engage. Therefore, new meanings are creatively produced, carrying some aspects of the previous activity, and reinvented throughout the new ones.

Critical collaboration as research methodology

Within the above-presented theoretical frame, our research team organized a long-term intervention and research project in six middle and high schools in São Paulo City, Brazil, with the aim to jointly produce critical collaborative curricular proposals through reflection afforded by the use of multiple media in the process of planning, developing and discussing curricula. The first phase of the project took place from June 2013 to June 2014. The second phase began in August 2014 and lasted until June 2015. To encourage the engaged participation of all members and to establish a social and critical education of learners, educators, and university researchers, labor has been divided in a way every group has been responsible to lead some kind of task, making everybody feel as a real part of the project development. The various types of participation and the roles they imply are described below:

The project coordinator, Dr. Liberali, has been responsible for the project's overall organization. Together with other researchers, she has also been responsible for maintaining the coherence with the theoretical and methodological framework. The organizational staff also included master, university, and high school students. The whole group has worked as a team in proposing and carrying out actions – planning and developing workshops, observing classes, participating in meetings and in reflective sessions – that aimed to develop the partnered schools from the Municipal Department of Education and their participants. Each partnered school has participated in workshops with two to four students, two to four teachers, one or two coordinators, and sometimes a principal. The coordinators and school principals have followed the process of development and implementation of the project, supporting researchers, teachers, and students, conducting meetings, monitoring and promoting follow-up activities with the staff of the schools. They have taken responsibility for the in-depth study of the central concepts of the multiliteracy linked to issues of curriculum in their own everyday realities.

Two or more teachers from each school have formed a teacher support group. They take the lead, along with school coordinators, to support the development of the staff within their workplace. As colleagues, they have supported and coached the other teachers, creating binding moments of collaboration. Furthermore, about four students from each school have participated as *student-educators*. They have provided examples and suggestions of ways to use media to the teachers and school coordinators. Besides, they have analyzed and evaluated the curriculum proposed by the teachers and coordinators and they have shared responsibility for mobilizing and monitoring their peers and teachers in the use of media as to make it more effective, creative, and applicable in class.

In order to collect material for the collaborative analytical work, three workshops held in 2013 were video recorded and the material gathered was organized for transcription. The data was produced originally in Portuguese and translated into English by the researchers. Before watching the videos, the researchers discussed the criteria for selection and drew a list of categories that could be helpful for watching and analyzing them. Through viewing and discussion, episodes from the workshops were selected to exemplify knots in the creative chain and the categories used for analysis were revised.

Data analysis was conducted from an argumentative perspective, which considered contextual, discursive, and linguistic aspects in the understanding of the episodes chosen for discussion. The contextual characteristics focused on the circumstance of the utterance, specifically in the dialectical relationship among place, moment, participants, objectives, contents, and vehicles of communication for the production, circulation, and materialization of the activity. In the data analyzed, emphasis was placed on the understanding of the process which led participants to produce meanings that would be intentionally carried out to other related activities, forming a creative chain. The analysis focused on the tensions created and the means participants found to deal with them in order to make it possible not only to convey their ideas but mainly to jointly produce meaning through questions that led them to develop creative answers (Liberali, 2013).

The discursive characteristics were analyzed by the way turns were articulated in the events. According to Liberali (2013), it is essential, especially in schools, to both understand and develop forms of introducing, refusing, accepting, opposing, questioning, asking for, mirroring, presenting, contrasting, supporting, explaining, exemplifying, expanding, interconnecting, enforcing, concluding, and clarifying ideas. This raises possibilities for the construction of meaning that interlocutors are creating together in the activity.

The research data was organized into three links of the project chain of activities:

- Binding Moment 1, the first contact between researchers and the school communities;
- Binding Moment 2, a workshop in which all participants from schools had the opportunity to perform different subject tasks from a cross-curricular teaching unit, developed by researchers, based on multiliteracy concepts; and
- Binding Moment 3, a meeting in which each school prepared tasks focused on the same multiliteracy related concepts to develop the themes they chose.

These binding moments will be discussed below.

Binding moment 1

Following previous episodes of collaboration with the Municipal Department of Education of the City of São Paulo, in 2013, the researchers sent an email about this research project to some schools and invited them to join it. Six of them decided to participate. The first two meetings were held in June, 2013, while collaborating researchers from Greece, UK, and the Netherlands were visiting the Pontifical Catholic University of São Paulo. The objective of the meetings was to invite students, coordinators, and principals to share their views on the use of multiple media at school and on the way this could help improve teaching-learning processes. The meetings also involved presenting the project's objectives and layout, both in its international and local instances, in order to raise everybody's interest in joining the research and intervention project in the second semester.

After this introduction, students were separated from school staff and divided into three groups of approximately 15 participants. The aim was to have them interact with people from different institutions and explore their views on the use of multimedia at school. Students discussed the questions posed by the researchers about their media usage inside and outside the school. The researchers actively participated in the discussion by asking provocative questions, which led students to expand their ideas on the topic. After that, the students were invited to perform their ideas using some sort of media.

Subsequently, the students were invited to use improvisational theatrical performance to convey their perspectives on the use of media at school – which was a means to express their views about the topic in a creative way. This procedure was preferable once students could be freer to express themselves without being led by researchers. All the discussions and performances were video recorded for further analysis. While students discussed and created their performances with some of the researchers, school coordinators, principals, and teachers held a discussion on the same issues.

In the first group, students performed and recorded a classroom scene in which a teacher, unable to control her students in order to deliver a class, asks a couple of them to take over the leading role in the activity. They, then, resort to the internet to gather the information they needed to deliver to the class. Afterwards, the participants watched the recording and suggested different ways they could have used to perform the same scene. In another room, a second group was divided into two smaller teams. One team chose to film an interview on how young people use media at school. The other team set up a blog with impressions of the group on the same topic. The third group was also divided into two smaller teams. In one of them, students discussed environment exploration and capitalism and presented their conclusion with the help of a song played on an iPhone, a video presented on an iPad, and a poem found on the internet. In the other team, students decided to record a TV news program in which a reporter interviewed people about the use of media in classroom.

Analyzing what the groups presented, one could say that there was a strong reproductive perspective on the teaching-learning process in which students used gadgets as a means for the pure reproduction of pre-established knowledge. This can be illustrated by the performance of a student who was obliged by the teacher to "teach" something to his colleagues and stated: "Ah, then I'll teach about the ... the discovery of Brazil. I'll research very quickly on the internet." He moved to the side and in less than 5 seconds he started talking about it.

Likewise, media was seen as a substitute for the inefficacy of the teachers' approach. The same student told the performing teacher that he did not need her help and, at the end of the performance, he stated that he had taught his classmates because the teacher had been unable to do that. In a way, he simply reduced the potential use of media (in the case, the internet accessed through a cell phone) to a single mode (reading about the discovery of Brazil), reiterating practices that impose fixed, unquestioned contents upon students with a lack of multicultural perspectives. The reproduction of *banking patterns of education* (Freire, 1970), disregarding the possibility of other ways of considering the same content or of discussing it or its implications, was also present in most of the other interactions. Although, in another group, the use of different media as sources of knowledge was suggested for building different perspectives, qualities and/or uses in a subject area, the view of knowledge presented by students was still mono-cultural. For instance, students did not evaluate different media based on their potentiality, considering the printed dictionary and its crystallized meanings as more *reliable* than the internet and its variety of *unreliable possibilities*.

In a similar mode, the school coordinators, principals and teachers reported on important long projects using digital media in order to deal with their subject areas. But still, this was done only as part of certain areas and in very specific and special projects. In the everyday life of schools, things seemed quite different. Besides, the idea that using media would guarantee better results was not necessarily accompanied by a theoretical, critical, or methodological awareness of issues such as: how this was used, with what purpose, how contents were worked with or even which aspects could be addressed once the use of different media was proposed in classrooms.

The results of this initial contact with students, coordinators, principals, and teachers brought to light a need to consider what the use of media in schools' everyday lives was. This created the basis for researchers to start studying more about the use of multiple media in schools, its main aspects and considerations. It also led the researchers (most of whom had a background in applied linguists) to decide that they needed to broaden their studies in the area of multimodality to work with various media in the different area contents.

Based on these initial results, researchers concluded it was important to challenge the *banking patterns of education* being reproduced among participants as well as to implement and expand the use of multiple media at schools. Pursuing to address these issues, the researchers decided to organize follow-up meetings to focus on three aims:

- To work with improvisational theatrical performances as a means to live, analyze, evaluate, criticize, and propose new creative possibilities of acting out in school contexts.
- To organize didactic units based on multiliteracy.
- To use argumentation in the critical collaborative perspective outlined in the introduction above.

Binding moment 2

The second meeting, held on October 8, 2013, was designed by the researchers as to offer the experience of multiliteracy practices through the performance of a cross-curricular teaching unit previously constructed by the researchers. For the creation of the unit, researchers used the topic *public demonstrations,* widely discussed at that time due to the large number of people who were going to streets to protest against the increase in bus fares. The researchers also reflected on how the issue could be worked in different disciplines: history and Portuguese language were chosen as focal subjects.

The didactic unit was organized for the 9th year of the school programme based on the Municipal Curriculum Guidelines, which present the learning aims for all the years of basic education. The teaching unit aimed at sensitizing students, teachers, school coordinators, principals, and other participants for the theme, departing from everyday situations. In Portuguese language, the focus was to critically read, evaluate, and criticize news, articles, and reports. Besides, participants also had to analyze the entailments of oral, verbal, and written language, still and moving images, framing, tone of voice, etc. Through a set of media such as songs; plays on YouTube; printed magazines, photos, books; articles on webpages; among others (see Figure 8.1), participants were invited to discuss, analyze, evaluate, and construct concepts of demonstrations/protests in the area of history.

During the meeting, for the first task, participants, acting as "students," were supposed to observe images that represented different scenes of violence from a video. In relation to this video, "students" answered controversial questions (e.g.: "What does the video bring to your mind?", "How do you feel about it?"); furthermore, they could reflect on the theme and present their impressions and opinions about what was shown. Linking this task to the theme "demonstrations," they were encouraged to reflect on how they would react to those situations.

In the second part of the task, the "students" had to respond to statements based on their daily-life experiences such as the ones below. The researchers deliberately chose situations that had been vented by the social media. They clearly pointed at controversial issues, which could trigger students' emotions and encourage them to react:

- Teachers suspended physical education classes because students were not behaving appropriately.
- Students have to pay a toll to the group of drug dealers in order to enter school.
- Policemen stop a group of young people but search just the two black guys.

Figure 8.1 Various media presented in a didactic unit suggested by the researchers

Enhancing multimedia use in schools 135

In this task, two different kinds of media were used: the video and then snippets with statements. Both were used to enhance critical reflection, based on the multimodal aspects of media (cf. Bezemer & Kress, 2017). The multiple choice of sound, images, positions, gestures, words, and the various ideas conveyed by them offered the "students" the opportunity to express their positions and support them, based on analyses and interpretation, guided by the "teacher," a role played by one of the researchers, hence forth researcher-teacher. In order to better visualize the process of argumentation conducted in the group as to generate critical collaborative discussion, an excerpt from this event is presented here. In the performance, the "students" were presenting their opinions on the issue: "Teachers suspended physical education classes because students were not behaving properly." After the "students" presented their initial ideas, a researcher performing the "teacher" (researcher-teacher) started questioning about ways to deal with the situation presented, by posing a controversial question: "Do you think that this would work, people, this collective work to deal with this situation?"

Researcher-teacher[2]:	Do you think this would work, people, this collective work to deal with this situation?
Student 1:	There are possibilities.
Researcher-teacher:	Yes, there are. Yes, why are there possibilities?
Teacher 1:	There would be others.
Researcher-teacher:	Right.
Teacher 2:	This is a way.
Researcher-teacher:	You.
Student 1:	Because sometimes this student that messed up and was responsible for the cancellation of the physical education class, everyone's going against him. Then he'll feel that everybody's leaving him aside, that he's hated by everyone. So he'll start, stop, he'll think, I think that he'll even get better, then he'll try to do something.
Researcher-teacher:	Do you agree with student 1, people?
Researcher 2:	I'd like to say something, I don't know, because if I had messed up, but I think that this is no big issue so I won't stop doing this. Do you think that just because I did this, everyone is gonna miss the class? And, isn't there any other choice for the school? Won't anyone defend me? Can't we talk to the school to do something else? Oh, I think we should try to do something else, people.
Teacher 3:	I think that if it continues to be like this we should do nothing in all the classes. Not only in physical education. We do not participate in any class.
Researcher 2:	That is it! I agree with him. We shouldn't participate in any other classes anymore, people! I put my foot down! Let's have a revolution in this school! If we cannot go to

136 Liberali et al.

	physical education classes, then we won't go to any class at all. The teacher gets in and we don't do anything.
Teacher 2:	I don't think it's fair because I want to go to class and **they** were the ones who disturbed the class so I think that only **they** should miss classes. Why should everyone miss classes?

To respond to the researcher-teacher's question, student 1 gave a short answer ("There are possibilities.") The researcher-teacher agreed with his point of view and introduced a controversy question ("Why are there possibilities?"), that could create possibilities for student 1 to reorganize his ideas and support them with the use of arguments. Besides, the new question stimulated others to participate in the conversation. Teacher 1 and teacher 2 answered the question but didn't develop their points of view. The researcher-teacher invited one of the students to talk.

Student 1 answers with an explanation initiated by an explanatory connective "because," stating that "everyone" will go against the student who didn't behave well. In his opinion, the student is the culprit and the fact that he will be punished by his colleagues will lead to his transformation and improvement. In order to announce his position, he uses the third person pronoun (*he/his*) to refer to the guilty one and the indefinite pronouns *everyone/everybody* to the antagonists, the ones who will impose their value on the others. Moreover, his lexical choice (*messed up, going against, leaving aside, hated, get better*) indicates his view of the need to follow and subjugate to school rules without questioning. Hence, reinforcing traditional patterns of power relations in school.

This position, however, is confronted by researcher 1 when she answers researcher-teacher's question ("Do you agree with student 1, people?"). In order to intentionally challenge largely accepted punishment practices – a goal established after the analyses of Binding Moment 1 – researcher 1 proposes talking to the school about finding another solution and thinking about the situation as a minor issue. The researcher intentionally chooses to bring a different stance from the one expressed by the previous student. She assumes the attitude of a possible disruptive student, who could have misbehaved, in order to question the position of power assumed by the school and accepted by student 1 ("Can't we talk to the school to do *something else*?"). She asks for support from the group ("Won't *anyone* defend me?") and gets it from teacher 3 who suggests a movement of nonparticipation in other classes through the use of a threat with a conditional phrase ("**if** it continues to be like this we **should do** nothing in all the classes"). However, a third participant, teacher 2, presents an opposing idea ("I don't think it is fair") by presenting another option ("I think that only **they** should miss classes. Why should everyone miss classes?"), reinforcing the stance that misbehavior at school should be punished, this time addressing it only to the culprits ("marked by the pronoun **they**").

In the next sequence of the discussion, another student presents a situation that he experienced in his real school as a support to his idea on the topic under discussion. His utterance leads to a temporary abandonment of the performance and suggests that he is more concerned with the theme in discussion than with the mode of interaction proposed for the activity. It also implies that he is not fully acquainted with this type of activity, which is essential for this research group.

Student 2: In May, my teacher died and another one came to substitute her. I think that the problem was that she said right off the bat that she was against sending students to detention and then her class became a mess. Nobody talks (. . .)³, they sing, and change the lyrics of the song inserting bad words, they keep singing and speaking here and there, she scolds them. Then she asked me: "but why do they make such a mess?" and I said: "Have you tried to impose yourself a little more?" Then, she sent fifteen to detention in one day in one single class.

Researcher 1: See, but that is what I'm talking about. You must have presence, not to send students to detention. If you have presence, you don't need to send anyone to detention. It's different, it's different.

Student 2: She already found herself in a difficult situation and everybody keeps . . .

Teacher 2: So, we . . .

Researcher 2: Can't we solve the problem in the classroom? Why does everybody need to be out and miss class? Isn't there any way of making someone solve this in the classroom?

Teacher 2: We thought about a way to solve our problem. That was another problem, but I think it's good for this one, too. Student 3 was telling us that in his school there are assemblies and that we have to bring some problems for the whole group to discuss.

Researcher 2: That is what I think.

Teacher 2: (. . .) So, let's discuss everyone and try to find a rule, an agreement, I don't know, something (. . .) about what mess is, what it isn't, what leads to detention, what doesn't, I don't know.

Student 2 expressed his discomfort by narrating a situation that exemplified the school culture of punishment. It also suggested that personal relationships should not be part of what was dealt with in the classrooms once problems should be solved outside class in detention. This recovered the position expressed by student 1 and teacher 2 who also talked about the power relations at school. Researcher 1 brings the discussion back to the environment of the performance by accepting the contribution made by student 2 as part of it. Researcher 2 created a counter point to the idea of sending students out when she questioned participants about the possibility of solving relational problems in the classroom. Her questioning invited participants to find different, non-traditional solutions. This led teacher 2, who previously had assumed a reproductive form of interaction, to bring up a discussion held in her group about the proposition of assemblies as a form of involving the whole group in solving the problem. She mentioned student 3 who had told them his experience and suggested discussing "what mess is, what it isn't, what leads to detention, what doesn't." By doing so, she also leaves the context of the performance, focusing exclusively on the theme of the discussion, also showing lack of acquaintance with this type of activity. According to the theoretical background that supports the research group, by distancing from the performance, participants do not get fully emotionally involved in the experience in order to go through a transformational process.

In the discussion presented, it is possible to see the clashes of opinions and ideas supported and opposed by arguments. Different participants had the opportunity to present their views in the discussions. The researcher acting as a teacher offered the group a chance to express their views and agreement or disagreements. As students, researchers proposed less traditional views and triggered a context for a multicultural perspective of the situation. This way, participants could rethink their previous ideas and new creative solutions could be thought of. The performance of the task, prompted by the use of media, provided the group with a locus for reflection on a school life situation. This grounded them to present and support ideas through collaborative argumentation. In this performance, participants could go beyond their immediate possibilities and go through critical reflective development. This binding moment was the basis for the units schools were invited to create and share in November. They were supposed to use media to build a didactic proposal to address the themes of violence and/or quality of life, within a multiliteracy perspective.

Binding moment 3

For the fourth workshop, held on November 9, 2013, researchers proposed that each school develop their themes bearing in mind what had been discussed about multiliteracy. Coordinators, principals, teachers, and students from each school were supposed to engage in the development of a didactic task. Together, they were responsible for selecting and bringing different media to be used in their unit. The results of this work were to be presented to other participants during the workshop. The presentation should contain objectives, subject areas and contents involved, and detailing of the didactic proposal. After the presentations, participants debated how multiple modes of presenting content conveyed and influenced our perspectives of the world. For the purpose of this chapter, one of the presentations was selected as it fulfilled the goals set for the task (collectively preparing the unit and working with the whole staff from the school in pedagogical meetings).

Participants from one of the schools[4] chose to talk about violence against animals. The unit they presented had as its objectives the *construction of meanings about violence*. This would be done in order to transform pedagogical practices in the classroom by the use of different resources that could favor critical framing, redesign the views of the people involved, and motivate the transformation of everyday practice. Their unit focused on Portuguese language, history, and arts. Focusing on *news* as a major content, the language area worked with the use of animals for testing in labs. In the tasks, students had to build groups working with TV news, magazine articles, and blogs, and discussing the ways ideas were

Enhancing multimedia use in schools 139

presented by relating image and verbal text ("What is the relationship between what is seen and what is said?" and "Is there a relationship between the image and the written text? Justify your answer"). The final evaluation was an opinion essay about violence against animals.

The contents dealt with in history focused on the comparison between animal and slave treatment in order to lead students to evaluate and discuss animal and human rights. To do so, the students compared newspaper ads about the slaves from the 19th century and internet ads about animals. In groups, the students had to search images of slave-related topics on the internet in order to construct a panel to guide the class discussion. After that, they were supposed to write an argumentative article, using what they had learned from their colleagues' presentations, answering the controversial question: should there be a difference between animal and human treatment?

In arts, the unit proposed dealt with artistic performance, videos and photography through the production and analysis of images and discussion and creations of posts about artistic productions on the topic of violence against animals. In the tasks, the students were supposed to compare the media presented ("What is the difference between the photos and the video? Justify your answer." And "What artistic language was used? Justify your answer.") and were invited to post their own comments on a real news website platform. Besides, they had to create and film their own artistic performances to be posted on a school blog. The myriad of pictures (Figure 8.2, with colors in original) below exemplify the media prepared by the group and used in the unit.

The tasks proposed included the use of diverse media and the contrast among them, the comparison among various modes and the argumentative discussion of different opinions. Their presentation during the workshop focused on the

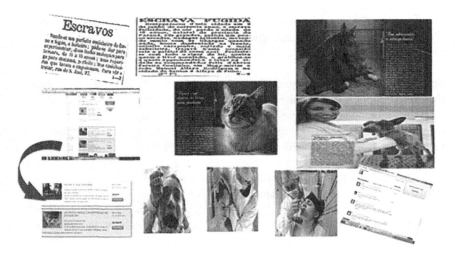

Figure 8.2 Various media used by one school in the didactic unit presented

narration of the path they took in order to put together the didactic unit. They mentioned the importance of the participation of all members in the production of the task as well as the role of discussion among them. One of the most important issues in the project was the students' participation as teacher-educators. The researchers considered that the students had an essential contribution to rethink the tasks created in schools. This engagement was also reflected in the speech of the school's coordinator and teacher as seen below:

Coordinator: The paths we followed to build this project, right (...) that's why I said to my team (...) we carried out the project as a group (...) teachers, students, coordinator and then (...)

In her speech, the coordinator brought about the idea that they had worked collaboratively through the lexical choices she made (*my team a group, teachers, students, coordinator*). She assumed the enunciative responsibility for what she was saying (*I, my*) and simultaneously shared it with the group (*we*). Besides, she individually quoted each participant's role, her tone of voice and intonation expressing her pride in the participation of all different members of the group. Others also presented support to this idea such as the ones below.

Teacher 2: In fact, *we* (...) when she talked about this discussion process, I mean, *we* have done this week, for example, *we* had to wrap up, to gather material, *the kids* did research, brought magazines, it's crazy when it's time to wrap up, when *we're* discussing with *them* it is (...) *we* are discussing; "but, people, is this what *we* are going to do in class?" (...) "no, but wait," and then *we* look at one another and ask "what are *we* really doing here?" *We* had a taste of it *ourselves*.
Director from directory of education: Sensational, sensational!
Teacher 2: The great truth is to construct it, even the terms **we** use, because there is **our** pedagoguese[5] that is extremely complicated while talking to **them**. (...)

Teacher 2 interlaced his utterance with the coordinator by recovering the process they went through ("when she talked about this discussion process") and recurrently attributed the collective responsibility of the group for their actions using the pronoun *we*. Besides, this teacher clearly presented the division of labor established in the group and the difficulties in attuning to it ("it's crazy when it's time to wrap up. We had a taste of it ourselves"). He commented on one important issue which pointed to the difficulties and contradictions the activity created. When teacher 2 discussed the jargon used ("pedagoguese") by the teachers and students' obvious difficulties in understanding it, he necessarily recognized the need to find a different way to convey their knowledge. This illustrates how the need to challenge questions of power in school were intentionally thought of and carried out in the actions of this group.

The second aspect that was viewed as necessary for the constitution of a critical collaborative group was the critical participation of all the school members in the process of decision making, as exemplified by the excerpt below.

Coordinator: And then we brought (. . .) There was a long discussion to get to the conclusion about what we were going to present, wasn't there, teacher 1?

Teacher 1: There was a long discussion.

Coordinator: Because it was like this: part of the group thought we had to present the performance of the class immediately; (. . .) part of it thought that we should present the steps followed to build the unit. (. . .) After a long discussion, we decided to present the steps of what had happened. There were the discussions, the work itself, to reach the final result, ok?

The argumentation that took place in the school was expressed by teacher 1, when he described how teachers and students brought different ideas about the topic to be dealt with and how they collaboratively reached a final topic.

Teacher 1: Let me just say something else before starting. It is important to mention that students (. . .), actually the girls, was student 3 in already or not? Student 2 and student 1 certainly were (. . .) they (. . .) when we asked what the theme would be, what they thought would be relevant (. . .) for us to work, they came up with the proposal of working with bullying, you know? At first, then, I mean, they connected to the idea of bullying, and we were thinking about violence. I, the coordinator and teacher 2, were considering violence and they came up with bullying (. . .) then we asked: Can we use violence? They said: "perfect because," you know (. . .)

Teacher 2: It broadens.

Teacher 1: (. . .) exactly, we have a (. . .) have more, have more, have a greater range of options, so we could come up with this broad proposal. Then we thought of a number of activities that we could work within that theme of violence, trying to bring a current topic. Then, the proposal was to work something still alive in the flesh, which was still bleeding, that was very much alive in the memory of people. And that's when we came up with (. . .)

Coordinator: There were (. . .) sentences from a magazine article about violence against animals, ok? That came out in Veja Magazine.

The process of decision making is presented here from the perspective of the teachers and the coordinator. Up to this point, although students talked when in small groups, they were still very reluctant to make assembly presentations.[6] In the teachers' description, one can see that students' initial position about bullying as a form of violence was contested by the educators' suggestion of discussing violence in general. However, it seems that students agreed with their position and even gave support to it by stating that this topic could *broaden* their possibilities of topics for the project. The interplay between *we* (teachers and coordinator) and *they* (students) which ends in a *we* (teachers, coordinator, and students) in the format of a question ("Can we use violence?") sets a different perspective for the hierarchical perspectives of school organization. In this extract, different ideas were introduced, dwelled, and supported. In a critical collaborative perspective, the curriculum was being co-designed by the participants, not through simple acceptance but by joint agreement and co-responsibility.

Finally, whenever researchers introduced a new concept or task, they used performances. When the school group presented their unit, they did the same. They started their presentation by inviting the whole group of participants to act as students and do the following task: "Well, to start, we brought some sentences and we'd like you to read and reflect about them. After that, you should tell us what they're about." Participants were supposed to read the following sentences: "I almost starved; I got stabbed blind; I was abused and run over; nobody knew how to take care of me." By suggesting to the group of researchers, teachers, school coordinators, students, principals, and director of the Directory of Education of São Paulo that they engage in the activity as students and try to accomplish the task, this school group recreated a typical school situation in which all participants debated their ideas and had to present their views and support their opinions. They used the theoretical knowledge about multiliteracy as the basis for creating the tasks and this gave the whole group a chance to reflect on the issues they had experienced. Besides, the group reported how they organized the work with teacher education with the whole staff in the school and this also served as an example for other schools.

Reflective remarks

Assuming that the use of multiple media can contribute to participants' development, our project aimed at the construction of curriculum proposals to challenge the encapsulation of knowledge within a multiliteracy perspective. The objective was to involve the various participants in the school context so that they jointly construct new ways of working through multiple media. In this sense, using media at schools is not only related to choosing content and what media to use. Rather, it is fundamentally related to thinking how contents and the use of media can foster reflection and transformation.

The project we presented in this chapter shares some essential ideas with the Echo Park Film Center, a Los Angeles nonprofit media education organization, presented by Rosales (2013). We believe that media literacy educators should promote media comprehension amongst children and young people. Kids and teens should appropriate the knowledge and have the choice to define their own conceptions of media literacy and how they will engage with them. However, media are not transparent tools. They carry ideologies and feelings which turn them into mediational artifacts. Hence, the choices for what media to use, how to use them, and what meaning effect to entail need to be negotiated and discussed. Moreover, media should be seen as means to develop children's and adolescents' collaborative attitudes that involve trusting others and taking risks. Finally, our project shares with the Echo Park Film Center the idea that a project must be simultaneously linked to participants' reality and detached from it. We assume that these dialectics create the possibility to take the participants from where they are to where they can be, as discussed by Vandewater (2013). Departing from where they are, students have the chance to move beyond their immediate realities to go the distance.

Another piece of research which also brings about a design that correlates to ours is that presented by Chee (2011). Her article describes funded research directed toward the development and evaluation of innovative technology-enhanced pedagogies that incorporate new media literacies in classrooms in Singapore. The challenge of this project, based on American pragmatism, was designing game-based learning to enact a pedagogy of "learning as becoming." Our project shares with the Singapore project the importance attributed to personal agency in investing on the learning process. Although from a somewhat different perspective, we also center our project on the idea of play and performance as essential to lead people beyond their immediate possibilities and to trigger critical, reflective, and conscious development. In addition, we recognize the idea of dialogue as central to human development and its connection to media.

Since we base our work on critical collaboration and argumentation, we claim that everybody's opinions deserve to be placed, supported and discussed; there is no hierarchy among students', teachers', and coordinators' voices; we believe that each participant has some responsibility in the totality that can be reached. We insist on constructing our paths according to the contexts and demands of reality and people involved. This creates flexibility in the way we act. The focus of our work in involving different participants of the school context is to create an environment to jointly rethink schools and communities.

The beginning of these transformations can be seen mainly through three results achieved when analyzing this chapter's data. Firstly, participants critically reflected on the issues they had experienced based on theoretical knowledge about multiliteracy. In the first binding moment, it was possible to visualize participants' level of literacy and of media use. This triggered the need to a study of how to deal with different media, modes, and cultures. Based on the study of multiliteracy, in Binding Moment 2, researchers created a didactic unit, using distinct media and exploring different modes in dealing with diverse area contents. The types of questions and variability of materials and positions brought to discussion were central to creating a multiplicity of possibilities of knowledge production. In Binding Moment 3, school participants used our example as support and went beyond, creating their didactic unit based on the analysis of the schools' needs. They integrated the demands of the reality to the new theoretical and practical concepts they were introduced to.

Secondly, argumentation was essential for creating critical collaboration. In Binding Moment 1, students could present their positions and support them by performing different roles, creating different products, using media and the modes they afforded. In the unit prepared for Binding Moment 2, the tasks demanded that students support their positions in relation to questions posed. Besides, during the discussions, different views were collaboratively presented. When ideas were too reproductive, the researchers intervened, posing contradictions that allowed participants to expand their points of view. Finally, in Binding Moment 3, as reported by the participants of school analyzed here, they also experienced argumentation as a means to develop as a team. They had to reconfigure modes of talking to one another, overcoming limitations of their ways of acting. We noticed that participants were all involved in the process of decision making, there was less hierarchy in the relationships among students, teachers, and coordinators. In other words, the work was co-designed by the participants in the creative chain.

Thirdly, based on the analysis of the performances created by the students, we noticed in Binding Moment 1 the need to challenge pre-established relations at school, which reiterate the teacher as the sole authority responsible for controlling contents and students. In Binding Moment 2, during the performance proposed, we could also see a discussion that triggered a reflection on commonly accepted authoritarian practices at school, namely, punishment. When looking at Binding Moment 3, we perceived the engagement of all participants in the construction of the unit. It seems that the whole group had some responsibility in the totality of results. In this sense, new possibilities were developed in the creative chain of activities. The very possibility of having students and educators jointly working to discuss and produce curricula is a first step in the creation of the new afforded by this creative chain.

Finally, we argue that learning is dialectical and involves mutual interdependence between self and society, which establishes a need for co-responsibility and development of new forms of participation. The creative chain, present in the project discussed here, emphasizes not only the transformation of individuals but, as a result, the transformation of the whole community. It is not enough that the immediate participants become efficient and effective in the project's objective. It is essential that the whole community is involved as a springboard for the transformation of everyone's life.

Notes

1 Comitê Gestor da Internet no Brasil (Internet Management Committee in Brazil), see: http://www.cgi.br/noticia/cgi-br-divulga-resultados-da-pesquisa-tic-educacao-2012/336
2 In the transcript, names have been omitted – instead all participants were represented according to their real functions in the project (researcher, teacher, or student), even though all – except the researcher-teacher – acted as if they were students.
3 (. . .) = hesitation or pause.
4 Eda Terezinha Elementary Municipal School.
5 *Pedagoguese* as a neologism for the language related to how people in education talk.
6 In the last event of the research group on May, 17 2014, those three students, responsible for participating in a round table together with the teachers and coordinator, exposed their position and expressed their views on these same episodes.

References

Bezemer, J., & Kress, G. (2017). Young people, Facebook, and pedagogy: Recognizing contemporary forms of multimodal text making. In M. Kontopodis, C. Varvantakis, & C. Wulf (Eds.), *Global youth in digital trajectories*. London: Routledge.

Brown, S. (2010). From VLEs to learning webs: The implications of Web 2.0 for learning and teaching. *Interactive Learning Environments*, 18(1), 1–10.

Chee, Y. S. (2011). Learning as becoming trough performance, play and dialogue: A model of game-based learning with the game Legends of Alkhimia. *Digital Culture & Education*, 3(2), 98–112.

Dafermos, M., Triliva, S., & Varvantakis, C. (2017). Youth tubing the Greek crisis: A cultural-historical perspective. In M. Kontopodis, C. Varvantakis, & C. Wulf (Eds.), *Global youth in digital trajectories*. London: Routledge.

Emmel, B., Resch, P., & Tenney, D. (Eds.). (1996). *Argument revisited: Argument redefined*. Thousand Oaks: Sage.

Freire, P. (1970). *Pedagogy of the oppressed*. New York: Herder and Herder.

Hillman, T. (2014). Finding space for student innovative practices with technology in the classroom. *Learning, Learning, Media and Technology*, 399(2), 169–183.

Liberali, F. C. (2009). Creative chain in the process of becoming a totality: A cadeia criativa no processo de tornar-se totalidade. *Bakhtiniana: Revista de Estudos do Discurso*, 2, 1–25.

Liberali, F. C. (2013). *Argumentação em contexto escolar*. Campinas: Pontes.

McCormick, R. (2004).Collaboration: The challenge of ICT. *International Journal of Technology and Design Education*, 14(2), 159–176.

Mosca, L. L. S. (2004). Velhas e novas retóricas: Convergências e desdobramentos. In L. L. Mosca (Ed.), *Retóricas de ontem e hoje* (pp. 4–54). São Paulo: Associação Editorial Humanistas.

New London Group. (1996/2000). A pedagogy of multiliteracies: Designing social futures. In B. Cope & M. Kalantzis (Eds.), *Multiliteracies: Literacy learning and the design of social futures* (pp. 9–32). New York: Cambridge.

Ogan-Bekiroglu, F., & Aydeniz, M. (2013). Enhancing pre-service physics teachers' perceived self-efficacy of argumentation-based pedagogy through modelling and mastery experiences. *Eurasia Journal of Mathematics Science & Technology Education*, 9(3), 233–245.

Rosales, J. A. (2013). Participatory culture at the Echo Park Film Center. *Journal of Media Literacy Education (JMLE)*, 5(1), 349–356.

Vandewater, E. A. (2013). Ecological approaches to the study of media and children. In D. Lemish (Ed.), *The Routledge international handbook of children, adolescents and media* (pp. 46–53). London: Routledge.

Vygotsky, L. S. (1930/1978). *Mind in society: The development of higher psychological processes* (Ed. M. Cole, V. John-Steiner, S. Scribner, & E. Souberman). Cambridge: Harvard University Press.

Warwick, P., & Mercer, N. (2011). Using the interactive whiteboard to scaffold pupils' learning of science in collaborative group activity. *Conference presentation: EARLI*, University of Exeter, September 2, 2011. Retrieved from http://iwbcollaboration.educ.cam.ac.uk/publications/Scaffolding-symposium-paper-for-website.pdf (date of access: 30/03/2014).

Instead of an epilogue
Iconophagy: Impact and impulses for global youth and education

Norval Baitello Jun.

1) Contemporary society, to a great extent, is based on visuality and visual images. According to Christoph Wulf (2009), images have achieved a ubiquitous presence; they are everywhere ("Bilder haben eine ubiquitäre Präsenz erlangt", cf. also the introduction by Kontopodis, Varvantakis & Wulf, 2017). This means that human sociability is constituted and organized by obeying the logic of images and of visuality, with a huge supremacy of perception of what is on the superficial, at the expense of everything that involves density, volume, depth, and weight. In turn all dimensions of corporality (gesture, presence, slowness, the kinesthetic complexity, multisensoriality) are losing ground in life and in contemporary interactions. Furthermore, the most complex operations involving the world of reading, do also lose because these require time and immersion in varying depths. Harry Pross (1990) with great precision called this ability to immerse and take time and give attention during reading *lange Weile des Lesens*; i.e., the slow languor of reading.

2) Contemporary image, spread by the various mass media, requires lightness and promotes lightness. As it is the cause and the consequence of smooth and simple technologies, it spreads very easily and quickly, has a high degree of capillarity, optimized in its ability to irrigate and occupy the environments in which it circulates. This means that contemporary image is absorbed very easily, but is also consumed and discarded quickly, promoting the rapid replacement by new images. Moreover, it doesn't require prior learning for its mild reception. Decoding is immediate, does not require mediation in learning for its understanding (cf. Daryan & Wulf, 2017).

3) By being lightweight, easy and quickly replaceable, it is also cheap. Contemporary image belongs to an economical logic of the perishable and disposable, that only leaves room for objects (imagery) of low or insignificant individual cost. Thus, economy doesn't move by the individual value of the product but by the massive scale of its production and, above all, by being quickly replaced. The obsolescence, or in other terms, the rapid death of the product when loses its glitz, appeal or information, is incorporated a priori into its project.

4) Every project is the design of a future scenario. Therefore, the future is now also designed as lightweight, superficial, ephemeral, and cheap. These

Iconophagy: impact and impulses 147

image characteristics determine the future as an image and encourage furthermore the disposal of the present. Since the future will not have weight (density), volume, durability, and cost, it is not necessary today to reserve strength and energy for it. It has no worth as a promise or as a horizon of expectation.

5) Now, nothing that is durable is worthwhile, we move past things, leave them behind as disposal, as garbage. We do not use memory anymore as ballast for the future. Even the storage media no longer memorizes for eternity, as did the rupestrian paintings, sculptures in stone and bone, the mummification and burial rituals, paintings on canvas, written on durable materials and even preserved books in suitable environments conservation.

6) While writing (secondary media) was designed to outlast its authors and served to carry them forward into a much larger symbolic longevity than their own physical life, technological memory supports (in tertiary media) are scheduled to phase out long before their users. They carry within much of the memory of their users, registering images in great profusion that could not be transferred to other latest gadgets. As record and store is superficial and free, also the loss is superficial and free, this is seen as a magical cycle of disappearance/appearance. There is another sense of *re-imagining* the world and life itself, as announced by Vilém Flusser already in 1972.

7) These lost memories go to waste, further thickening the already thick layers of litter being deposited under our floor. Such garbage, consisting of rich memory material, not used in its fullness, dropped before it has exhausted all its possibilities of use, will become a valuable source of means to feed the voracious need of the consumer society, to produce new objects, new images. Again, according to Flusser, a third kingdom, the realm of garbage appears next to the realm of nature and the realm of culture (which now defines us much more than the historical awareness of realm of culture).

8) Since we live in an age of image and visuality, the accelerated production of images requires a lot of raw material to feed the hysterical flow of media images. It finds such raw material in the deposits of discarded and buried images. Recycles junk-images and conveys them to new vehicles, new media, to be consumed again as cheap, light and ephemeral surfaces, to be quickly forgotten, discarded and buried again and again. This is the dynamics of contemporary media images as primarily exploited on television in North American, Italian, and Brazilian models. Such reality was portrayed accurately, humorously and artistically by Federico Fellini in his classic film about television "Ginger and Fred".

9) The consumer society is the one that cannot consume everything it produces, as announced by Flusser. Today we know that its remains and trash are intentional and unavoidable. This garbage is going to feed the machines that engender the fleeting, fast, and shallow future. The image machines are the most successful inventions of the last century.

10) The image machines are also those most developed and demanded investments in the late nineteenth century and the twentieth century as a whole: photography, cinema, television, personal computers, mobile phones,

tablets, laptops, and e-book readers. These technological innovations have become rapidly accessible to the great public. The media image industry – small, shallow, ephemeral, and free – has flourished and transformed quickly habits that were before enshrined: the face-to-face conversation, visitation, proximity, gestures, rituals of encounter, sociality of physical presence.

11) Also the educational processes are profoundly affected. Writing and reading as a form of appropriation of a vast body of knowledge suffer from the hasty greed that assimilates only fractions of what is offered. There is always an urge to pass on, to go to the next step without having completed the latter step. As argued by Dietmar Kamper (1994), the greatest difficulty of man today is living entirely on today (in our own present). Leakages to the future are irresistible. We are never entirely on the present. And therefore we never live it fully, always just fragments.

12) Today we read texts as if they were images, jumping, with random comings and goings, fast and fleeting. Weightlessly and without density, with no linearity and totally fragmentary. The texts are partially devoured. We skip some parts and they are untouched by swift and eager eye of the future, in a rushed and inattentive matter. A new kind of literacy will have to be practiced, the literacy of presence, which rescues itself from shelters of the future, from the voracious maw of an easy future.

13) The omnipresent media image does not only provide itself as a light and cheap antipasto. It reverses the vectors of action and hijacks us to idealized and promising future scenarios, devouring our presence and corporality. I call both operations *iconophagy*: when we feed the images and when they feed on our lives, our time, our space, and our bodies (cf. also Baitello, 2008). Iconophagy occurs when we feed ourselves with images, devouring their attributes, appropriating its main qualities, approaching its two-dimensional, superficial, light and ephemeral reality, many times we turn into images and even feel as such. But iconophagy is also the reverse operation, in which images are the ones that appropriate our gestures, our embodiment, our time and our space, reducing our multi-sensorial, multi-sensory sociability, and our wealth inside imagery, our complex experience of space and time.

14) Iconophagy becomes a regulating principle of traffic between humans and images, the ownership of each other. The iconophagy is the process of a hasty and incomplete digestion of the other, i.e. a metabolic process that does not properly break the molecules to be assimilated and incorporated. The residue of the devoured is therefore indigestible; it becomes part and defines the future nature of the devourer. In this sense, iconophagy is the opposite of cannibalistic ritual, devouring the enemy to take ownership of their qualities.

If above assumptions are correct, if we consider them as a diagnosis (which means, a portrait of an illness – and this may not be consensus or unanimity!), we, educators and social scientists, have a task in front of us: the transmutation of impacts into pulses. If the invasion of images and image machines is irreversible, what remains is learning how to use them in favor of the young people, reversing their use as support rescuing gestures and presence, corporeality, and multisensoriality. By this I mean, a better balance between:

- primary media (Harry Pross has argued since 1971 that all communication begins and ends in the human body),
- secondary media (must regain the slow languor of reading and relearn the slow time) and,
- tertiary media (the world of new objects of desire, the new image technologies, today loaded in each pocket).

Maybe the solution is to promote education through images, encouraging multimodal dimensions of literacy, while reflecting on its deeper layers of historical senses, as Bezemer and Kress as well as Liberali et al. suggest in the studies presented above (2017). According to Hans Belting (2001), the image will always be the traffic between its external manifestation and its internal existence. If external images are inflated, the internal images and their world, the world of imagination, can be harmed in its heart, i.e., in its creative ability. The alchemical garbage transmutation of the excremental images is in our hands – and is also in the hands of the young people as the fascinating studies by Dafermos, Triliva and Varvantakis (2017) as well as by Rubtsova and Ulanova (2017) demonstrate. Accordingly to Flusser, the animal that best represents this operation is the worm, because it transforms waste into humus. Updating Zarathustra, who praised the cows for their ability to ruminate, we should claim today: "if we do not become like worms we won't enter the kingdom of heaven".

References

Baitello, N. (2008). *La era de la iconofagia*. Sevilla: ArCiBel.
Belting, H. (2001). *Bildanthropologie: Entwürfe für eine Bildwissenschaft*. München: W. Fink.
Bezemer, J., & Kress, G. (2017). Young people, Facebook, and pedagogy: Recognizing contemporary forms of multimodal text making. In M. Kontopodis, C. Varvantakis, & C. Wulf (Eds.), *Global youth in digital trajectories*. London: Routledge.
Dafermos, M., Triliva, S., & Varvantakis, C. (2017). Youth tubing the Greek crisis: A cultural-historical perspective. In M. Kontopodis, C. Varvantakis, & C. Wulf (Eds.), *Global youth in digital trajectories*. London: Routledge.
Daryan, N., & Wulf, C. (2017). Digital identity building: A dialogue with Berlin technology & computer science students. In M. Kontopodis, C. Varvantakis, & C. Wulf (Eds.), *Global youth in digital trajectories*. London: Routledge.
Flusser, V. (1972). *A consumidora consumida*. Rio de Janeiro: Comentário.
Kamper, D. (1994). *Bildstörungen*. Stuttgart: Cantz.
Kontopodis, M., Varvantakis, C., & Wulf, C. (2017). Exploring global youth in digital trajectories. In M. Kontopodis, C. Varvantakis, & C. Wulf (Eds.), *Global youth in digital trajectories*. London: Routledge.

Liberali, F., Magalhães, M.-C., Meaney, M.-C., Santiago, C., Canuto, M., Amaral, F., Cababe, B., & Santos, J. (2017). Enhancing multimedia use in state secondary schools in São Paulo: A critical collaborative perspective. In M. Kontopodis, C. Varvantakis, & C. Wulf (Eds.), *Global youth in digital trajectories*. London: Routledge.

Pross, H. (1971). *Medienforschung*. Darmstadt: Carl Habel.

Pross, H. (1990). Die lange Weile des Lesens. In V. Rapsch (Ed.), *Über Flusser* (pp. 141–149). Düsseldorf: Bollmann.

Rubtsova, O., & Ulanova, N. (2017). Digital filmmaking as a means for the development of reflection: A case study of a disabled university student in Moscow. In M. Kontopodis, C. Varvantakis, & C. Wulf (Eds.), *Global youth in digital trajectories*. London: Routledge.

Wulf, C. (2009). *Anthropologie*. Köln: Anaconda.

Index

activism: digital technologies and 110; Facebook and 112; filmmaking and 128; television news and 113, 118, 122n18
activity: digital technologies and 53; mediated 53–4, 62–3, 67, 74; mediating 53–5, 63–4, 67, 73–4, 76, 82–4, 92; physical 43; signs and 54, 66; text making and 32–3; tools and 54, 66
actors/actants 41–2, 48
adolescence *see* youth
agency: body and 40; designer and 26, 37; digital technologies and 40; knowledge production and 36; of learners 37, 143; meaning making and 25; nature of 49; of objects 12; social 37; youth and 70
anthropology: educational 40; symmetric 41
Appadurai, Arjun 1
app generation 1
argumentation 128–9, 138, 141, 143–4

Bakhtin, M. 98–9, 106
beauty ideals 100, 103
body: agency and 40; communication and 149; concepts of 40; culture and 49; extended 4; images and 46, 48–50; movements of 42, 46; on-screen/off-screen 39, 42–3, 46

campaigns: anti-rape 116–17; Facebook and 111–12, 116, 120; media-generated 120; television news and 111, 113–15, 117–18, 120; YouTube 97–8, 100–4, 108
case study: disabled student filmmaking 55–66; Dove YouTube campaign 100–8; Facebook text making 27–35; Nintendo Wii bowling 46–8; Nintendo Wii shadow boxing 44–6
coding schemes 99–102, 106–7

cohesion: cross-modal 27; social 69–70; text making and 33, 35
collaboration: argumentation and 129, 138; critical 128–44; defining 128; multimedia use and 143
collaborative learning 82, 128
comments: Facebook 34–5; news media 139; Nintendo Wii 48; YouTube 97–108
communication: civic 110; content analysis and 97; digital technologies and 18–19, 23–4, 127–8, 131; gestural 49; non-verbal 83; protest and 91; reflective 63–4, 67; semiotic theory of 25; text making 25; youth and 71
community: digital 13; imagined 71; transformation of 144
competence: defining 17; design and 26; digital media 13; filming and 35; media 18; social domains and 24; text making and 35–6
computer science, students of 13–14
conflict: inner role 89–90; reflective communication and 63; social media and 97, 106–7
content analysis: coding schemes for 100–2; of digital technologies 97; traditional 97–9
control 81–3, 86, 88, 92
creative chains 129, 131, 144
crisis 73–5; *see also* social crises
cultural-historical theory: concepts of 73–5; cultural signs and 53–4, 66, 73; cultural tools and 53, 66; development and 71–2, 90–1; reflection and 59; video-making and 78–9
cultural signs: development and 53–4, 73, 81; mediating activity and 54, 66, 82–3; resistance and 84, 91; social meaning and 83
cultural texts 78

152 *Index*

culture: body and 49; digital 5, 19, 48; ethnography and 41; learning 13; meaning and 128; online gaming 5, 39, 43, 47, 50; participatory 91, 128; of rioting 70–1; school 137; text making 23; youth 4, 69–70, 88, 90
curriculum: critical collaboration in 129–42; development of 130–8, 142; multimodal 24; proposals for 130

design: innovation and 37; signs-as-texts and 26
development: crisis and 74–6; cultural 88–9; digital technologies and 53–5, 67; process of 72–3; real/ideal forms and 75; social interaction and 59
dialogism 98–100
dialogue: argumentation and 128; classroom 127; development and 143; media and 143; online discussions 98–9, 108
didactic units 133–8
digital culture: hypersphere and 12; politics and 5; technography of 48
digital identity: egocentricity and 15; formation 14–19; media competence and 18; online/offline world and 6, 14; sustainable 18
digital identity formation 14–19
digital literacies 2
digital media competence *see* competence
digital natives 12–13; hyperspherical practices 20; Net logic and 18; public/private sphere 14, 18
digital public spaces 81–2
digital role models 16–17, 19
digital technologies: access to 148; body and 19; brain and 1; developmental processes and 53–5, 67; disabled students and 55–9, 66–7; everyday lives and 12, 14–15; globalization and 15; learning and 13, 53; memory and 147; protest and 91; as signs 54–5, 66; social relationships and 19–20; as tools 54–5, 66; youth and 1–5
disabilities: defining 55; digital technologies and 19, 55–6; redefining 4
disabled students: challenges of 57; digital technologies and 55–67; reflection and 57, 59, 64, 66; support for 56–7
Dove beauty products 100, 102–6, 108
drama 59, 92

Echo Park Film Center 128, 142–3
education: banking patterns of 132–3; digital technologies and 148; images and 149; *see also* pedagogies; schools
educational anthropology 40
engagement: argumentation and 129; collaboration and 140, 142, 144; interest and 31; participatory culture and 91–2; political 82; social relationships and 36; text making and 24, 35; texts and 26, 30
everyday life: gaming culture and 39; interactivity and 41; modalities of 3; schools and 133; surveillance and 85; technography and 41

Facebook: anti-rape protest coverage *117*; corruption coverage and *115*; learning and 13; News Feeds and 34–5; posts on 27–34; protest and 110–11, 113–14, 116, 120; shared links 28–9; status updates on 28–32; television news and 113, 120–1; text making on 24, 26–35
filmmaking: disabled students and 57–67; mediated activity and 62, 66–7; mediating activity and 63–7; process of 59–66; *see also* video-making
focus group discussions 13–17, 99

gaming culture: interface 47; mirror imaging in 50; research on 39; socio-technical involvement in 47–8
gender: internet use and 110; media coverage and 116, 118–19
gender violence: Facebook pages on *117*; media coverage of 116, 118–20; middle class and 118–20; protest and 116–18; victims of 118
gestural communication 49
girls: beauty industry pressures on 100–3; cultural signs and 83; social crises and 82–3; *see also* women
globalization: digital technologies and 15; protest and 91
Greece: educational system 87–8; political occupation of 84–5; rioting culture in 70–1; social crises and 75–6, 81–91; social world of 84–8; youth in 69–71, 76–91

Hazare, Anna 113–14
higher psychological functions 53, 55, 67
homogeneous mediality 15, 18–19

Index 153

hypersphere 12
hyperspherical practices: competence and 18; youth and 12–16, 20

iconophagy 148
identity: digital 1, 6, 14–19; Facebook and 29; group 129; youth and 70
images: body and 46, 48–50; impact of 149; indexical 19; modes of 22, 25, 27; production of 147; society and 146; use of 22–3
imagination: concepts of 40; image production and 49; socio-technical interactivity 50; youth and 91
imagined communities 72
indexical images 19
India: corruption coverage and *114–15*; criminal law in 118; internet use 110–11, 121n1; middle class and 118–19; protest and 110–18, 121; social media and 110–11, 113, 116–*17*
India Against Corruption (IAC) campaign 112–15
information and communication technology (ICT) 128
Instagram 13
interaction: design and 25, 34; media 15; online discussions 107–8; sequential analysis and 107–8; social 59, 73; video 36
interactivity 41, 49–50
inter-agency 41–2
interconnectedness 1
interest 31
intermediation 47
international/intercultural digital collectives 15
internet: access to 110; mass media and 120; protest and 110; public spheres and 120
iPhone camera 30, 32

Kavafi, Konstantinos 83, 92
Kazantzakis, Nikos 84–5, 92
knowledge: mono-cultural 133; multimedia as 132–3; multimodal 129
Koodankulam Nuclear Plant campaign 112–13

Lall, Jessica 118–19
Language in Activities in School Contexts (LACE) 127

learning: agency and 143; dialectical 128, 144; digital technologies and 53
literacy skills 23, 149

mass media: beauty ideals in 100, 103; discourses of 111; internet and 120; oppression and 81–2, 86, 90
Mead, George Herbert 49
meaning: argumentation and 129; communication of 25–6, 78, 97, 128; construction of 46, 138–9; creative chains and 129, 131; dialogism and 98; digital technologies and 42; interpretation and 42; modes of 25–6; signs and 25, 83; text making and 22; youth and 26
meaning makers 25–6, 33, 37
media competence 18
media literacy 56, 142–3
mediated activity: defining 74; filmmaking as 62, 66–7; tools and 54, 66, 74
mediating activity: filmmaking as 63–7; reframing and 83; signs and 54–5, 66, 74, 82
mediation 74, 82
mimetic learning 17
mobile interfaces 2
mobile phones 1, 34, 147
modes: arrangement and 27; defined 25; ensembles of 33; functions of 33–4; highlighting and 27; meaning and 26; representation and 22, 25, 36; selection and 27
multiliteracy practices 133, 138, 142–3
multimedia use: collaboration in 128, 130–1, 143; didactic units and 133–8; knowledge and 132–3; school 128, 131–6, 139–41; students and 131–3, 139–40; teachers and 132–4
multimodal communication: education and 149; media and 135; text making and 23–35, 78–9; youth and 4, 23–5

neoliberalism 70–1, 83
News Feeds 34–5
news media: gender violence and 116, 118–19; middle class and 119; protest and 110–14, 116
Nintendo Wii 39, 42–8
non-human 12, 40–1
nonsequential analysis 100, 102–4

occupation: political 84–5; resistance and 92
online discussions: dialogue and 98; interactions in 107–8; nonsequential analysis 102–4; sequential analysis and 98–101, 104–8; systematic observation 99
online/offline world: boundaries of 2–3; digital identity and 6; methodologies for 41
oppression 81–2, 85–90

Pandey, Jyoti Singh 116, 118–19
participatory culture 91, 128
pedagogies: conflicts of 36–7; technology-enhanced 143; text making and 36–7; of writing 37; *see also* education
perezhivanie 60, 66, 73–4, 85
performance: movements and 47; presentations and 142, 144
Piaget, Jean 48
platforms: filming and 36; multimodal text and 24; resources and 25; text making and 22–3, 31
politics: digital culture and 5; engagement and 82; in Greece 84–5; video and 81–2, 84–7; YouTube and 81–8
posts: Facebook 27–34; social media 97, 139; YouTube 84–92, 98–107
Programme for International Student Assessment (PISA) 23
protest: digital technologies and 91; Facebook and 111, 113, 116, 120; news media and 110–16; social media and 110–11, 114; television news and 111, 113–16, 118, 121
public/private sphere 14, 18, 72, 120
public spaces: digital 81–2; virtual 5; women and 123n20

Rammert, Werner 41
reading 147–9
reflection: critical 143; developmental processes and 59; disabled students and 57, 59, 64, 66; mediating activity and 63–5
reflective communication 63–4
representation: augmentation of 29; modes of 22, 25, 36
resources: platforms for 25; text making and 31
rhetorical interest 25–6, 37

scaffolding 128
schools: collaboration in 131, 139–40; discourse in 131; information and communication technology (ICT) 128; multimedia in 127, 130–41; student-educators 130, 132, 140; *see also* education
sensuous: technologies 41; video gaming 39–40, 46, 50
sequential analysis: behavior and 100; coding schemes for 106–7; interactions in 107–8; online discussions and 98–101, 104–8
sequentiality 35
signs: -as-texts 26; cultural 53–4, 66, 73, 81–4, 91; defining 54; internalization of 54; -making 25–6; mediating activity and 54–5, 66
smartphones 30–1
social cohesion 69–70
social crises: cultural signs and 83; development and 75–6; experimentation and 69, 92; social relationships and 89; youth and 75–6, 81–92; *see also* crisis
social interaction 59, 73
socialization 40, 42
social life: digitization of 72; fragmentation of 92
social media: protest and 110–14, 116, 118; television news and 111, 118; user interactions 107–3; user opinions 97
social movements 70, 91
social networking platforms 110
social relationships 81; digital technologies and 19–20; social crises and 89; youth and 89–90
social semiotics 24
society 146–7
socio-technical interactivity 49–50
space: discussion 98–101, 105–8; imaginary 50; networked 71, 86, 92; occupation of 80; protest 111, 120; public 5, 81–2; social 47, 72; technical 47
student-educators 130, 132, 140
students: internet use 139; multimedia use 131–3, 139–40; teachers and 141–2
symmetric anthropology 41

teachers: argumentation 141; collaboration and 140–1; multimedia use 132; students and 141–2

technography 39–42
technology *see* digital technologies
television news: anti-rape protest coverage *116*, 118; corruption coverage and *114*; Facebook and 111, 113, 120–1; protest and 111, 113–14, 116, 118, 121
tertiary media 149
text: analysis of 27; content analysis of 97; as image 18, 148; multimodal 23–4, 26, 35, 139; multimodal analysis of 78; reading 148; semiotic work and 25; sequential analysis of 101; significance of 78; video 80
text making: changes in 22–4; cohesion in 33; engagement and 35; Facebook and 24, 26–35; interest and 31; meta-language for 35; modes of representation and 22; multimodal 23–35; order of elements in 32; pedagogies for 36–7; platforms for 31; repertoires of 36; resources and 31; semiotic resourcefulness and 24; social semiotics and 24–5; users-as-interpreters of 25; youth and 36
texts-on-texts 78, *79*, 84
text types 29, 31–2
tools: cultural 53; defining 54; mediated activity and 54, 66
transformation: creative chain and 144; crisis and 74; multiliteracy and 143
Twitter 111

unemployment 69–70

video: cohesion in 33–4; inclusion and 35; mediation and 74; mimetic references to 16; modes of 27; News Feeds and 35; as a political tool 81–2, 84–7; real/ideal forms 75, 86; sequentiality and 35; social world and 76, 85–7, 90, 92; writing and 32–3; *see also* YouTube
video games: body and 39–40; research on 39
video-making: analysis of *77*, 77–86; as a developmental tool 75; mediating activity and 75, 82–4, 92; *see also* filmmaking

videosphere 12
violence 134, 138–9, 141–2; *see also* gender violence
virtual: communities 3; digital natives in communities 12–13; hypersphere and communities 12; literacies 2
visuality 146–7
Vygotsky, L. S. 54, 59, 72–5, 79, 82–3, 88–91, 128

WhatsApp 31
Wii console 42–3, 46–8
women: body ideals for 100–3; internet use 121n2; middle class 119–20; protest and 118, 122n18; public spaces and 123n20; violence against 116–19, 123n20
writing 147; modes of 22, 25–7; multimodal design of 37; pedagogies for 37; text making and 22–4, 36; use of 22

youth: authority figures and 86–8; cultural development 88–9; daydreams and 90–1; development and 81; digital identity formation 14–15; as digital makers 4; digital technologies and 1–5; future plans and 88, 90; mobilization of 70–1; multimodal communication 4; neoliberalism and 70–1; networked technologies and 71; oppression and 81–2, 85, 87–9, 92; participatory culture and 91; rioting culture and 70–1; social crises and 75–6, 81–92; social relationships and 89–91; social world of 84–8; unemployment of 69–70; video-making 71, 73, 76–92
YouTube: collaborative learning and 82; comment-response sequences 101–8; Facebook links to 28–9; Greek youth and 71, 73, 78, 81–91; mediating activity and 92; multimodal analysis of 78–92, 97; nonsequential analysis 102–4; participatory culture and 91; as a political tool 81–8, 90; sequential analysis and 98–101, 104–6; user opinions 97

zone of proximal development 73–5, 89, 92